Nash, Helen, 1944–
Complete guide to water
garden plants /
2003.
33305211723014
la   11/03/06

complete guide to

water garden plants

Helen Nash
with Steve Stroupe

Special Photography by Perry D. Slocum & Bob Romar

Sterling Publishing Co., Inc.
New York

Designed by Judy Morgan

1 3 5 7 9 10 8 6 4 2

Published in 2003 by Sterling Publishing Co., Inc.
387 Park Avenue South, New York, NY 10016
Originally published in hardcover under the title *Aquatic Plants & Their Cultivation*
Also published under the title *Plants for Water Gardens*
© 1998 by Helen Nash
Distributed in Canada by Sterling Publishing
^c/o Canadian Manda Group, One Atlantic Avenue, Suite 105
Toronto, Ontario, Canada M6K 3E7
Distributed in Great Britain by Chrysalis Books
64 Brewery Road, London N7 9NT, England
Distributed in Australia by Capricorn Link (Australia) Pty Ltd.
P.O. Box 704, Windsor, NSW 2756, Australia

Printed in China
All rights reserved

Sterling ISBN 1-4027-0954-4

For Perry D. Slocum
and
Steve Stroupe

Contents

Introduction

I tried to ignore Steve Stroupe's urgings that this book was needed. I knew he was right, since I had gone through years of frustration looking for the information now conveniently compiled here. Fortunately, Steve is a persistent sort, and together we planned this book. It's not that the information wasn't out there, it just wasn't readily available. It could be found in college textbooks or tucked away in the experience of growers in many areas. Gathering it all was only half the job; the information needed "translation" into a usable format for the backyard pond keeper. While my mother still considers me a klutz (with good reason), I hope all of you know me as practical. Steve is a practical fellow, too. And so we hope you'll find herein all the information you need to grow and propagate the plants within your ponds.

Scientists and horticulturists will note that we have not covered *all* the aquatic plants out there in lakes, ponds, and streams. They may also rue the absence of technical jargon. But our goal is practicality. We cover only those plants easily bought or acquired in the trade or marketplace. We do cover some of the newest plants available at this time. We hope we've covered the plant families in enough detail that you can tend subsequent plant introductions.

While we discuss everything as non-technically as possible, you can refer to the glossary for the Latin that goes with what you've picked up in these chapters. You'll then have a good basis for launching into real science.

You don't need a botany degree to grow, propagate, hybridize, or simply enjoy aquatic plants. Just as the moving and serene waters of your garden enhance your life, becoming familiar with your plants also enriches life. Enjoy!

Helen Nash and Steve Stroupe

chapter one

AQUATIC PLANTS

WHAT IS AN AQUATIC PLANT?

Although all the earth's plants grow under conditions ranging from very dry (xerophyte) to very wet (hydrophyte), an aquatic plant is one that is *normally* found growing in water at or above the surface of the soil. Aquatic plants, while unique in their habitats, are *not* separately classified by botanists from other plants on earth. For example, in the United States an approximate 1,300 species of aquatic plant are assigned within 65 plant families. Only 12 of these families are entirely aquatic.

Plants, whether terrestrial or aquatic, share the same structures, forms, and functions. The difference between aquatic and terrestrial plants lies in the *adaptations* made by some species to allow their growth in water.

Types of Aquatic Plants

The degree of these adaptations depends on the way the plant grows in water: emergent or only partially submerged, such as cattails; fully submerged, such as "water weeds" or anacharis; floating and attached with roots anchored in soil beneath the water, such as water lilies; or fully floating and with roots free in water, such as water hyacinths.

Leaf Adaptations in Aquatic Plants

Terrestrial leaves feature two different surfaces: the upper surface, usually covered with a waxy cuti-

TYPES OF AQUATIC PLANTS

emergent roots growing in soil

free floating

fully submerged, anchored or rooted in soil/substrata

floating leaves, roots growing in soil

Above: A well-planted water garden includes a variety of aquatic plants. Photo by Carol Christensen.

cle, and the lower surface, bearing pores (*stomata)* that allow the plant to breathe. This breathing process allows carbon dioxide in the surrounding air to enter the plant and oxygen produced within the plant to leave during the daylight process of photosynthesis that creates the plant's food. At night, the process is reversed, as oxygen enters the plant and carbon dioxide leaves it. (This nighttime, reversed process is known as respiration.)

Terrestrial plant leaves and leaves on emergent or marginal aquatic species are quite similar. Yet, most emergent plants start their growth in soil that is either underwater or saturated with water. There is a period of time when the young emergent plant leaves must grow in water. Somehow, during the nighttime hours they must have oxygen supplied underwater. Since plants have a limited capacity to store oxygen, aquatic plants may have adapted to use this stored oxygen during the brief time it takes the leaf to emerge from the water and to begin breathing air as terrestrial leaves do.

Floating leaves present unique adaptations. Leaves that float on the water's surface expose their upper side to the atmosphere and their under side to the water. These leaves often grow in a circular form with a smooth edge. This shape offers maximum protection from tearing by wind or by waves. A tough, leathery texture also pro-

Hardy water lilies display adaptations that ensure their survival: smooth, round edges and a leathery surface coated with a protective, waxy cuticle.
Photo by Ron Everhart.

tects against damage. A heavy, waxy cuticle covering on the surface of the leaf lets the water roll off and helps prevent the leaf from sinking. Floating leaves have their breathing pores on the upper surface, where they contact the air, and also large air spaces inside the leaves that help them float.

During the growing season, water lilies continually send up new leaf growth. The leaves may live 3 to 4 weeks at the peak of the season. This photo shows the rosy new growth color, the mature green and cream color, and the aging and yellowing "old" leaves of *Nymphaea* 'Arc-en-Ciel.'
Photo by Ron Everhart.

Stem Adaptations in Aquatic Plants

The petiole is the stem that attaches the leaf to the plant. Terrestrial plants have air touching all sides of the leaves, while floating plant leaves touch the air on only one side. The stems of aquatic plants that root in the soil below and have floating leaves are usually longer than necessary to reach the water's surface. This is Nature's way of allowing these plants to survive where water levels rise and

The petioles, or leaf stems, of water lilies grow extra long to accommodate fluctuating water levels. Photo by H. Nash.

fall. With extra long stems, the leaves easily adjust to changing water levels. If the leaves become submerged with a rapid rise in water level, the stems begin growing until the leaf again reaches the surface. Water gardeners who place a potted water lily in water deeper than where it was taken from often notice this. Long stems also allow the many leaves of an individual plant to spread out on the water surface for sunlight and air.

Submerged Leaf Adaptations

Submerged leaves have adapted to obtain oxygen and carbon dioxide from water rather than air. The leaves are either long and extremely thin with smooth edges or are deeply dissected or compound. Because water offers support, the more rigid tissue that is found in

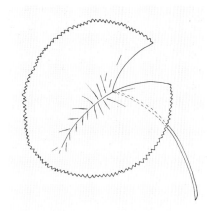

While hardy water lilies usually have smooth edges, tropical water lily leaves may display jagged or dentate leaves.

Tropical water lily leaves may also display convolutions in a gently ruffled and more deeply dentate form.

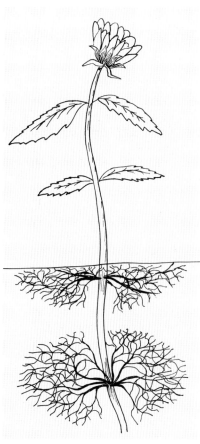

A common leaf adaptation in aquatic plants is the presence of submerged leaves along with floating or emergent leaves.

terrestrial leaves is replaced by spongy tissue full of air pockets. These air pockets make the leaves buoyant and prevent their hanging straight down. The absence of the waxy coating enables dissolved gases and solids to move in and out of the leaves. A common adaptation in aquatic plants is the presence of floating leaves or leaves that rise up out of the water along with submerged leaves on the same plant.

Submerged Root Adaptations

Terrestrial plant roots bring nutrients into the plant. In some submerged aquatic plants, the primary function of the roots is to anchor the plant. Many of these plants take their food directly from the water through their leaves. If the leaves and stems are the main means of acquiring

food, the plant is considered a "sink" plant. Plants that get their food primarily through their roots are considered "pumps."

Both types of submerged plants are commonly called "oxygenators." Since plants give off oxygen in sunlight as part of photosynthesis, the name makes sense. However, during the night hours of plant respiration, oxygen is taken up and carbon dioxide is produced. For that reason, we refer to these plants as "water clarifiers" since it is their direct uptake of nutrients from the water that starves free-floating algae and often results in clearer water.

PHOTOSYNTHESIS

water + light + carbon dioxide gas (in the presence of chlorophyll)

↓

carbohydrates + oxygen gas

RESPIRATION

carbohydrate + oxygen gas

↓

energy + water + carbon dioxide gas

The Ultimate Adaptation —*Lacunae*

Just as humans have blood vessels, terrestrial plants have a system for moving gases and fluids through the plant. These are called vascular structures. Since aquatic plants live in a world of water instead of air, they have developed a unique system for transporting gases—*lacunae*. *Lacunae* are simply air-filled spaces between the tissues of plant stems. The *lacunae* provide open channels for gases to move through the plant.

They begin as tiny cracks among the tissues near the growing tips and enlarge with time and growth to extend from the tips of

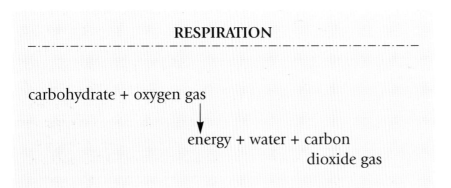

Cross section of an aquatic plant stem: The dark areas are typical plant vessels for moving plant fluids; white spaces are *lacunae*, used for storing and moving gas.

individual leaves down through the stems and into the buried rhizomes and roots. This is how bubbles escape from a severed water

lily leaf or flower. *Lacunae* can be found in nearly all submerged growing portions of aquatic plants.

TYPES OF AQUATIC PLANTS

True aquatic plants grow in water, be it shallow water barely covering the plants' crowns or in deeper water. Other plants that will grow in the shallow waters around the edge of the pond or water garden may be found in nurseries. These plants are commonly called marsh

True aquatic plants, such as water lilies, grow completely within water. Marginal or emergent plants grow with their leaves emerging from the water in which they are rooted. Fully submerged plants remain beneath the water's surface.
Photo by H. Nash.

The pitcher plant, a carnivorous bog plant, is one of the few bog plants that can be grown in standing water. It tolerates "wet feet and dry ankles" but still requires acid enhancement of its soil.
Photo by H. Nash.

plants, marginal plants, or emergent plants. Generally soft-stemmed, these plants (such as cattails, sweet flags, water irises, grasses, and sedges) may even tolerate periodic dry spells in the wild. Often, these plant names are used interchangeably with the term "bog plants."

This term is misleading since real "bog" plants grow in acidic, saturated, peaty conditions. Carnivorous plants, such as sundews or pitcher plants, are bog plants that require both moisture and acidic soil. Although they grow in very moist soils, they are not true aquatic plants and do not grow well in the typical water garden. (Pitcher plants, however, can be grown successfully with "wet feet/dry ankles" in the water garden.)

"Moisture-loving plants" is yet another descriptive term. These plants thrive in the presence of

very moist, unsaturated soils. Some, such as daylilies, may thrive in the shallows of a pond if the water does not extend above the plant crown. Siberian iris and gar-

"Moisture-loving" plants, such as daylilies, can be adapted to shallow water culture during their growing season. Winter such plants outside the pond in a well-drained location. Photo by Ron Everhart.

den cannas are other examples of such plants. Usually best used in the damp areas around natural ponds and streams, they can be planted in containers for seasonal use in the water garden. However, remove them from the pond and bury their containers to the rim in the terrestrial garden for the winter months.

THE WATER GARDEN AND AQUATIC PLANTS

When you create a water garden, you must cope with the needs of the plants, the chemistry of the water, and the needs of other liv-

ing things—fish, frogs, and so on. While controlling the number of creatures that live in your water garden impacts the overall condition of the garden, the number and type of aquatic plants you select also affects the condition and quality of your garden.

Ideally, days are sunny. During those sunny days, photosynthesis by your plants creates oxygen within the pond waters. At night, respiration produces an approximately equal amount of carbon dioxide as oxygen is removed. What happens during a period of very cloudy days? Daytime photosynthesis slows and less oxygen is produced. Nighttime removal of oxygen and production of carbon dioxide continues at the same level. The balance of the pond's production of oxygen relative to that of carbon dioxide is thrown off; more oxygen is used than is produced. This can also occur when the pond water is very green with free-floating algae.

Reduced oxygen levels also result if too much of the pond's surface is covered by floating plants such as duckweed, water hyacinth, water lettuce, or water lily leaves. Not only do excessive numbers of these plants shade the plants below and slow plant growth, they also limit the area of surface water in contact with the air where oxygen enters the water.

Aquatic plants can affect oxygen levels in the water in yet another way. Even pond owners who regularly remove dying vege-

On sunny days, green plants and their process of photosynthesis produce a maximum amount of oxygen within the pond waters. Photo by Greg Jones.

On cloudy days, photosynthesis slows and lesser amounts of oxygen are produced within the pond by the green plants. Photo by H. Nash.

water. This results in less combined hydrogen and carbon dioxide (carbonic acid) in the water and a corresponding rise in the pH reading. During nighttime respiration when oxygen is removed from the water and free carbon dioxide is produced, carbonic acid

Too much coverage by plants reduces the amount of gas exchange at the water's surface. Supplemental oxygen helps both fish and plants in these conditions. Photo by H. Nash.

tation and surface debris from their gardens are amazed at the amount of sediment that collects on the pond bottom. Floating plants continually shed dead roots. Likewise, natural die-offs from disease, weather, winter, and normal aging add to this organic matter or "bio-load" of the water garden. Bacteria that decompose this organic matter use oxygen and can affect the water's oxygen level.

Reduced oxygen levels in the water may not seriously affect your plants, but they can cause life-threatening conditions for fish and can result in a "fish kill."

Plants can also impact the water's pH. During the daylight hours of photosynthesis, free carbon dioxide is removed from the

is added to the system. This in turn lowers the pH. Aquatic plants tend to lower the pH of water during the night and raise it during the day. Dr. Dean Earlix refers to this ebb and flow as "the breath of a pond."

PLANT NUTRIENTS IN AQUATIC ENVIRONMENTS

Green chlorophyll makes plants appear green and helps with photosynthesis, which produces plants' growth foods.
Photo by H. Nash.

Beyond oxygen and carbon dioxide for photosynthesis, plants also require essential elements to complete their life cycles. The essential elements known for plant survival are divided into two groups, macronutrients and micronutrients. Macronutrients, needed in measurable quantities, are carbon, hydrogen, nitrogen, phosphorus, sulfur, potassium, calcium, and magnesium. Micronutrients, often called "trace elements," are iron, manganese, boron, zinc, copper, molybdenum, and chlorine. With terrestrial plants, these nutrients are supplied by the soil in which the plant grows or by enhancing that soil with fertilizers, either inorganic or organic.

The natural pond or lake may offer all the nutrients needed by plants. In the water garden, however, in creating mini-aquatic habitats, sparkling clear *(and sterile)* water is desirable. Regularly supplying essential elements, in the form of fertilizer, is necessary for healthy pond plants.

ALGAE

The most common aquatic plant is the least desirable in the water garden—algae. Within your pond, algae may be the single-celled, free-floating type of green water; the stringy, filamentous type (blanketweed) that entangles plant growth; or the mossy growth that covers the sides of the water garden and pots. The mossy type

Green-water algae is a single-celled, free-floating plant that can turn a garden's water pea-soup green.   Photo by Bill Marocco.

is of no major concern since it functions much as submerged grasses within the garden and provides nibblings for fish and tadpoles.

Green-water algae typically appear in the early spring as the air and water warm before most aquatic plants break their winter dormancy. Some water gardens may be plagued by these algae at other times during the growing season. The growth requirements of green-water algae are the same as those of other green plants: light and nutrients.

Since most ponds are constructed to receive at least three or four hours of sunlight daily, light is readily available for algae growth. One way to discourage algae growth is to cut down on the water's sun exposure with floating plants and floating leaves.

Another way to shade the water is to use water dyes. A drawback is that aquatic plants growing below the water surface are also deprived of light. Move submerged grasses and potted water lilies closer to the surface to avoid slow or stunted growth. Since the dye does not evaporate from the water, it must be removed through water exchanges.

Prevention is the easiest remedy for green water algae. Check that nutrients are not entering the pond through runoff from surrounding lawn and grounds. Ensure that aquatic plant fertilizer is not leaching into the water. Monitor your fish population; too many fish

Botanical gardens like Longwood Gardens in Pennsylvania frequently use black water dyes to shade the water and prevent green-water algae growth. Photo by H. Nash.

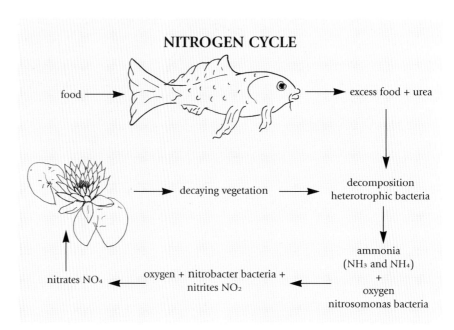

NITROGEN CYCLE

food → [fish] → excess food + urea

decaying vegetation → decomposition heterotrophic bacteria

excess food + urea → decomposition heterotrophic bacteria → ammonia (NH_3 and NH_4) + oxygen nitrosomonas bacteria

nitrates NO_4 ← oxygen + nitrobacter bacteria + nitrites NO_2 ← ammonia (NH_3 and NH_4) + oxygen nitrosomonas bacteria

result in the production of excess nitrates that brings on an algae bloom. Mechanical filtration and good pond hygiene aid somewhat.

Although biofiltration establishes nitrifying bacteria to aid in waste processing, nitrate is the end-product of that process. Ideally, the way to control the level of nutrients is to provide plants that access the nutrients before the algae. Submerged plants, such as *Elodea* or anacharis, at a ratio of one bunch per one-to-two square feet (0.09 to 0.18 sq m) of water surface, effectively compete with algae in a pond not overburdened with fish or great amounts of decomposing organic matter.

Controlling the growth of green water algae with algicides introduces chemicals that may also inhibit the growth of desirable aquatic plants or harm the fish

Too many fish for the size of the pond can create problems if too much waste is being added to the water. Photo by H. Nash.

population. One such chemical, copper sulfate, removes the slime coating from fish and leaves them more susceptible to parasites and disease. Some water lilies, particularly dwarf forms, are inhibited or killed by such chemicals, as are the lower plant forms of submerged grasses.

Algae can be killed with ultraviolet sterilizers. These lights are set up after the filter unit so that all water passes within a specific distance to kill any microscopic plant or animal life within the water. UV lights sterilize the water, not necessarily desirable in the true aquatic plant water garden. This means of algae control also presents a "cleanup" problem. If the dead algae collect on the pond bottom as sediment, the cycle of decomposing organic matter produces more nutrients for more algae. A coagulant or flocculant, such as Acurel-E, assists in the collection of this dying matter by causing the single-celled plant forms to clump together. They can then be netted with a fine skimmer net, vacuumed, or filtered.

UV sterilizers can kill green-water algae. Use a coagulant to clean up the dead algae if your filtration system cannot remove it from the water. Photo by Oliver Jackson.

Filamentous algae present a unique problem for the water gardener—they do not seem to be dependent on the same water chemistry as free-floating algae. In fact, filamentous algae usually occur in clear waters. Interpet Ltd., a British company, has developed Pond Balance, a product that with regular use adjusts the water chemistry to lessen or prevent blanketweed growth. It does not affect the growth of aquatic

Filamentous or "string algae" can literally choke pond plants. Photo by Ron Everhart.

plants. The product has only recently been approved for sale in the U.S. Pond Balance applied in a solution in the early spring discourages blanketweed in the pond. While some water gardeners have reported the need to use the product in midsummer, most use it only in spring and fall applications.

The generally accepted means of controlling blanketweed or filamentous algae is simply to twist a stick or a bristle brush in the water and remove the blanketweed. Many water gardeners like to keep a bit of algae in the pond for tadpoles to eat.

ECO-BALANCE IN THE WATER GARDEN

The concept of eco-balance within a pond is organic water gardening at its best. It involves having the number and types of aquatic plants within a range that renders water relatively clear and algae-free. Approximately 60 percent of the water surface is covered with a combination of floating plants

Establishing a balance among all the life forms in your pond produces a clear and beautiful garden. Photo by H. Nash.

and floating leaves. This cuts down on the amount of sunlight entering the water that might encourage algae growth while still allowing enough sunlight to penetrate for the plants growing below. In practice, many water gardeners have discovered that, regardless of surface coverage, submerged plants in a quantity of one bunch per one to two square feet (0.09 to 0.18 sq m) of the water's surface provide enough nutrient control to result in clear water, as long as the amount of decomposing organic matter and the number of fish are controlled.

Important to the concept's success, though not a part of the eco-balance formula, is the number and size of the fish within the garden. Fish grow and multiply. If their stocking level goes beyond what the garden can reasonably handle, excess nutrients can feed algae blooms.

Water quality also suffers with elevated levels of ammonia and nitrite, and these put fish at risk. Keep your fish population no more than one inch of goldfish per square foot of water surface or per five gallons of water, or one inch of koi per two square feet of water surface or per ten gallons of water. Likewise, feed only what the fish will eat in five to 10 minutes and then remove any remaining food to prevent it from decomposing and affecting the water quality.

Feed fish only what they will eat in 5-10 minutes. Net out any excess food to prevent it from decomposing and adding to the pond's bioload. Photo by Carol Christensen.

Phyto-filtration

Understanding how plants function within the water garden, particularly with respect to their uptake of nutrients from the water, enables the water gardener to create a mini-ecosystem that functions naturally. Frequently,

Using plants to help remove excess nutrients from water is known as "phyto-filtration." Photo by H. Nash.

Robert Mixon's vegetative filter for his koi pond is beautiful enough to be a separate water garden. Photo by Carol Christensen.

this can be combined with bio-filtration, the provision of a filter, a home for nitrifying bacteria that enhance the nitrogen cycle within the pond. Some water gardeners grow efficient nutrient-removing plants, such as water hyacinth or water celery, in the top of their biofilters or in a special container pond known as a "vegetable filter." Using plants to remove excess nutrients from water is known as phyto-filtration.

Richard Schuck's Ten Percent Solution

Maryland Aquatic Nurseries' Richard Schuck devised a system some years ago that uses the principles of vegetative- or phyto-filtration. Essentially a pond-within-a-pond, Richard's solution offers a 12-to-18-inch deep area equal to 10 percent of the pool's total surface. With the water recycled to enter at one end of the 10-percent-pond, particle settlement occurs with water flowing gently over pots of marginal plants. Gravel or rock topping on the plants in containers provides a home for nitrifying bacteria that aid in water-quality control. Floating plants, such as water hyacinth and water lettuce, help remove both nutrients and particulates from the water. This same principle is applied in the form of a slow-moving stream planted with appropriate aquatic plants. (See Appendix for plant list.)

An adaptation of Richard Schuck's Ten-Percent Solution is to include nutrient-absorbing aquatics within a stream bed. Photo by H. Nash.

PLANT NAMES

Although plants have common names, these names often vary from one region to another and become confusing. This problem dates back to the time when Latin was the language of scholars. Hence, the universal, binomial plant-naming system was developed, using Latin for the scientific names of plants.

A plant name consists of two primary words. The first word always begins with a capital letter, as it is the plant's family name. The second word is the species name and is not capitalized. Ideally, these names are italicized; otherwise, they are underlined. (Example: *Nymphaea odorata*) In technical writing, this binomial name is also followed by the person's name or the standardized abbreviation of the person's name who officially described the plant. This name is not italicized. (Example: *Nymphaea odorata* Aiton)

A genus is a family or group of plants with very similar characteristics. The genus is divided first into individual species with even finer subdivisions as necessary: subspecies (ssp.), form (f.), and variety (var. or v.). While subdivisional names are also italicized or underlined, the reference word of subspecies, form, or variety is not. (Example: *Nymphaea odorata* var. *gigantea* Tricker) Once the full name of a plant is used in a discussion, other references to it may abbreviate the genus name. (Example: *N. odorata*)

Hybrid plants are produced

from two different species, from two hybrids, or from a species and a hybrid crossing. They may occur naturally in the wild or be produced deliberately by plant breeders. They may be identified by either a formula name or by a collective name. Formula names indicate the parentage of the hybrid, with the seed parent listed first and the pollen parent listed last. (Example for *Nymphaea* 'Cherokee': *N.* 'Colonel A.J. Welch' × *N.* 'Aurora') An "x" listed before the second name of a plant indicates the plant is a member of a group of hybrids of a particular cross. (Example: *Nymphaea* x*laydekeri* 'Alba') Alternatively, a collective name may be written in parenthesis following the genus name. (Example: *Nymphaea laydekeri* 'Alba')

A cultivated hybrid that displays significant enough characteristics to distinguish it from other hybrids of the same parentage may be designated as a cultivar. Often the cultivar is given a special name that is preceeded by the abbreviation "cv.", or the plant's special name is enclosed within single quotation marks. Hence, a hybrid water lily of the genus *Nymphaea* with a given name Mary may be written as *Nymphaea* cv. Mary, or more commonly, as *Nymphaea* 'Mary' or *N.* 'Mary'.

COMMON LATIN HORTICULTURAL TERMS AND THEIR ENGLISH TRANSLATIONS

alba	white
atropurpurea	dark purple
aureum	golden
compacta	compact
esculentus	edible
fastigiata	erect
floribunda	free-flowering
glauca	with white or gray coating
grandiflora	with large or showy flowers
horizontalis	horizontal
nanus	dwarf
occidentalis	from the Western Hemisphere
officinalis	medicinal
pendula	hanging
rotundifolia	round-leaved
rubrum	red
semperflorens	ever (*semper*)-flowering (*florens*)
stellata	starlike
tuberosum	bearing tubers
variegata	variegated
vulgaris	common

chapter two

GROWING AQUATIC PLANTS

PLANTING CONTAINERS

The typical water garden is artificially constructed as a preformed unit, as a concrete-formed pool, or as a membrane-lined structure. Plants included in the garden are potted in containers, usually in pots with or without holes.

Mesh-type pots are commonly called "laundry basket"–type containers. Homemade versions are constructed of chicken wire, but these oxidize and deteriorate in one season. Plastic basket planters of this type originated in England. Depending on the size of the holes in these containers, the pot may require lining with natural burlap to retain the soil. Gardeners who prefer this type of container feel that the plants' roots need to "breathe" and find nutrients. In ponds lined with pea gravel, soil, or sediment buildup, this practice can result in healthy plants.

For the water gardener who keeps a "clean pond," few nutrients are available to the wandering roots of an aquatic plant outside its container. Consider that if a pond is free enough of excess nutrients to prevent the growth of green-water algae, how many nutrients can be present for higher plant forms? Also, in nature only certain submerged and free-floating plants obtain most of their nutrients directly from the water. Most aquatic plants, such as water lilies and emergent or marginal plants, grow from water-saturated soil from which they get their food.

In recent years, growers have experimented and learned that aquatic plants grow well in containers made without holes. Lerio Corporation has developed 30 different container sizes in response to the needs of aquatic plants. (Standard terrestrial pots with drainage holes can be used, but the hole in the bottom should be plugged with stone, untreated burlap, or wadded newspaper. Plugging the holes helps keep plant roots and fertilizer within the container, as well as preventing soil from building up on the pond bottom.)

Mesh-type molded containers are called "laundry basket" pots. These containers are available in square- or round-cornered styles. Untreated burlap linings help contain the soil. Photo by H. Nash.

Above: Aquatic plants need containers suited to their habits for the most successful growth.
Photo by H. Nash.

Lerio Corporation has developed over 30 different containers in response to water gardening needs. Containers with no holes range from very small to very large and can accommodate plants within the water garden or plants such as lotus that might be grown in their own "pond pot."
Photo by H. Nash.

Many other options exist for containerizing aquatic plants: plastic shoe boxes, plastic bowls, plastic oil changing pans, and wooden boxes. If you use wooden planters, avoid chemically treated wood that can leach harmful chemicals into the water. Likewise, avoid woods such as oak that can leach tannic acid into the water.

Most shallow-water aquatics are happy growing in ordinary garden soil. True bog plants such as bogbean (*Menyanthes*) or the calla family (*Zantedeschia*) grow better if acid is added to their potting soil. Photo by H. Nash.

Using black containers lessens their visibility, particularly if the water is clear. Since most aquatics are shallow-rooting plants, select wide-mouthed containers that are wider than they are deep. UV-stable materials ensure the longevity of the container.

PLANTING SOIL FOR AQUATICS

The most commonly recommended soil for planting aquatics is "heavy garden loam." This term can mean different things to gardeners in various regions. Florida soils, for example, contain a much higher sand content than the heavy clay soils of other regions. The term, however, does convey two requirements in aquatic planting soil: some clay content to make the soil "heavy," and fertility such as is found in a garden. The heavy clay subsoil found beneath topsoil is not suitable for growing aquatic plants because it lacks nutrients and soil bacteria. Likewise, additives such as peat are not recommended for several reasons. Most obviously, these additives are lightweight and can easily disperse into the water of the pond. Peat additives also acidify the soil. While such acidity is desirable for true bog plants like carnivorous plants, it is not desirable for most aquatic plants. (Bogbean, *Menyanthese trifoliata*, and the callas, *Zantedeschia*, are two species native to boggy areas

that have been adapted to water garden culture. Both plants grow better with acid added to their potting mix, as does Louisiana iris.)

Many water gardeners do add compost to their potting soil. In mixing a wheelbarrow full of soil, one or two shovels of compost are added. This may be cow manure or leaf compost, always well rotted. Michael Duff, a knowledgeable and avid water lily hobbyist, uses well-rotted chicken manure. Other growers have stopped using manures due to a risk of contamination.

Prominent hybridist Dr. Kirk Strawn uses a heavy garden loam covered with a shallow layer of sand. Kirk plants his water lily

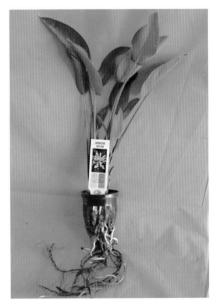

Florida Aquatic Nurseries has adapted a hydroponic technique to grow marginal aquatics in a rockwool medium in two-inch (5 cm) net pots. The plants are then transplanted into soil for growing within the water garden.
Photo by Brad McLane.

An alternate way of growing aquatic plants is to build planting troughs within the pond and plant directly in them.
Photo by Eamonn Hughes.

tubers on top of the loam layer and completes the filling of the container with coarse sand. Joe Tomocik of the Denver Botanic Gardens prefers a heavy clay loam for his hardy water lilies and a lighter mix with more loam for tropical water lilies. Richard Sacher of American Aquatic Gardens in New Orleans uses a local product called "spillway sand," a mixture of fine alluvial silt and sand collected from a spillway adjacent to the Mississippi River. Davis Creek Nursery uses a mix of 70 percent topsoil and 30 percent sand. Florida Aquatic Nurseries uses rockwool, a hydroponic growing medium, to grow marginal or emergent plants in two-inch (5 cm) net pots. Joe Villemarette of Patio Garden Ponds in Oklahoma reports good results using Americo filter media as potting soil. Other experts recommend slight variations, such as adding one part 10–10–10 granular fertilizer to five parts heavy soil. Even

generic cat litter has been used successfully, as have variations of soil-less media.

Although the in-pond planting trough is easily constructed around the pond perimeter for marginal aquatics, troughs can be built anywhere in the pond for growing water lilies, too.
Photo by Eamonn Hughes.

AQUATIC PLANT FERTILIZER

Generally, if aquatic plants are repotted each year in roomy containers with fresh soil, fertilizing is not needed for their survival. But for the plants to thrive and bloom, supplemental feeding is advised.

Perry D. Slocum notes that in the days before tablet forms of aquatic plant fertilizers were avail-

able, he used a granular 10–10–10 food of 10 percent nitrogen, 10 percent phosphate, and 10 percent potash. The remaining 70 percent was an inert filler, such as sand. Perry mixed two or three cups of this fertilizer in the bottom half of a planter along with a couple of shovels of well-rotted cow manure.

After moving to Florida in 1963, Perry met Mr. Bachman, who shared his fertilizer formula that included dried blood meal, steamed bone meal, and 10–10–10 granulated fertilizer. Perry mixed two or three cups in the potting soil in the bottom half of the container, along with a ring of the mix about halfway down the inside wall of the planter. He still recalls Bachman's advice: "Make the plant hunt for it!" Placing the fertilizer too close to the plant roots risks burning. Since then, Perry has experimented with various formulas with his water lilies. An experiment with 15–30–15 fertilizer resulted in the plants' death. Perry advises never to go higher than a 10 percent nitrogen content.

Following a regular program of fertilizing your water lilies guarantees the biggest blooms of these spectacular flowers. Photo by Ron Everhart.

In recent years, the industry has addressed the specific needs of aquatic plants. Fertilizer was formed into tablets for insertion into the soil around plants at a dose of two tabs per gallon of soil every two to four weeks, depending on the particular plant. Tropical water lilies, for example, which bear more flowers than their hardy cousins, need more frequent feeding to maintain their healthy vigor. Likewise, plants in small pots may require more frequent feeding with the dosage cut in half.

Time-release aquatic plant fertilizer tabs, such as are manufactured by AgSafe, formerly SK Research, Inc., are an exciting development. These tabs are formulated at 10–15–10 with added micronutrients. Time-release doses avoid problems created by too rapid dissolution in soil, leaching into the surrounding water, and the burden of frequent feeding.

The first step in potting aquatic plants is to place fertilizer tabs in the bottom of the pot, where they will be accessible once the plant's roots have established themselves.
Photo by H. Nash.

Organic Sources of Fertilizer

Nitrogen is supplied by dried blood, cottonseed meal, coconut, bean and peanut shells, bone meal, composted garden soil, and finely ground phosphate rock. Organic sources of potassium are plant residues such as wood ash, hay, leaves, well-rotted manures and compost, and natural mineral sources such as granite dust, green sand, and basalt rock. The problem with mixing your own organic fertilizer is that nutrients may or may not be readily available. Rock powders and organic materials release their nutrients over an extended period of time depending on the soil type, bacterial conditions, moisture, and acidity. Phosphate rock, for example, provides about 1.5 percent available phosphate in the first year, even though it has a total of 28 to 30 percent that it gradually releases over three or four years. Super phosphate is rated at 19 to 21 percent that is highly available for a very brief period of time before it leaches out of the soil and leaves behind salt deposits that inhibit soil bacteria.

Plant Talk

One trait aquatic plants share with their terrestrial family cousins is the ability to communicate their needs. Nitrogen produces green leafy growth. If a plant suffers from a nitrogen deficiency, growth will be stunted and the leaves yellow. Excess nitrogen produces an overabundance of leafy growth, often with decreased flower production.

Phosphorus is part of the plant's genetic material and is important for proper seed development. A deficiency causes stunted growth and seed sterility.

Potassium helps form carbohydrates and is necessary for making proteins that promote early growth and improve stem strength. Plants deficient in potassium are usually stunted and have poorly developed root systems. Older leaves may be spotted, curled, or mottled, and may even appear burned around the edges.

CONTAINER SELECTION

How you pot an aquatic plant depends primarily upon the individual plant's root type, growth habit, and particular cultivation needs. Select pots best suited to the plant's habit. If the plant is rhizomatous (growing from a thickened root), such as most hardy water lilies, pickerel weed, sweet flag, or irises, the cut edge of the plant is placed against the container's wall to provide maximum growing room across the pot. These plants need a container wider than it is deep. Clumping-type plants, such as rushes, are planted in the center of their container. Likewise, fast-growing rhi-

Rhizomatous plants need to be planted in pots that are wider than they are deep to avoid their "jumping" out of the container.
Photo by Ron Everhart.

zomatous plants, such as cattails or bulrushes, are also planted in the pot's center, as the pot fills up rapidly, regardless of where the plant is positioned. Although widemouthed containers allow maximum growing space, they are not crucial for the clump-growers. Plants fare better and you save time by selecting as large a pot as you can handle.

GENERAL POTTING GUIDELINES

Consider the plant's soil and planting-depth requirements. Because containers of wet mud are heavy, use the least amount of soil necessary. Lotuses, for example, used to be planted in large pots of soil that are difficult to manage by oneself. In recent years, both Davis Creek Nursery and Maryland Aquatic Nurseries have discovered that the shallow-rooting lotus does not require as much soil depth as it does breadth of area in which to grow. Both nurseries successfully grow lotus in only 2–3 inches of soil.

Most aquatic plants are rapid growers. By placing fertilizer tabs in the bottom of the pot, the fertilizer is available when the plant's roots reach it. The same principle holds true with the use of granular fertilizer—the layer of soil containing the granular mix is placed in the bottom of the container to await the roots' access.

If you use dry soil for potting, air is likely to be trapped within the soil. Firmly tamping the soil does not remove all the air. Either

Shallow-rooting aquatic plants do not need depth of soil as much as regular feeding. Photo by H. Nash.

water the soil before placing the container in the pond or lower the planted container into the water very slowly to allow the air to escape gently and to avoid "bubbling out" the new planting. Potting with dampened soil alleviates this problem, but slow, gentle placement in the pond is still advised. Using mud is messier than it is worth, because the soil eventually settles, leaving the plant sitting lower in the pot than you wish.

One-to-two-inch-diameter river rock tops the planting, with the rocks kept away from the plant's growing tip. Many water gardeners use pea gravel or coarse sand for this topping. Pea gravel, however, is often too small to discourage fish from rooting, in search for larval tidbits. A common recommendation is to use stone no smaller than the nose of your largest fish. This proves impractical with very large fish. Select flat stones to discourage fish from disturbing the plants.

HOW TO POT SPECIFIC AQUATIC PLANTS

THE POND BURRITO

Scott Bates of Grass Roots Nursery in New Boston, Michigan, shared this clever planting technique with the readers of *Watergardening Magazine.*

1. Assemble the materials, which should include the following:

> **Plant, such as parrot feather**
>
> **Large square of porous landscape fabric**
>
> **Loamy soil**
>
> **Fertilizer tab**
>
> **String**

2. Heap the soil around the root ends of the plant in the upper center of the landscape fabric. Tuck in the fertilizer tab.

3. Roll up the fabric like a burrito and tie it with string. Tuck the burritos into moist nooks and crannies of streams or waterfalls.

Refer to the following procedures for potting particular aquatic plants. Note that these guides are for bare-root plants that are either received that way by mail or that have been divided from your own plants. See Chapter 3 for directions to divide and/or propagate the plants.

Most aquatic plants can tolerate a strong hosing away of soil from their roots. Excess fibrous roots can be trimmed to reveal the root form as you determine what type of pot is best suited to the plant's growing habit. Photo by Ron Everhart.

New plants ordered by mail are usually sent bare-root with the roots already washed clean. In repotting plants, your first task is to remove the plant from its container and hose the soil from its roots. Most aquatic plants have sturdy roots that hold up to a forceful jet of water. For pot-bound plants, you may need to free the roots by hand as you spray away the soil. Losing fine roots in this process does not harm the plant as long as some rootstock remains. However, just as with terrestrial plants, if the rootstock is significantly cut back in the repotting process, the leafy part of the plant should be pruned correspondingly.

POTTING A LOTUS

A shallow kettle tub provides enough depth and growing breadth for the dwarf lotus 'Momo Botan.'
Photo by Bob Romar; © Maryland Aquatic Nurseries.

Lotuses are usually potted in wide, shallow containers because of the vigorous running nature of their tubers. Dwarf varieties such as 'Momo Botan' or 'Chawan Basu' should be planted in a container at least 24 in. (60 cm) in diameter with 10–12 in. (25–30 cm) of depth. Standard-size lotuses do best in a container 3 feet (90 cm)

1. Space six aquatic tabs (10-15-10) evenly around the bottom of a 23-inch (60 cm) wide and 10-inch (25 cm) deep pot. (Lerio BP2310). Place 5 inches (12.5 cm) of dirt in the container. Any more dirt than this is unnecessary and may result in a container that is too heavy to move.

in diameter. Planting these gorgeous plants in smaller containers crowds them and results in fewer or no blooms. (These suggested sizes of container will accommodate lotuses for one to two years, depending upon variety, fertilizer, and growing conditions.) Because these containers are much larger and less manageable than containers used for other aquatic plants, lotuses are often planted in individual containers that also serve as their "ponds."

The following procedure describes the potting of a dwarf-type lotus, 'Momo Botan.' The same method is used with standard-size lotuses.

The primary cause of lotus tuber failure is transplant shock caused by water that is too cold. Ideally, the container should be placed on top of the ground in a sunny location until the plant

2. Place the lotus tuber on top of the dirt with the cut edge of the rhizome against the edge of the pot.

3. Place a flat rock on top of the tuber and gently fill the container so that 2-3 in. (5-7.5cm) of water covers the tuber. Keep the container in a warm, sunny place as the plant establishes itself. Add water as necessary to compensate for evaporation. Once the lotus has produced several leaves, a shallow layer of soil may be added to cover the tuber, always with care not to cover the growing tip. Gravel topping may also be added in the same manner, if desired.
(Photos by H. Nash)

raises five to six leaves above the water, at which time the container can be moved into the pond just below the water's surface.

Another cause of tuber failure is either breaking the growing tip or planting the tuber in a square or corrugated-sided container that allows the tip to grow into a corner and break. Smooth-sided, round containers avoid these risks.

Most printed sources characterize lotuses as heavy feeders. However, when potting a new, single rhizome, too much fertilizer can easily burn the plant. When this happens, the plant's leaves turn yellow around the remaining green veins (interveinal chlorosis). An established plant of a year or more can be fed heavily, as often as the recommended every 3–4 weeks during the growing season, with minimal danger of burning. Because the growing tips of lotuses are brittle, Perry Slocum does not recommend feeding them during their most active growing period, because inserting fertilizer tabs can break and kill tender new growth.

In another planting method, cover the tuber with a shallow layer of soil, leaving the growing tip free of soil. A flat rock may still be necessary to hold the rhizome in place until roots grow to anchor it in the soil. Keep the water very shallow to prevent the freshly planted tuber from floating free. Established lotuses may have several inches of water over their crowns.

The flowers of hardy water lilies usually float upon the water's surface while tropical water lily flowers are usually held up in the air above their leaves. Photo by H. Nash.

POTTING WATER LILIES

Division, propagation, and potting of hardy water lilies vary according to the type of rhizome or rootstock of the particular variety. Four types of rootstock are found in this family of *Nymphaea*: mexicana, odorata, tuberosa, and marliac. If the distinction is not clear, the root type is described with the prefix "semi" preceding the type it most resembles. If a rhizome is a cross between two types of rhizome, the rhizome type is hyphenated with the name of the type it most resembles listed first.

Odorata rhizomes grow into thick, fleshy, horizontally extended forms with growing eyes along the length of the tuber that develop into thick branches if not trimmed away. Leaves and flowers are produced from growing tips.

Tuberosa rhizomes are characterized by broomstick-thin horizontal growths with rapidly growing eyes along the length that easily snap free. Leaves and flower stems are produced along the rhizome rather than from a specific growing tip or eye.

Marliac-type rhizomes, while tending to horizontal growth, are less vigorous than the odorata or tuberosa types. Plantsmen often characterize their growth as more "clumping" than "running." Marliac rhizomes display a more horizontal growth and a thicker, fleshier nature such as is found in the odorata rather than the spindly-type growth typical of a tuberosa. A variation of the marliac rhizome is distinguished by

The five types of hardy water lily rhizomes, as displayed by Perry Slocum. Photo by Perry D. Slocum.

some growers as a fifth type of rhizome, the "thumb" or "finger" rhizome, the name reflecting the miniature version of the rhizome.

Tropical water lily hybrids and some hardy water lilies grow from rhizomes with an upright growth habit, often compared to a small pineapple form and called a mexicana type. New plants form from tubers either immediately under or immediately adjacent to the tuber.

GENERAL POTTING PROCEDURE FOR HARDY WATER LILIES

Preparing the water lily rhizome for potting:

If horizontally growing rhizomes, such as the odorata, tuberosa, and marliac types, are not purchased bare-root and are repotted from your own mother plant, use pruning shears or a sharp knife to trim away all roots

and cut the leaf stems close to the rhizome. (Some fresh roots may be left on the rhizome to help anchor it and give it a head start in establishing growth.) Trim the rhizome to no more than 2 or 3 inches (5 or 7.5 cm) long. Discard the oldest portion of the rhizome that appears hollow and dead. Keep the roots and any leaves left attached to the rhizome covered with damp towels or wet newspapers to prevent them from drying out. If mail-order plants are received with some roots and leaves still attached, check that they are still fresh and without evidence of injury and/or rotting. Rather than wasting the plant's energy nourishing leaves and roots that are certain to die, trim them away to direct the plant's energies into healthy, productive growth.

Trim the water lily rhizome of excess roots and all furled leaves before potting. Photo by H. Nash.

Method One for Odorata and Tuberosa-type Rhizomes.

(Also use for *Nuphar* and *Aponogeton*, water hawthorne.)

Among the most vigorous of growers, the odorata rhizome requires a large pot. Its fleshy rhizome can punch a hole through a 5-gallon (20 l) heavy-duty container.

1. Space one aquatic tab per gallon (4 l) of soil evenly around the bottom of the container. (If using extend-release tabs, use two per gallon of soil.)

2. Fill the pot three-quarters full of your selected and dampened potting mix, mounding the soil slightly for the rhizome. Place the cut edge of the rhizome against a side wall of the pot, tilting the rootstock at a 45-degree angle so that the growing tip is at the anticipated soil level.

3. If the rhizome has viable roots attached to it, spread them across the soil.

Mound the soil in the container and set the water lily rhizome at a 45-degree angle with the cut end at the container's side.
Photo by Ron Everhart.

4. Fill the remaining space in the container with soil, tamping it to ensure root contact and minimal air spaces. Leave the growing tip free of soil.

5. Top with an inch (2.5 cm) of river stone kept free of the growing tip.

6. Gently lower the potted plant into the pond water to the desired depth. Usually a freshly

Gravel topping keeps the soil from muddying the pond water. Photo by Ron Everhart.

potted water lily is placed in shallow water until leaf production indicates roots have established, and the plant is then moved to its normal depth.

Method One for Tropical Water Lily and Mexicana-type Rhizomes.

(Also use for *Nymphoides*, Water Snowflakes, and Floating Hearts.)

1. Both the mexicana type and the tropical water lily rhizomes are planted in the center of the container since they tend to grow somewhat vertically rather than horizontally.

2. Follow the same procedure given in the prior section for odorata rhizome planting, the only dif-

An alternate way to plant the mexicana or upright rhizome (such as those of tropical water lilies) is to fill the container and then scoop a space from the center in which to place the rhizome. A flat rock may be placed over the rhizome, avoiding the growing tip, to hold it in place until growth is established. This "scoop method" works well with rhizomes that are well trimmed of roots. Photo by Perry D. Slocum.

ference being that tropical lily tubers are planted with the crown of the plant just *above* the soil level. These rhizomes usually do well in five-gallon (20 l) containers.

Tropical water lilies should not be set out in the water garden until the water temperature has stabilized at 70° F (20°C) or above.

Method Two for Planting Water Lilies and Other Aquatic Plants: The Plug Method.

This high-speed "plugging" method was developed at Davis Creek Nursery and is particularly suited to mass production. It also provides a quick and easy method for the home gardener to plant both water lilies and marginal aquatics.

In high-speed "plugging," first prepare the pond (with no water) with soil-filled containers. (Fertilizer tabs are placed at the bottom of each container.) Photo by H. Nash.

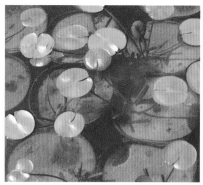

1. With water lily rhizomes, trim all roots and furled leaves from the rhizome, leaving the unfurled leaves intact; with marginal aquatics, trim excess roots and prune back the top of the plant. Place the appropriate number of fertilizer tabs in the bottom of the container, evenly spaced, and fill the pot with the desired soil mixture. Fill the pond with water to a depth of 2–4 in. (5–10 cm) over the top of the pots.

2. For horizontally growing root-stock, place the cut edge of the rhizome at the edge of the pot and wiggle the rhizome down into the mud to leave the crown just level with the soil line. Mexicana-type, tropical water lily rhizomes, and upright-growing non-rhizomatous marginal plants are wiggled into place in the center of the pot. The wiggling settles mud around the rhizome and/or roots.

3. After the plant is established, as determined by leaf production, gravel or coarse sand topping may be added to the container, if desired. Keep the topping free of the plant's growing point. The plant can then be moved into deeper water.
Photos by H. Nash

Potting Submerged Plants

Submerged plants are typically bunch plants or rooted plants. Examples of bunching plants are anacharis, *Elodea*, and *Cabomba*. Usually sold in bunches of stem cuttings with a lead strip wrapped around the base, they may be simply tossed into the pond and allowed to sink. As long as they sink to the bottom of the pond, they will grow, since they take their nutrients primarily through their leaves. Problems can occur if the plants are not anchored and end up floating at the water's surface. While it may be that the water is too warm at the surface or that too many of the plant's leaves are exposed to the air in floating,

it is just as likely that the strength of the sunlight at the water's surface is harmful to them.

As with any plant, you want to duplicate as closely as possible its growing conditions found in nature. These submerged plants do form roots, even if they are for anchoring the plant beneath the water's surface. While they can be potted, soil is not their primary source of nourishment. They can be potted in pea gravel, for example. Fill a container two-thirds full of gravel and lay the cut stems in the pot. Add more gravel to securely anchor the plants.

Hornwort (*Ceratophyllum*) is the one exception to both the lead-

Since *Elodea* and anacharis use their roots primarily for anchoring, they can be done up in pots of gravel instead of soil.
Photo by Oliver Jackson.

weight and gravel-potting methods. During the growing season, the plant floats just below the water's surface. In winter it settles to lower depths, where it survives in dormancy, often anchoring itself to the bottom. It also returns in spring from tiny tubers that break free from the stem tips in the autumn.

Other submerged plants such as tape grass (*Vallisneria*) or dwarf Sagittaria *(Sagittaria natans)* are shallowly rooting plants that take nutrients from both the soil and the surrounding water. As colonizing plants, they send out short runners to form new plants. *Vallisneria,* particularly the popular shorter form, *V. spiralis,* is sturdy enough to establish itself in the water garden with goldfish. Simply fill a shallow container with your usual aquatic potting soil and tamp a shallow layer of it

Dwarf Sagittaria, *Sagittaria natans, (S. subulata)* can be difficult to start in the presence of fish. Provide protection until the tender plantlets are established. This pond shows the plant growing directly in a 2-inch (5 cm) layer of gravel on the pond bottom. Photo by Ron Everhart.

around the roots. A thin layer of pea gravel, stone, or coarse sand discourages fish from rooting directly into the soil. (Once the plants are established, that layer of

Black predator netting provides an inconspicuous barricade to separate nibbling fish from tasty plants. Photo by H. Nash.

protection can be increased.) Lower them gently into the water. Note that *Vallisneria* appreciates an initial feeding.

Dwarf Sagittaria (*Sagittaria natans*) requires care in planting in the fish-populated water garden. If the plants are mature and are several inches high, the fish are less likely to nibble them away. Newly purchased plants, however, may be tender young plants only a few inches high. Plant them on the surface of a shallow container of soil as you would *Vallisneria,* lightly covering the roots with soil, gravel, or sand. If the pond has fish, provide a fiberglass screen protection over their container, grow them in a netted-off section of the pond, or actually grow

them to mature size in a fish-free container of water. It is not necessary to fertilize these plants, although some growers give them a half dose of fertilizer upon planting to get them off to a fast start. A taste treat for goldfish, *Sagittaria* is often irresistible to koi.

Potting Marginal or Emergent Aquatic Plants

Marginal or emergent aquatic plants typically grow in shallow water an inch or two (2.5 to 5 cm) over their crowns, but may grow with 4 to 6 inches (10 to 15 cm) over their crowns, depending upon species. Generally shallow-rooting plants, the best containers for them are squat and wide-mouthed. Although fresh, heavy topsoil provides enough nutrients to start, it is still recommended to fertilize initially and then regularly throughout the growing season. One tab of regular aquatic plant food or two tabs of time-release food per gallon or two (4 to 8 l) of soil each month keeps them healthy.

Emergent plants are of two basic growing habits: upright or clumping and horizontal. The growing habit determines the method of potting. Most upright emergents grow from short rhizomes which "clump" rather than run, such as bulrush (*Scirpus*) or thalia. Settle the plant in the center of the container with the plant crown at the soil's surface. It is not as important that their pots be wide-mouthed as it is with plants of running growth habits.

Fast-traveling horizontal rhizomes, such as are found in water irises, pickerel, or sweet flags, need as wide a container as possible to contain their vigorous growth. Standard nursery containers are usually "jumped" before the end of the growing season. In the wild, their rhizomes creep along the surface of the soil. To containerize for the water garden, supply fertilizer tabs and fill the pot nearly full with heavy garden soil. Place the rhizome with its cut end up against a side wall of the container. The rhizome should have some anchoring roots extending from it that are covered with well-tamped soil or coarse sand. (Growing points along a rhizome can be encouraged to send out roots by exposing them to water for a few days.) If the rhizome has few anchoring roots, hold it in place with a flat stone. Use an inch of gravel topping to prevent soil disturbance by the fish.

Another form of horizontal growth is a scrambling habit in which plants, although anchored in soil, grow and spread from runners. These are often invasive plants that take over large areas of the water garden. Plants such as floating heart, water snowflake, and water poppy grow in depths of several inches to 2 feet (60 cm) of water. Runners spread rapidly across the surface of the water,

The *Nymphoides* family can blanket a pond with unchecked running growth across the water's surface.
Photo by H. Nash.

anchoring themselves by roots in other pots and producing new plants at their leaves.

Plant them by covering the roots in the center of a shallow container of heavy garden loam prepared with fertilizer tabs in the bottom. Secure the plants with flat rocks or a layer of gravel or coarse sand. Monitor their growth and thin as necessary. Some of these plants, especially the hardy form of floating heart, *Nymphoides peltata*, are especially vigorous and invasive.

Bogbean (*Menyanthes trifolia*) is a scrambling plant that grows in nature along the edges of still waters, especially in true peat bogs. Long runners send out roots to anchor the plant in its travels. If

you purchase the plant by mail order, you will receive long stems with a few growing points from which clean, white roots extend. Simply lay the section across a wide-mouthed, shallow pot of heavy garden soil and anchor the roots into the soil. A flat rock may be needed to hold it in place. Place the pot in very shallow water. The plant may be slow-growing for the first year or so, but once established, it can become quite lush and invasive. Because bogbean is a true bog plant, enriching its potting medium with peat or acidic fertilizer produces lusher and faster growth.

Parrot feather (*Myriophyllum aquatica*) is often classified as a submerged plant or as an "oxygenator." The plant produces two different forms of leaves, one submerged and the other of delicate, ferny rosettes at the water's surface. The submerged leaves, however, are not as efficient as other submerged plants at removing nutrients from the water. A lush and invasive plant of bright green, it can become so invasive in the wild as to be considered a weed. Because the submerged leaves access nutrients directly from the water, it is not necessary to plant it in soil. It can be anchored in pots of pea gravel or heavy garden soil as you would bogbean or other running plants. Pieces allowed to float free in the pond usually find a pot in which to anchor themselves. Like the stems of water lilies, the plant will grow to the water's surface. It can be placed with only a few inches of water over the top of the pot or in depths up to 12 inches (30 cm). Likewise, it can be tucked between rocks in a stream or waterfall and is a perfect candidate for the burrito planting method illustrated earlier in this chapter.

GENERAL MAINTENANCE OF POTTED AQUATIC PLANTS

1. Fertilize monthly according to the directions of your aquatic plant fertilizer. Use one tab per gallon (4 l) of soil of standard fertilizer or two tabs per gallon (4 l) of soil of time-release fertilizer. Push the tabs into the soil with your finger to a depth about 3 in. (7.5 cm) from the plant's crown. If the soil is compacted or filled with plant roots, use a wooden dowel or broomstick to poke the hole. Insert the tablet and cover it with soil to prevent it from leaching into the water. Most aquatic plants require only monthly feedings, but some flowering tropical plants may be fed every two to three weeks during their growing season.

2. Prune away dying foliage and spent flowers to keep the plants looking their best and to avoid adding decomposing organic matter to the pond.

3. Check for insects and disease periodically and treat as necessary.

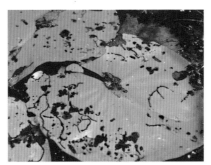
Summer maintenance involves pruning yellowing leaves from your plants and inspecting them for insect attacks. Photo by H. Nash.

If the plants are kept pruned regularly, you will notice problems when they first appear and can be easily controlled. If you must use soaps or chemical treatments, remove the plants from the pond to a separate treatment container to avoid endangering your fish. (See Chapter 10 for specific pests, diseases, and controls.)

Wintering Aquatic Plants

WATER LILIES

Move **hardy water lilies** to the deepest, ice-free portion of the pond. In Zone 5 or colder, water lilies that have mexicana parents should be removed from the pond and stored in their pots of soil in airtight plastic bags in a cool but non-freezing place. Check them occasionally to be sure they do not dry out. Hardy lilies grown in shallow ponds or tub gardens that might freeze should be stored in

the same manner. You can also hose away the soil and wrap the rhizomes in living sphagnum moss. Enclose the wrapped plant within an airtight plastic bag and store in a cool, non-freezing place. (Living sphagnum moss seems to prevent mildew and fungal rotting.)

Cold-zone ponds benefit from being covered for the duration of the winter with plastic tents. Photo by Ron Everhart.

Tropical water lilies can be left in the pond in Zone 10. In Zone 9, many can also be left in the pond, particularly blue and viviparous varieties, although they may have to brought inside or be covered temporarily in plastic tents for the occasional cold night. In Zones 8 and colder, remove tropical lilies from the pond before the first hard frost signals it is time to die. Tropical water lilies can be wintered in several ways:

1. Move the tropical water lilies into a greenhouse pond in full sun. Since growth will be slower than in the summer months, do not feed them. Once the water

Larger ponds, such as the Styler pond in Colorado, make use of PVC-formed tent structures to protect pond plants and fish. Photo by Nancy Styler.

MARGINAL AQUATIC PLANTS

Hardy marginal aquatics are trimmed back an inch or two (2.5 to 5 cm) above the water line to prevent their rotting in the water. Some gardeners do not trim them back until spring, although this leaves dried foliage in which insects may overwinter. Simply leave the pots in the usual place in the pond for the winter. Semi-hardy plants in your zone can often be moved to the deepest non-freezing part of the pond along with the hardy water lilies. Do not prune back these plants until you have brought them back up to shallow waters in the spring.

Tropical marginal plants can usually be wintered indoors as houseplants. Bring them inside

temperature outside has stabilized above 70° F (21° C), repot them and return them to the pond.

2. Remove the potted plant from the pond after the second frost. (This allows the developing tubers to "harden" in anticipation of winter dormancy.) Hose the soil from its tuber and allow it to air-dry for two days. Remove any remaining soil and root fragments as you separate the mother tuber from the smaller attached tubers before storing them in jars of distilled water at a temperature of 50–55° F (10–12° C). Repot them in the spring in small pots about four weeks before the pond water temperature is likely to stabilize above 70° F (21° C). Prior to repotting, you may wish to treat them with an anti-bacterial, an anti-viral, and a fungicide, such as Phy-San. Grow them in a sunny,

well-lighted location in warm water. (Use an aquarium heater to maintain the temperature, if necessary. See the end of this chapter for growing under artificial lights.) Transplant to summer-sized pots as growth requires and return them to the pond when the water is warm enough.

3. Follow the procedure above, but store the tubers in airtight plastic bags of damp, but not wet, sand. Store in a cool, dark place at 50–55° F (10–12° C) Some water gardeners report success with storing the bagged tubers in the refrigerator door or vegetable crisper, although this is somewhat colder than their preferred winter storage temperature.

Deep-dish plastic saucers maintain the water level for marginal aquatics kept outside the pond or wintered indoors. Photo by Oliver Jackson.

before the first frost sends them into dormancy. Set them in a saucer of water in a well-lighted window. Do not feed, as they require a period of rest. Since most tropical plants are "day-dependent," they are assured a healthy wintering with supplemental lighting to give them 10–12 hours of light. If they are set in a sunny window, you may only need to supply additional light for a few hours in the early morning and a few more in the late afternoon and early evening. Running the lights on an automatic timer makes this an easy chore. (See the end of this chapter for more information about indoor lighting.)

SUBMERGED PLANTS

Hardy submerged plants such as *Elodea* and anacharis, as well as parrot feather, can be safely wintered below the ice level in the pond. If the plants have growth extending up into the possible freeze zone of the pond, prune them back in the fall to an ice-free height. Although parrot feather is reputed to be frost-tender, it is known to winter over in nothing more than mud in Zone 5. When in doubt or if the plants are grown in shallow ponds or aboveground ponds, winter a sample in a lighted aquarium.

Tender or tropical submerged plants can be wintered outdoors in Zones 9 and 10. In temperate-zone ponds, winter samples of the plants indoors in lighted aquariums.

FLOATING PLANTS

Tropical floating plants such as water hyacinth and water lettuce are frost-tender. Water lettuce, especially, burns and begins to rot with frost exposure. Most water

Tropical aquatics can be wintered in ponds set up inside a greenhouse or sunroom. Photo by H. Nash.

gardeners grow these plants as annuals, although they may be wintered over indoors or in greenhouses. Basic indoor wintering requirements are water temperatures over 60° F (15° C), preferably into the 70s F (21–26° C). They also need 10–12 hours of light per day. Some gardeners in zones as cold as Zone 5 have successfully wintered water hyacinth in outside containers supplied with heaters and enclosed within polyhouses. Others report winter-

ing hyacinths successfully in small containers, enriched with liquid fertilizer, and under 10–12 hours of light. Adding soil to their containers increases the rate of success. Water lettuce is particularly difficult to winter over indoors.

Since these tropical floating plants are inexpensive to replace, most water gardeners simply discard them after the first frost. Allowing them to rot in the pond can foul the water and contribute to the generation of fish-toxic gases within the winter pond.

The Hanging Basket Method of Wintering Tropical Aquatic Plants

Often used by aquatic plant nurseries, the hanging basket method of wintering certain tropical plants makes creative and aesthetic use of indoor space. Lerio Corporation now makes a hanging basket planter without holes, although you can also line a regular hanging basket with plastic to make it watertight.

With the plant potted in the container, the soil should be kept approximately 2–3 in. (5–7.5 cm) deep to allow enough containment of water. Hang the basket in a sunny window or in a greenhouse or sunroom.

Plants to winter over in a hanging basket include parrot feather (*Myriophyllum aquatica*), *Neptunia aquatica*, *Bacopa*, and water poppy (*Hydrocleys*).

Watertight hanging baskets provide a space-saving way to winter tropical plants indoors.
Photo by H. Nash.

Wintering Plants Indoors

Before you consider wintering a tropical plant indoors, be sure the plant will continue to grow. Allowing the plant to be touched by frost and temperatures in that low range signals the plant that life is ending. The plant shuts down. Even ideal growing conditions following exposure to autumn's cold temperatures may not convince the plant to change its mind. Always bring your tropicals indoors *before* temperatures push them into irreversible shutdown. Water gardeners with fish switch to high carbohydrate foods and fewer feedings when water temperatures hover around 50° F (10° C); coordinate your pond-

keeping efforts and bring in your tropicals then, while they are still healthy and growing.

Northern gardeners who bring tropical plants indoors must be prepared to maintain the plants for several months. Without an elaborate lighting or greenhouse setup, the primary goal is to keep the plants alive and in good enough health to resume active growth outdoors the following season. Fortunately, even tropical plants experience a period of slowed growth during the winter season. Withholding fertilizer during this time allows the plants to "rest."

Growing Plants Indoors with Artificial Lights

The two primary factors to consider in growing plants indoors are light intensity and light duration or day length. Horticulturally, light intensity may be referred to as a measurement of foot-candles—the illumination of a surface one foot (30 cm) from the light of a standard candle. (A comfortable light for reading is 50 foot-candles and a bright summer day yields about 10,000 foot-candles.) This system of measurement has been replaced by the metric lux. Serious artificial-light gardeners may wish to fully explore these measurements, but most of us wish only to know how to keep the plants going. The critical consideration is to provide enough light so that the plant maintains

its green leaves. If the plant's leaves begin to yellow and the stems turn weak and spindly, we know that insufficient light is forcing the plant to burn its stored food. Plants thrown into such stress need more light.

Where do we put our tropical plants indoors? By a sunny window! South-facing windows offer the brightest and longest duration of light in northern latitudes. East- and west-facing windows provide an intermediate amount of light,

Most tropical aquatic plants can be kept indoors near south-facing windows. Photo by H. Nash.

although in the western U.S. west-facing windows are comparable to south-facing windows. North-facing windows receive no direct light. Factors such as overhanging eaves, buildings or fences, shrubs or trees, curtains, and tinted windows can affect or block light. As a general rule, flowering tropical plants require bright light. Place them no farther than 3 ft. (1 m) from a southern window or 2 ft. (60 cm) from an east or west window. The more light they receive, the healthier they remain.

The other part of the equation is duration of light. Plants growing happily during the summer in northern latitudes experience as much as 15 hours of daylight. In the depth of winter, daylight may be reduced to only nine hours. Even constantly sunny days cannot compensate for those lost hours. Casual experiments growing tropicals indoors in sunny windows with no supplemental lighting have resulted in acceptable plant maintenance until only January or February. To get them the rest of the way through the winter, we need to extend the available daylight with artificial lights.

The Makeup of Light

Light energy is divided into wavelengths with only three—ultraviolet, visible, and infrared rays (heat)—contained in solar radiation and of significance to plant growth. Ultraviolet light is not necessary for plant growth. Infrared waves transmit heat necessary for plant growth, but that is not necessarily supplied by a light fixture. Only visible light is necessary for plants, and not all visible light is necessary. Light in the orange-red and blue-violet portions of the spectrum are the most important for plant growth. Both of these ranges are used in the plant's production of food (photosynthesis).

Types of Artificial Lights

Incandescent lights, the lightbulbs used in household lighting fixtures, emit light in wavelengths of orange-red but low in blue-violet. Plants grown exclusively under these lights are pale, thin, stringy, and lanky. (The plants are consuming their stored carbohydrates and burning themselves out.) These lights also produce considerable heat that can burn plants grown too closely to them.

Fluorescent lights are long tubes coated with phosphorescent material. Electricity flows from the electrodes at each end and reacts with mercury to stimulate the phosphorescent coating to give off light. Giving off almost no heat and producing up to five times as much light from the same wattage, fluorescents are less expensive to operate and have a longer life than incandescent lights. Available in various types, cool white is used most often for growing foliage plants. Since they are low in the orange-red range of the spectrum, combine cool white fluorescents with incandescents.

Special plant lights provide light in both blue-violet and orange-red wavelengths. More expensive than fluorescents, they are acceptable for small setups. If you require a larger setup, combinations of household tubes can be used to supply both essential wavelengths.

WAVELENGTH EMISSIONS OF HOUSEHOLD-TYPE FLUORESCENT TUBES

Tube Type	Blue-violet	Orange-red
Cool white	Good	Poor
Cool white deluxe	Good	Fair
Warm white	Fair	Poor
Warm white deluxe	Good	Fair
Daylight	Excellent	Poor
Natural white	Good	Fair
Soft white	Fair	Fair

Setting Up Supplemental Lighting

Experienced light gardeners commonly use at least two and usually four light tubes placed side by side. Generally, tubes of 40 watts or more are best, placed not more than 3 in. (7.5 cm) apart. A homemade fixture can be created with a shop light fixture containing two tubes and a built-in reflector. Mount the fixture on a metal stand or in a shelving unit and use a lamp timer to regulate operation.

Growing Plants under Lights

Both the distance from the tubes where the plants are grown and the number of hours per day the lights are used determine the success of your efforts. For 40-watt household tubes, blooming plants should be about 2 in. (5 cm) from the bulbs. With higher-wattage bulbs, the distance can be increased up to 6 in. (15 cm). Since fluorescent lights do not give off heat, you need not worry about heat damage to the plants. Foliage plants can be grown as much as 2 ft. (60 cm) from the lights.

Since most tropical plants are day-dependent, leave the lights on 12–16 hours per day. If you are growing the plants in a sunny, southern-exposure window, you may wish to run the lights a few extra hours before the sun hits them in the morning and for a few extra hours after the sun has

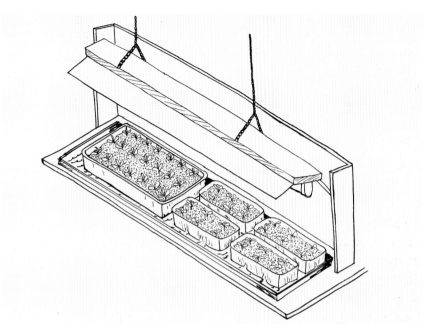

Suspend fluorescent lights very close to the plants or seedlings you grow indoors. Foliage plants may be up to 2 ft. (60 cm) from the lights. Be sure your supplemental lights supply both the orange-red and blue-violet ranges of light. Leave the lights on 12-16 hours per day.

left them in the late afternoon and evening. Automatic timers make this easy to do.

Maintaining Fluorescent Lights

Fluorescent lights lose intensity slowly over their lifetime of 12,000 or more hours. After the tubes have reached 75% of their life, their intensity has decreased by 15 to 20%. If you replace them before they have lost too much intensity, you can avoid shocking the plants with sudden intensity increases upon replacement. Bulbs should be replaced every 3 to 4 months. Plants brought in during October may require one replacement in January.

Returning the Indoor-Wintered Plants to the Pond

Abruptly moving the indoor-wintered plants back outside to increased light intensity can result in the leaf surfaces burning. Since sunburned leaves do not heal, you must remove them. To avoid losing the carefully maintained growth of the winter months, first move the plants to a sheltered outdoor location where they are protected from winds and midday sun. After a week they can be returned to the pond. Tropicals should not be set out in the pond until the water temperature has reached 70° F (21° C).

PROPAGATION

VEGETATIVE PROPAGATION

Aquatic plants are typically vigorous growers, if only because they are an all-or-nothing–type plant. With an adequate source of nutrients and light, the third requirement of growing plants—water—is not a factor. It is either present in the pond, or the pond is not a pond. Because these plants flourish in their unique environment, the hobbyist's most common way to increase their number or propagate is plant division. In its most basic form, division simply requires sectioning the plant into rooted pieces and repotting. The plant's roots are hosed clean of soil to determine points of division that include growing points or growing eyes along with supportive root growth.

Akin to division is separation, which involves separating bulbs or corms from the mother plant. The most obvious example of this propagation method is with tropical water lilies.

Plant division is vegetative propagation. Other means of vegetative propagation are stem, leaf, leaf-bud, or root cuttings. These

Outdoor propagation ponds may be in-ground with the propagation accomplished in individual containers or in a bed of soil. Shown here are earthen propagation beds at Perry's Water Gardens in Franklin, North Carolina.
Photo by Perry D. Slocum.

Above: Propagation involves both increasing the number of plants and creating new plants. This unnamed beauty was listed only as FTL 797 at the IWLS Water Lily Trials in 1997 at the Denver Botanic Garden. Photo by H. Nash.

other methods are performed in the same manner as with terrestrial plants, but they are not used much with aquatic plants since division and separation are so much easier to perform.

PICKEREL PROPAGATION

1. Using the Davis Creek Nursery speed-plug method of propagation, excess roots of *Pontederia* (pickerel weed) are trimmed away.
Photo by H. Nash.

2 The pruned pickerel division is ready for planting. Photo by H. Nash.

3. With very shallow water covering the top of the pots, the trimmed plant division is wiggled into the soil. Photo by H. Nash.

4. Note that the pickerel division is planted with the cut end of the rhizome near the edge of the pot to allow maximum growing room.
Photo by H. Nash.

Vegetative Propagation of Hardy Water Lilies

As discussed in Chapter Two, hardy water lily rhizomes are of four basic types: marliac, odorata, tuberosa, and mexicana. All these rhizomes produce growing eyes or growing points of some form, whether very nubby as on the marliacs or odoratas or as brittle appendages on the tuberosas. The mexicana rootstock produces tubers like bulbs or corms at the base or even embedded within the mother plant. When a potted water lily is divided in its second season, many of these growing points will be developed enough to produce blooms. Only a 2–inch (5 cm) section of rhizome with a

Along the living portion of a water lily rhizome, growing "eyes" produce growth that may be severed and potted in small containers for propagation. If the growing eyes have produced enough growth, they may be snapped free of the mother rhizome; otherwise, they must be cut off. Photo by Ron Everhart.

growing tip can be potted individually. Smaller eyes may be cut from the rhizome, especially if they are producing some roots, and potted into 4-inch (10 cm) pots and grown to flowering size. While cultivars vary in their degree of growing-eye production, odorata and tuberosa rhizomes typically produce the most propagative growth.

Understanding how a rhizome produces its propagative growth enables you to produce more plants than would normally occur. At the beginning of the growing season, the plant's energy is focused on the existing growing points. Think in terms of the plant sending a chemical message to grow to its growing points. As the season progresses, and especially toward the latter half of the season, the plant generates propagative growth as a survival mechanism. This is a stressful period for

the plant. By increasing the stress level of the plant, it can be forced to produce even more reproductive growth.

Commercial growers create stress in these plants by exposing the top portion of the rhizome to the water or air, crowding the plant, and decreasing the water depth in which it grows. Kirk Strawn notes that hardy rhizomes grown in earth-bottom ponds can be forced to produce more growing eyes along the rhizome by severing the growing tip from the rhizome. The growing tip need not be removed from the pond; simply interrupt the message to grow. In fact, each scaled-appearing section on a living rhizome has the potential to produce a growing eye or plant division. (This method also stimulates production in pickerel, Louisiana iris, and sweet flag.)

Even greater production of growing points results by "wounding" the rhizome. This technique involves scoring the rhizome, much like slashing a hot dog for broiling. Do not cut all the way through the rhizome; simply wound it in various places.

Pot the growing-eye divisions with enough time left in the growing season for the plants to establish healthy root systems prior to winter dormancy. Winter the young plants along with your other water lilies. Move them close to the water's surface in the spring for faster resumption of growth.

Vegetative Propagation of Tropical Water Lilies

Dr. Kirk Strawn recommends starving most day-blooming tropicals in a gallon (4 l) or smaller container to produce overwintering tubers. He explains "starving" as feeding the plant upon initial planting and perhaps only the first month or so of growth. Use a container with no holes to prevent the roots from escaping the pot and seeking nourishment elsewhere.

If you are propagating from the tubers produced before autumn, remove the plant from its pot and hose away the soil. Firm tubers will be found around the bottom of the mother tuber. Rinse them clean and store them through the winter in barely damp sand or in distilled water at 50 to 60° F (10 to 15° C).

If you are starting out in the spring and plan to propagate from your mother tuber, plant your overwintered tubers in one-gallon (4 l) containers with no drainage holes. Fill each pot with loamy soil covered with about an inch (2.5 cm) of sand. The top of the upright tuber is set at the bottom level of the sand. If you cannot tell which end of the tuber is the top, plant it on its side. Two or three crops of little plants will be produced in one growing season.

When the first crop has two or three surface leaves, rinse away the soil and repot the small tubers in small pots submerged in shallow water. Another crop may be harvested during the season, or you can leave it attached to the mother plant until you lift the plants for wintering in the fall. Because harvesting the small tubers weakens the mother plant, you may wish to leave the second or third "crop" attached to nourish it back to vigor before winter. (See Chapter Two for winter storage of tropical water lily tubers.)

Follow the same procedure with tropical night bloomers, although note that the tubers produced by the mother plant are found embedded in the mother plant's rhizome.

Viviparous Propagation of Water Lilies

Characteristic of some day-blooming tropical water lilies is viviparous reproduction—the production of tiny plant clones at the

Some tropical water lily leaves produce tiny plantlets. This reproduction is known as viviparity. Photo by Perry D. Slocum.

Viviparous leaves accept water onto the leaf at the leaf's sinus, where developing nodules grow into tiny plantlets. Photo by H. Nash.

Nymphaea **'Colonel A.J. Welch' is one of the few hardy water lilies that reproduces viviparously. Plantlets form from spent flowers.** Photo by H. Nash.

center connecting point of the two lobes of a leaf (at the leaf's sinus). Some plants, such as *N.* 'Dauben' produce these tiny clones on every leaf. The tropical species *N. lotus* and some of its progeny occasionally reproduce viviparously from the flower. *N.* 'Colonel A.J. Welch' is the first hardy water lily known to reproduce in this manner, forming clones from spent flowers rather than from the leaves. Perry D. Slocum has used this plant as a parent in some hybridization efforts and developed some varieties of hardy water lilies that

Once the plantlet has grown roots, it can be potted in its own container as a new plant. Photo by H. Nash.

occasionally, perhaps five percent of the time, reproduce viviparously at spent flowers.

The tiny viviparous plantlets produce miniature leaves and some roots, but they do not display much growth until the parent leaf begins to yellow and die. Remove the tiny plantlets once you notice root growth. Pot them in small containers and treat as

A surprising viviparous plantlet forms from a flower on Kirk Strawn's recent hybrid, *N.* 'Colorado.' Photo by H. Nash.

any other seedling—place them in shallow water of 2 to 3 inches (5 to 7.5 cm) of water over the soil, protect them from strong direct sunlight, and begin feeding appropriately reduced amounts of fertilizer once mature growth begins.

Water Lilies that Reproduce Viviparously

Note: Viviparous reproduction occurs at the leaves unless otherwise noted.

Tropical Species

N. micrantha

N. lotus (night-bloomer, occasionally from flower)

Day-Blooming Cultivars

N. 'August Koch'
N. 'Bagdad'
N. 'Bluebird'
N. 'Charles Thomas'
N. 'Daubeniana'
N. 'Edward D. Uber'
N. 'Isabella Pring'
N. 'Margaret Mary'
N. 'Mrs. Martin E. Randig'
N. 'Panama Pacific'
N. 'Patricia'
N. 'Paul Stetson'
N. 'Peach Blow'
N. 'Pink Platter'
N. 'Royal Purple'
N. 'Tina'

N. 'Bagdad' is a viviparous tropical water lily. Photo by H. Nash.

Hardy Water Lilies

Note: All are viviparous from flower.

N. 'Colonel A.J. Welch'
N. 'Cherokee'
N. 'Perry's Pink Delight'
N. 'Perry's Red Star'
N. 'Perry's Viviparous Pink'

Propagating Lotuses

Vegetative propagation is the most common and efficient way to obtain more of these plants. Lotus tubers attain significant growth during a single season. Lift the tubers after the plant has died back in the autumn and store them in a cool, non-freezing location until late spring. Storing them wrapped in living sphagnum peat moss helps prevent mildew and rotting. Since lotuses do not transplant well, they are best divided during their dormant period. In the spring, cut the tubers into sections of at least one growing eye per section of tuber.

CROSS SECTION OF LOTUS

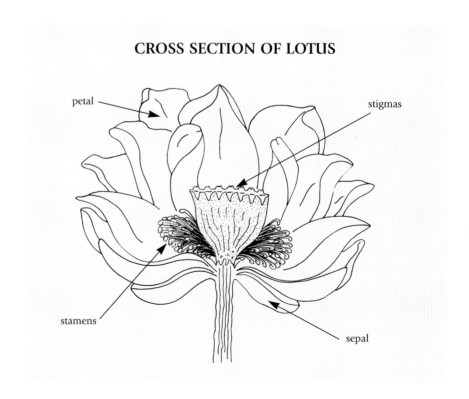

petal
stigmas
stamens
sepal

Mass production of lotuses in containers at Davis Creek Nursery.
Photo by H. Nash.

Vegetative Propagation of Other Aquatic Plants

Golden club, *Orontium aquaticum*, is propagated within individual containers in Davis Creek Nursery's propagation ponds.
Photo by H. Nash.

The *Cyperus* family offers a unique means of propagation besides the usual division of rootstock. In the wild, the plant's moppy heads frequently bend over and touch the water. New plants sprout from the flower heads. You can imitate this propagation by clipping the flowering heads while they are still fresh, with an inch or two (2.5 to 5 cm) of stem attached. The cut flower heads look like fancy parasols. Float them upside down in water. Within a short time, roots are produced and a new plant rises from the floating, upside-down head. Once ample roots are produced, pot up the new plant.

Most other aquatic plants can be propagated vegetatively by simple division. With the soil hosed from the roots, you can see what kind of roots you must divide. Often the plants will have a great quantity of fibrous roots filling out the container. As you hose away the soil, the bottom half of that fibrous mass can be pulled free and discarded to reveal the primary rootstock or rhizome. Clump roots are cut into squares.

As these containers of phragmites fill out, the plants can be divided and repotted for further propagation. Photo by H. Nash.

Rhizomes are cut into sections that each contain a growing tip and a supply of roots. The following drawings illustrate the rootstocks of various aquatic plants that you can propagate vegetatively.

Water mint, *Mentha aquatica*, **is propagated within holeless containers much like the self-contained lotus containers.**
Photo by H. Nash.

Nature's own method of propagation (the flower heads drooping into the water for viviparous reproduction) is duplicated by cutting the flower heads from members of the *Cyperus* **family and floating them upside down in water. Roots begin to grow and new plant shoots arise from the dying flower head.**   Photo by H. Nash.

Vegetative Propagation of Various Marginal or Emergent Aquatic Plants

▲ Arrowhead (*Sagittaria spp.*) May be divided; however, in the spring you may also find tubers growing at root ends. These tubers, which waterfowl devour, have earned the plant the common name of "duck potato." Plant the tubers in an inch of mud.

▲ *Eichinodorus* 'Marble Queen' forms divisible clumps within its pot. Propagate also from the viviparous plantlets that form at some stem tips.

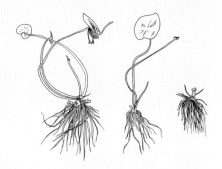

▲ Floating hearts and snowflakes (*Nymphoides spp.*) Can be divided vegetatively or started from viviparous plantlets that form on the floating leaves.

▲ Upon removing a taro (*Colocasia*) plant from its container, you may be presented with plantlets forming from the tip of the roots.

▲ Red-stemmed thalia, *Thalia geniculata*, grows through a thick mat of fibrous roots that form at the soil's surface. Hose the soil from the rhizome to reveal the knobby rhizomatous growth that can be divided.

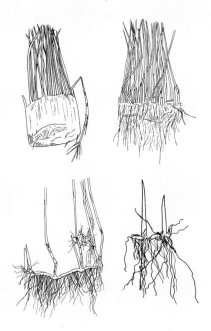

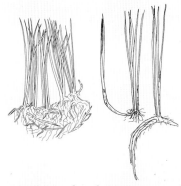

▲ Variegated rush, **Baumea,** and cattails, **Typha** spp., grow from horizontally spreading rhizomes that often circle the upper level of a container. Pull away excess fibrous roots to reveal divisible rhizome sections.

▲ Divide the **Thalia** rhizome into plants with both rhizomatous and leafy growth.

▲ Dwarf bamboo (**Dulichium**) produces dense, clumping growth.

1. Washing away the soil reveals fibrous roots that barely conceal the horizontally growing rhizome.

2. Pull away the fibrous mat to bare the rhizome.

3. Cut the rhizome into rooted sections and repot.

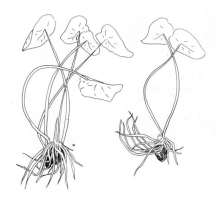

▲ Tropical day-blooming water lilies form tubers near the base of the mother plant. Separate and repot the new growing tubers in their own containers.

▲ Corkscrew rush (**Scirpus spiralis**) appears to grow from a tangled clump. Washing away the soil reveals a horizontally growing rhizome with many growing shoots along it. Cut rooted segments for propagation.

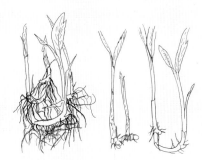

▲ **1. Canna** grows from thick, white, branching rhizomes.

2. Cut the rhizome into sections containing two or more growing tips.

PROPAGATING BY SEED

Even though vegetative division or separation is the easiest and quickest way to increase your bounty of aquatic plants, you may wish to try growing some by seed. With seed propagation, the backyard gardener discovers the means to create new hybrids or cultivars. If only for your own information, keep careful records—note and label seeds collected with the date and identification; record identification and dates of crosses on labels affixed to the seed pods and seeds produced. Make sure your tag identifications are weatherproof! Record data on plastic plant tags with indelible pen. If the tags will be underwater for any length of time, insert the written portion of the tag into the soil to prevent its turning brown and to prevent loss of the information. A diary or notebook keeps all records at your fingertips.

The Parts of a Flower

The flower is the reproductive organ of the plant. The outermost part of the flower, the *sepals*, appear to be an outer ring of petals, often green, that cover the young floral buds. Next come the *petals* of the flower. Often petals are colorful, to attract pollinators such as insects. Next to the petals are the *stamens*, the male reproductive part of the flower. The sta-

mens produce very fine, dustlike particles known as *pollen*. These particles divide to form the sperm cells that fertilize the flower's eggs to produce seeds. The very end of the stamen is made of specialized

The first-day bloom of a water lily presents its sweet nectar to attract insects for pollination.
Photo by Ron Everhart.

With the opening of the water lily bloom on the second day, the stamens enclose the nectar center of the flower. Photo by Ron Everhart.

tissue, the *anther*, that holds the pollen.

The innermost part of the flower holds the female reproductive apparatus, the *pistil*. Located at the tip of the pistil and often covered with a sticky substance to hold the deposited pollen is the

stigma. The stigma is held by a floral tube called the *style*. Deposited pollen from an anther sticks to the tip of the stigma, from where it grows down the style to meet with the eggs stored in the flower's ovary at the base. Within the *ovary* are one to many *ovules* containing *eggs* that can develop into *seeds* upon fertilization.

Pollen can be deposited upon the stigma by insects, wind, or splashing raindrops. Once the pollen's sperm cells have reached the ovules to unite with the eggs (fertilization), the entire flower structure is transformed into a *fruit*. Seeds must mature before removing them from the fruit for storage or planting. In the case of hardy water lilies, the fruit matures underwater. With most marginal or emergent plants, the seeds mature outside water. (Pickerel weed seeds, *Pontederia* spp., however, mature in water.) The natural evolution of the seed determines the method of collection and storage, as well as germination.

Seed Dormancy

Nature provides a slowed or stopped growth period (dormancy) to protect plant species. Seed dormancy may involve hard seed coatings or a chemical dormancy stimulated by water or soil exposure. A built-in dormancy prevents the seed embryo from full development at the time the seed pod

CROSS SECTION OF WATER LILY FLOWER

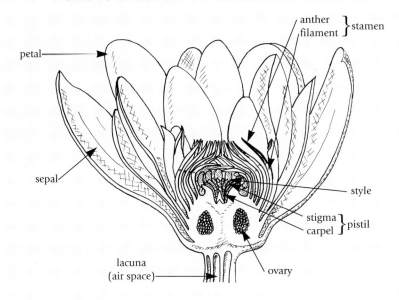

ripens to disperse the seeds. (Tropical species typically feature a functional dormancy requiring an extended period of very warm temperatures for germination to take place.) Most freshly harvested seeds of non-woody plants require either temperature or light for germination. Such seeds require one to three months of chilling to break the dormancy. Chilling the seed is referred to as stratification. Seeds are placed between layers of usually moist sand or soil in boxes and then exposed to chilling temperatures out-of-doors or in refrigerators. The storage temperature is kept comparable to the temperatures experienced by the species during winter and early spring in its native habitat. Commonly this involves temperatures in the 35 to 45° F (2 to 7° C)

range. Light-sensitive germination is required by seeds that are typically very small, such as *Lobelia cardinalis*, cardinal flower.

Refrigerated Stratification

Dry seeds are usually well-soaked in water before refrigerated stratification. (Cardinal flower, *Lobelia cardinalis*, and hibiscus are stratified dry, as are some others.) Seeds without hard seed coats require only 12 to 24 hours of soaking at warm temperatures. If a seed has a hard seed coating, it may require soaking for three to seven days, as well as scarifying. These seeds can be alternately soaked for 12 hours and drained for 12 hours throughout the peri-

od, or you can run water over them.

After soaking, mix the seeds with a moisture-retaining medium such as well-washed sand, peat moss, chopped or screened living sphagnum moss, vermiculite, or composted sawdust. Be sure the medium contains no toxic chemicals. Fresh sawdust, for example, may contain chemical preservatives. Suggested mixtures are one part coarse sand to one part peat or one part perlite to one part peat. These mixes should be moistened and allowed to stand for 24 hours before use. They should be moist, but not so wet that water can be squeezed out by hand.

Stratification involves mixing the seeds with one to three times their volume of planting medium or layering them between layers of the medium in containers such as boxes, cans, or glass jars with perforated lids to allow aeration yet without drying. Storing the seeds in a plastic bag without media is known as naked chilling. If desired, a fungicide may be added to prevent rotting of the seeds.

Stratification temperatures usually range from 32 to 50° F (0 to 10° C). The seeds may sprout prematurely at higher temperatures or be delayed by lower ones. Examine the seeds routinely during the stratification period to be sure they have not dried out. Remoisten the medium as necessary by spraying with a mister.

Most species require stratification from one to four months. Generally, consider the native habitat of the species. If the plant normally grows in a Zone 5, for example, and experiences full seasons, you can expect the stratification period to require an approximately four-month time-frame.

When sprouting begins, the seeds should be either planted or moved to lower storage temperatures to retard germination until you are ready for planting. Remove seeds to be planted from the medium. Avoid injury to the delicate, germinating seeds. One method is to use a screen that allows the medium to pass through and leaves behind the seeds. If you allow the seeds to dry out, they may revert to dormancy or die.

Storing Seeds

Generally, seed is stored in a manner approximating its natural habitat. Short-lived seed, for example, such as wild rice (*Zizania aquatica*), pondweeds, arrowheads, rushes, and hardy water lilies, are stored directly in water. (Recirculating, filtered water is ideal.) If you plan to store the seed over the winter until the next growing season, the seeds are stored in distilled water in glass jars in the non-freezing temperatures of a refrigerator. These seeds may be kept for a year or more. Watch that the water does not sour or turn bad. Seed stored in recirculating, filtered water does not face

this problem. Fouling of the water is more likely with seed collected early in the season and then stored at room temperature indoors before planting in the same season. Likewise, pond water may be subject to contamination. Distilled water is best. Generally, the seeds of tropical species are injured by being chilled below 50° F (10° C).

Seeds of tropical water lilies and most emergent aquatic plants can be stored dry in envelopes or small jars or vials. Baby-food jars are a popular container as are 35 mm film canisters. Before storing seeds, lay them out to dry for two or three days to lessen the chance of mildew or fungal attacks during storage. Store them under the same temperature conditions as listed above for water-storage. The tops of these containers are not perforated.

Scarifying Seed

Seeds possessing a very hard seed coat, such as lotus or canna seeds, should be scarified before attempting to germinate them; use a nail file to scratch the surface of the seed to the inner cream-colored material beneath. Many growers use needle-nosed pliers for this operation. (Nicking too deeply into the living material may kill the seed.) This allows water to access the seed more quickly and ensures germination. Scarifying these seeds greatly shortens the soaking period.

The Stages of Germination

Seed germination, whether of terrestrial or aquatic plants, occurs in three stages. In the first stage, water is absorbed by the seed to soften the seed covering and penetrate to the inner seed tissue. The seed swells and seed coats may break as the growth begins inside. The first visible evidence of germination is the emergence of the radicle, which appears as a thin white "tail" emerging from the seed. If a free-floating water lily seed germinates in water, it is often difficult to distinguish the radicle from the emerging first true leaves. However, the radicle functions as the plant's first root and is planted within the soil, whereas leaves grow above the soil.

During the second stage of seed germination, foods that are stored within the seed are digested and moved to the growing points of the embryo. The seed begins making protein and taking up oxygen to produce plant energy (respiration).

Cell division at both ends of the embryo axis occurs in stage three. One or more seed leaves grow from the "top" of the seed and the radicle grows from the base, or bottom.

▲ Cover planted seeds with plastic wrap to retain necessary moisture.

▲ Seed flats can also be enclosed within a tied plastic bag.

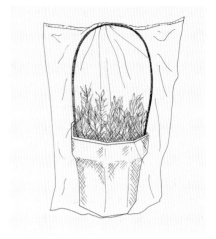

▲ Enclose individual pots in plastic bags and use a bent coat hanger to hold the plastic away from the seedlings.

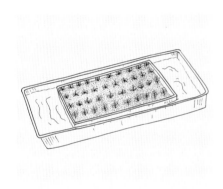

▲ Maintain the moisture level by setting the seedling flat in water halfway up the side of the flat.

▲ Once seedlings have two true leaves, they can be transplanted into individual pots.

▲ Always water seedlings from the bottom. Overhead watering can damage tender stems and leaves as well as making the tiny plants more susceptible to damping-off.

HYBRIDIZING

Hybridizing is the placing of pollen from one plant's flower onto the stigma of another plant's flower to produce seed of a new plant. This is known simply as "crossing." The parent plants may involve two species within the same family, a species and another hybrid, or two hybrids. The crosses must be performed, however, within the same plant family. Just as nature does not allow dogs and cats to interbreed, neither does she allow two plant families, such as water lilies and arrowheads, to interbreed. (In the case of many water lilies, particularly hardy varieties, the capacity to reproduce true to seed is lacking. These varieties must be propagated vegetatively by division. See the first part of this chapter.) Hybrids can occur naturally by wind, insect, or other means, including man. The term "cultivar," however, denotes a hybrid resulting deliberately from human cultivation, the product bearing significant differences from the parents and all other products of the same crossing enough to merit its being given a special name.

Certain basic procedures are recommended if you want to attempt hybridizing. Keep careful records and label all your efforts meticulously. Maintain a clean environment and sterile tools. This is especially important to protect the integrity of your product. Select your parents carefully with an eye towards desirable characteristics you wish to reproduce. Protect your efforts by ensuring that cross-pollination by another plant cannot occur. For example, while you may deliberately introduce the pollen from a selected parent to the stigma of another, your efforts can be ruined by an insect bearing pollen from yet another flower. Questions may arise, too, if the possibility exists of the seed parent self-pollinating.

If the seed parent can self-pollinate, carefully remove the stamens from the seed-parent flower before pollen can be produced to "contaminate" your efforts. Many hybridists also remove the immediate petals surrounding the stamens. The stamens should be removed as late as possible before the anthers erupt and release their pollen. This requires close observa-

tion of your subject plants to familiarize yourself fully with their habits. Use forceps, pointed scissors, or a single-edge razor blade to remove them. Sterilize your tools between uses to avoid transferring unwanted pollen. If you use alcohol for disinfecting, wipe it from the tool or dry it to prevent damage to the stigma.

Pollen can be collected from your selected pollen parent and stored in clean envelopes. This is helpful in case the seed parent is not in bloom or ripe for fertilizing at the time of pollen availability from the other parent. Likewise, as in the case of Louisiana irises which have early, mid-season, and late-blooming varieties, stored pollen allows crossing early-season varieties with late-season varieties.

You will notice that the flower is full of nectar on the first day it opens. The surrounding stamens are erect and allow insects easy access to the nectar. Once the stamens (capillary appendages) turn inward in subsequent days, the time for fertilizing that flower has passed. In water lilies, the seed parent is fertilized on the first-day flower with ripe pollen collected from the anthers of a second-day flower. (Self-pollinating flowers have pollen available on that first day; hence the need to remove the stamens from the seed parent.) Whether you use the entire anther or a soft brush to dust on collected pollen, once the selected pollen has been deposited onto the stigma of the receptive parent, protect

the pollenization by enclosing it within a gauze or muslin bag. Do not use plastic bags to enclose the fertilized flower as they work as a greenhouse and can overheat and cook the developing seeds. George Pring, the renowned hybridizer of Missouri Botanical Garden fame, recommended attaching a string to both the muslin bag and the flower stem to ensure easy location and identification of the developing fruit, since developing seed pods of water lilies are underwater.

Water Lily Hybridization

You know that fertilization in a hardy lily has occurred when the flower stem draws beneath the water's surface in a coiling spiral after the normal bloom period of three to four days. (Unfertilized flowers simply drift downward in the water, their stems remaining straight.) This is nature's way of ensuring the fruit is fully immersed in water to allow its development. Mature seed pods

Label your hybrid crosses on the developing fruit. Photo by Ron Everhart.

A ripe water lily fruit releases its cache of seeds to float upon the water's surface. Photo by Ron Everhart.

float back to the surface to release gelatin-enclosed seeds. Under normal conditions, these seeds float for a brief time, the gelatin dissolves, and the seeds then settle into the water to soil where they can germinate. Since the muslin bag confines the seeds, they can be easily captured and transferred

Shortly after the massed seeds float to the surface, the pod breaks up and the seeds float freely for a brief period before settling down into the water to possibly germinate in the soil below. Photo by Ron Everhart.

into a jar of distilled water. Within a week, the living seeds settle to the bottom of the jar. Those left floating are not viable. It is better to discard them than risk their rotting and fouling the storage water.

Challenges with Hybridizing Water Lilies

Flowers produced early in the season may not produce living seeds. Particularly with hardy water lilies, it seems that fertile flowers are produced later in the season as the plant approaches its natural dormancy period and goes all out to protect its future.

Another problem with hybridizing hardy water lilies is that many existing hybrids we might select as seed or pollen parents are not capable of producing fertile seed. Many of the familiar, standard hardy water lilies are the result of efforts by Joseph Bory-Latour Marliac, a French hybridizer of the late 19th century. Marliac furiously protected the parentage of his cultivars, as well as his methods of producing them. Most of Marliac's hybrids are sterile plants. N. 'Rembrandt,' however, does produce fertile seed. Odorata- and tuberosa-rhizomed plants lend themselves to hybridization efforts, as does the half-hardy species N. mexicana. (Consult the chart on page 53 for a list of known fertile parents.)

The true test of a hybrid water lily is whether it can be reproduced vegetatively. Using the tiny

species N. tetragona, for example, which does not reproduce vegetatively but only by seed, to produce a dwarf or pygmy variety often results in a rhizome that does not produce eyes to allow vegetative propagation. The "hybrid" is then lost if it cannot produce true to seed or if it dies.

If you hybridize water lilies, remember that most seedlings produced will be inferior to existing varieties. Often, the first gener-

Nymphaea 'Deva' is a Michael Duff hybrid produced with N. tetragona parents. Michael had to wait until the second year to determine if the new cultivar could be reproduced vegetatively. It cannot, but it does reproduce true from seed. It was shown at the Denver Botanic Garden's Water Lily Trials at the 1997 International Water Lily Society's symposium as a rare, dwarf, white cultivar.
Photo by H. Nash.

ation seedlings are crossed back with desirable parents to produce a second generation or more before a significant cultivar results. Ideally, a new hybrid or cultivar should be superior to its parents to be considered worth keeping and propagating. Confine your efforts to plants within the same species. Although Perry D. Slocum reports success in crossing a tropical and a hardy water lily, this is generally accepted as difficult or nonproductive. For the best hope of success, cross hardies with hardies, day-blooming tropicals with each other, and night-blooming tropicals with each other.

Over 50 years ago the Missouri Botanical Garden published an article, "Learning from the Bees," written by Edgar Anderson about George Pring, said to be the father of tropical water lily hybridization. (This article was reprinted in the December 1996 issue of *Water Gardening* magazine.) The article discussed Pring's efforts and methods of hybridizing with a breakthrough gained by observing the

Tiny bees are attracted to the sweet nectar of a first-day water lily bloom. Carrying pollen from other flowers, they provide the means for fertilization. After the flower's stamens have closed over the nectar, the bees still visit, picking up pollen that they deliver to other first-day flowers that are ready to be pollinated. Flower shown is *N. 'Bob Trickett' (George Pring)*. Photo by H. Nash.

Nymphaea **'Bill Yohn' was produced by William Frase by crossing *N. ampla* with *N.* 'Director George T. Moore.' Bill Yohn was a childhood friend of Mr. Frase.** Photo by Perry D. Slocum.

The same principles of hybridization are used with lotuses as well. Photo by Perry D. Slocum.

Kenneth Landon named his hybrid crossing of *Nymphaea flavorvirens* and *N.* 'St. Louis Gold' in honor of his mother, *N.* 'Ineta Ruth.' Photo by Kenneth Landon.

N. 'Helen Nash' was hybridized by Leeann Connelly of Tropical Pond and Garden in Florida. Photo by H. Nash.

tiny bees that visited the fragrant blooms early in the day. Until that point, Pring had hybridized, with inconsistent results, according to his own available time. He then tried to replicate what he saw in nature and gained increased productivity of fertile seeds. Many of his beautiful hybrids are fertile and have served as the parents of other more recent hybrids. Kenneth Landon in Texas, for example, frequently crosses a Pring cultivar with a species tropical lily. His seven-year efforts at crossing *Nymphaea flavovirens* as the seed parent with Pring's *N.* 'St. Louis Gold' as the pollen parent produced the unique tropical yellow star water lily *N.* 'Ineta Ruth,' named in honor of his mother. William Frase of Orlando, Florida, a water lily hobbyist for over 50 years, has hybridized tropical water lilies and named them in honor of dear friends and family members.

N. mexicana has been used as the pollen parent in several cultivars. Shown above, N. mexicana var. canaveralensis. Photo by Perry D. Slocum.

N. 'H.C. Haarstick' has been used as the pod parent of several night-blooming cultivars. Photo by Perry D. Slocum.

Hardy Water Lily Pod or Seed Parents

N. alba, N. alba var. rubra, N. 'Colonel A.J. Welch,' N. tuberosa, N. 'Virginalis,' N. tetragona (does not normally produce eyed-rhizomes), N. 'Escarboucle', N. odorata, N. odorata var. gigantea, N. 'Pink Opal', N. 'Vesuve', N. 'Perry's Pink', N. 'Gloire du Temple sur Lot,' N. tuberosa 'Richardsonii', N. 'Charles de Meurville', N. 'Rose Arey', N. 'Pink Starlet', N. 'Sulphurea Grandiflora' aka 'Sunrise', N. 'Texas Dawn'.

Hardy Water Lily Pollen Parents

N. mexicana, N. 'Aurora,' N. 'Sulphurea Grandiflora, aka Sunrise' N. alba var. rubra, N. 'Mrs. C.W. Thomas,' N. 'Splendida,' N. 'American Star,' N. 'Vesuve,' N. 'Perry's Super Red,' N. 'Atropur-purea,' N. 'Pearl of the Pool,' N. 'Charles de Meurville ,' N. 'Colonel A.J. Welch,' N. 'Gloire du Temple sur Lot,' N. 'Escarboucle,' N. 'Gladstoniana'.

Day-Blooming Tropical Pod or Seed Parents

N. colorata, N. 'Judge Hitchcock,' N. 'Blue Beauty,' N. 'Pink Platter,' N. ampla, N. caerulea, N. 'Castaliflora,' N. elegans, N. sulfurea.

Day-Blooming Tropical Pollen Parents

N. 'Mrs. Martin E. Randig,' N. 'Pamela,' N. 'William Stone,' N. colorata, N. 'Mrs. Woodrow Wilson,' N. 'St. Louis,' N. 'Director George T. Moore,' N. capensis var. Zanzibariensis, N. 'Mrs. Edwards Whitaker,' N. 'Castaliflora,' N. 'St. Louis Gold,' N. 'Pamela Pacific,' N. African Gold'.

Night-Blooming Tropical Pod or Seed Parents

N. 'H.C. Haarstick', N. 'Wood's White Knight,' N. 'C.E. Hutchings,' N. 'Mrs. George C. Hitchcock,' N. 'Red Flare,' N. 'Sir Galahad'.

Night-Blooming Tropical Pollen Parents

N. 'Emily Grant Hutchings,' N. 'Red Flare,' N. 'J. Sturtevantii,' N. 'Missouri'.

Planting Water Lily Seeds

Whether you have collected your water lily seeds from muslin bags provided for their containment or you have retrieved a fertilized pod approximately 10 days after its submersion to allow its final maturation in a container of distilled water, you can plant the seed at any time following its release from the fruit. If you plant seeds fresh, do not attempt to remove the gelatin coating.

Use shallow seed pans or margarine tubs filled with good garden soil. Spread the jellied seed or individual seed evenly across the surface of the planting medium. Lightly sprinkle sand over the seeds and gently water them in. Place the containers in an aquarium or bowl of water with no more than 2–3 inches (5–7.5 cm) of water over the soil's surface. Set them up in a well-lit, warm location. Bear in mind that in nature seedlings usually germinate beneath the protection of the mother plant's leaves overhead. Strong, direct sunlight can prove harmful, particularly in southern regions.

After three or four weeks, the first seedlings appear. You can almost see through the elongated, lance-shaped first leaves. When these first two or three leaves reach the water's surface, the plants may be pricked out in clumps, gently washed free of soil, and teased apart with toothpicks. Plant the tiny seedlings individually in small pots or margarine tubs and immerse them with 2–4 inches (5–10 cm) of water over the soil's surface. (Enhance your standard aquatic potting mix with a sprinkling of sterilized bone meal and aquatic plant fertilizer only in the bottom half of the container. Normal monthly feedings are not necessary.) It may take six months before the plants attain enough size to be planted in larger containers and moved into the water garden.

If you store your water lily seeds in a jar of water, you may be surprised by their speedy germination. Tease the plants apart and plant them two or three to a small butter tub or pot as described above. This situation presents you with the problem of determining which fragile stems coming from the seed are leaf-bearers and which is the radicle. The radicle should be covered by soil or sand since it is the first root of the tiny plant. The leaves should be left free of soil. If you place the tiny plant upon the soil surface, gently separate the fragile stems with a toothpick and determine which is the radicle. A drop of water from a pencil tip anchors the radicle to the soil so that you can sprinkle a fine layer of sand over it. Place the potted seedlings in very shallow water over their soil level in a brightly lit location. No fertilizing of seedlings is necessary beyond a sprinkling of fertilizer in the bottom layer of the container's soil.

As the young plants grow, watch them for growth of filamentous or string algae, which can easily strangle and kill them. Gently prick the algae away from the seedlings and twirl it around a toothpick. Even a dilute solution of algicide can kill the tender seedlings. Once the plants are several months old and attaining more mature growth, supply regular feedings of appropriately diluted or minimized fertilizer in accordance with the amount of soil in their containers.

Propagating Lotuses by Seed

Lotuses produce attractive seed heads that are often dried for winter floral arrangements. Seeds may still be confined within the dried seed head, protected by a hard seed coat that allows them to remain viable for many years. Tim Jennings, curator of aquatic plants at Longwood Gardens in

The center of a lotus flower bears a pod containing several seeds. After the pod has matured and turned brown, the seeds shrink within their pockets. Some may fall out on their own; others remain loose but still captive inside their space for years. Photo by H. Nash.

Pennsylvania, notes that starting lotus from seed is not as difficult as might be imagined.

Tim recommends first scarifying the brown, mature seeds by rubbing them gently on medium-grade sandpaper. Rub the hard seed coat until the creamy inner seed is visible. (Nicking into this living tissue may kill the seed.) Drop the seeds into a glass of non-chlorinated warm water. Seeds that float are probably not fertile and should be discarded before they can pollute the water. As you await germination, usually within one week, change the water daily.

The first sign of germination is the emergence of the primary root, the radicle. When you see

Victorias bloom at night. The first night's flower is white.
Photo by Perry D. Slocum.

this first root, pot up the seeds. Tim uses 4-inch (10 cm) pots without holes that he fills with good garden loam. Make a depression in the soil and put in one seed per pot, gently covering the

radicle and seed with soil or gravel. (If you wait too long and leaves start to emerge, keep them free of soil as you cover the radicle.) Set the potted seed no more than 2 in. (5 cm) deep in warm water of 70–80° F (21–26° C). Tim likes to use an aquarium for this stage of growing the lotuses.

As green sprouts—the first true floating leaves—begin to emerge, you may have to use a broad-spectrum fungicide to prevent loss of

On the second night of bloom, the Victoria flower opens a rosy pink.
Photo by Perry D. Slocum.

plants. Give the new seedlings as much light as possible (natural or artificial) until the water in your outdoor pond reaches at least 60° F (15° C). At that time, transplant the lotus into a larger container that doesn't have a hole. The plant is not likely to flower the first year but will produce tubers to survive the winter. Perry D. Slocum notes that at his Zone 7 home in North Carolina, he frequently has blooms the first year when seeds are started early enough.

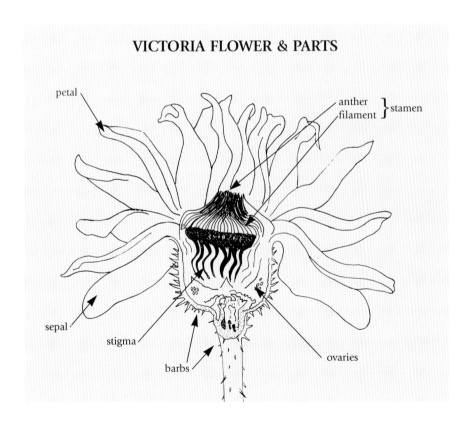

VICTORIA FLOWER & PARTS

petal

anther } stamen
filament

sepal

stigma

barbs

ovaries

PROPAGATING VICTORIAS BY SEED

Victorias are among the most spectacular of aquatic plants. They are huge, with leaves sometimes 8 ft. (2.4 m) across! A tropical annual, it cannot be propagated by division but must be grown each year from seed. While some of the larger aquatic nurseries sell the plants and/or seeds, acquiring them can be difficult. In the summer of 1996, for example, cooler than normal spring weather throughout the United States hampered many efforts to grow the plants from seed. Available seed was mostly confined to botanical gardens such as Longwood Gardens in Pennsylvania, where Patrick Nutt developed the *Victoria* 'Longwood' hybrid. Tim Jennings, who assumed curatorship of aquatic plants at Longwood following Patrick's retirement, kept the plants going at Longwood during that strange season of '96.

As you consider propagating *Victorias* by seed, remember that the 'Longwood' hybrid, acknowledged as the superior plant, results from crossing *Victoria amazonica* pollen with a *Victoria cruziana* stigma or flower. Reversing this to make the *Victoria amazonica* the pod or seed parent has not resulted in viable seed. The 'Longwood' hybrid, when crossed with either parent, does not produce viable seed, either, although crossing the hybrid with itself does produce a second generation true to seed. (A

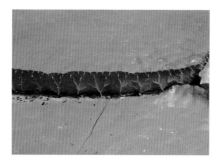

The edge of a *Victoria* leaf forms a ridge that displays both the spines and reddish color of the leaf's underside. Photo by H. Nash.

third generation crossing is unpredictable.) Both of the parent species can be crossed to themselves for viable seed production.

Tim Jennings, Curator of the aquatic collection at Longwood Gardens in Pennsylvania dons waders to fertilize the *Victorias*. Photo by Gail Perrone.

Pollinating *Victoria* Flowers

Victoria flowers bloom for only two days, opening at night. The first night's flower is white, and the second-night flower is pinkish-red. Pollen is collected from the second-night flower. Pollen is visible on the anthers of these flowers. Cut the anthers from the flower and place them in a plastic bag. The pollen can be stored in the refrigerator for up to 36 hours. (Pollen transported from off-site collection is successfully moved by storing it in sealed plastic bags and keeping it cool with ice or refrigeration.)

When the first-night flower opens, cut out the anthers along with the innermost row of flower parts, the stamenoids, that form a ringlike cover for the stigma. This fully exposes the stigma and makes pollinization easier. Tweezers help ensure no pollen-bearing anthers remain in the flower. Dust the stigma with the collected pollen from the anthers of the second-night flower. (Some growers use a small funnel to aim the pollen onto the stigma.) Use a soft camel-hair brush to spread the pollen all about the stigma. (If you are fortunate enough to have both a second-night and first-night flower open at the same time, you can simply cut out the pollen-dusted anthers from the second-night flower and place them directly onto the stigma of the first-night flower.) Fold the remaining flower petals around the now pollinated stigma and secure them with a rubber band. Tie a gauze or cheesecloth "bag" around the entire flower to prevent unwanted pollination by insects. If rain is possible during this period, temporarily cover the pollinated flower with a plastic bag to prevent the pollen from being washed away before it can begin growing down the style and forming seed. Do not leave the plastic bag on the flower for any length of time, however, as excessive heat may cook your efforts. The spent flower lowers beneath the water's surface after its second night of bloom like its water lily cousins, the stem of the pollinated flower coiling to draw the fruit under water.

Within two to three weeks, you will notice a swelling in the deteriorating flower beneath the water's surface. Keep the developing seed pod enclosed within the muslin bag to ensure capture of the ripened seeds when the mature pod ruptures about six weeks after pollination.

Collecting and Storing the *Victoria* Seeds

Place collected seeds in a jar of distilled water to allow the seed covering to dissolve slowly. Change the water as needed. After the seed covering has dissolved away, store the seed in distilled water at 60° F (15° C). The seeds may be stored until the following spring, when they can be planted.

Starting *Victoria* Seed

Disinfect seeds by dipping them in a 10 percent solution of bleach for three minutes. Sow the seeds about one inch (2.5 cm) deep in shallow pots. Several seeds may be started in any one pot. The first leaf is threadlike, with the next two leaves long and narrowly arrow-shaped (hastate). The next set of boat-shaped leaves is the first of floating leaves. Later, the *Victoria cruziana's* leaves are round with bluish purple coloration underneath, and the *Victoria amazonica's* leaves are somewhat elliptical and reddish purple beneath. The 'Longwood' hybrid has round leaves like its *cruziana* parent that are reddish purple underneath like its *amazonica* parent. After the germinated seeds have developed a second set of true leaves (the floating, boat-shaped leaves), transplant the seedlings into 3-inch pots with a soil mixture of three parts garden loam to one part sand. As the plants grow, transplant them into progressively larger pots—from a 5-inch (12.5 cm) to an 8-inch (20 cm) pot, for example. With each transplant, Patrick Nutt advises enriching the soil a bit more with well-composed cow manure. Many growers also follow a feeding regimen using Peters 20–20–20, as recommended by Longwood Gardens. Your young plants can be set outside when the water temperature has stabilized between 72 and 75° F (22–24° C). They should be planted in as large a container as is possible in your usual aquatic soil mixture or in a mixture of one part well-composted manure to three parts topsoil, along with 8–10 pounds of 10–10–10 granulated fertilizer. The Lerio 200S, a squat container that holds about 27 cubic feet (0.81 cu m) of soil, is recommended for this soil amount and formulation.

chapter four

SUBMERGED AQUATIC PLANTS

Often inconspicuous in the water garden, submerged aquatic plants perform a vital function in the water garden. By successfully competing with green water algae for the available nutrients in the water, they are the key to naturally establishing and maintaining clear water. One bunch of these plants per every one to two square feet (0.09 to 0.18 sq m) of water surface is the generally accepted formula for clear water. This formula

assumes, however, that the pond is neither overstocked with fish nor allowed to accumulate great amounts of decomposing organic matter such as leaves and debris.

Commonly called "water weeds," many submerged plants can become invasive and choke out other desirable aquatics, such as water lilies. The more tender-leaved species, such as anacharis and *Elodea*, may be kept in check by grazing fish. Both koi and goldfish enjoy the salad bar smorgasbord. Until the plants are established enough to survive fish consumption, you may wish to grow some in a separate container to replenish what is eaten, or you may wish to cordon the plants off from the fish with inconspicuous black plastic predator netting. Most of these plants available to the trade are readily propagated by stem cuttings or by separating young plantlets on runners from the mother plant.

Many of the trade-available species are hardy so long as they do not freeze. Since some of the species will grow to the water's surface in the shallow water garden, part of your autumn chores is to prune them back below anticipated winter ice levels to prevent their freezing, turning to mush, decomposing, and adding to the nutrient level of the water that will encourage a spring algae bloom.

Particularly if your pond's water is clear, you may wish to "landscape" the pool bottom by using a variety of these submerged plants. Besides enhancing the aesthetics of your pond, they also serve as spawning media for fish and cover for the tiny fry.

Submerged plants perform a vital nutrient-removing function within the pond water, lending to their common name of water-clarifying plants. Photo by H. Nash.

"Pruning" submerged grasses, such as *Elodea* or anacharis, is necessary to prevent their taking over the garden. Photo by Ron Everhart.

COMMONLY AVAILABLE SUBMERGED PLANTS

Cabomba caroliniana.

This subtropical species from the southeastern United States has bright green, fan-shaped, coarsely segmented leaves up to 1.5 inches (4 cm) in diameter. The surface leaves are linear with pointed tips up to 0.8 inches (2 cm) in length. Charming, white with yellow centers, the small flowers bloom on extended fine stems at the water's surface.

ℓℓ ℓℓ ℓℓ ℓℓ ℓℓ ℓℓ ℓℓ ℓℓ ℓℓ ℓℓ

Ceratophyllum demersum. Coontail, hornwort.

Frequently found free-floating or loosely anchored in the mud in both still and moving water. In autumn, the tips of the plant's growth shorten and thicken before breaking off and sinking to the bottom to overwinter as buds. Dark green, 0.6–1.5 in. (1.5–4 cm) long, forked leaves whorl about stems that grow 12–24 in. (30–60 cm) long. Inconspicuous flowers are borne within the axil of a leaf. Simply place in the pond to float freely and to offer shade, shelter, and spawning media for fish.

ℓℓ ℓℓ ℓℓ ℓℓ ℓℓ ℓℓ ℓℓ ℓℓ ℓℓ ℓℓ

Egeria densa. Anacharis.

Originally native to the warm and temperate zones of South America and now established in Central and North America, Europe, and Australia, this is the plant commonly sold as anacharis or *Elodea*. A vigorous grower with multibranched stems of whorls of mid-green sessile leaves that are linear with pointed tips usually bend backward and are 1 in. (2.5 cm) long and up to 0.1 in. (0.3 cm) wide. The brittle branchlets easily break off from the parent plant to form new plants. In water temperatures above 73° F (23°C), the stems become sparse and lanky. Tiny white flowers are produced atop thin stems that reach to the water's surface. Feeding primarily through its leaves, the plant produces roots to anchor itself. Bunches are often sold weighted for submersion in the pool. They may also be planted in pots of gravel or sand, since soil is not really necessary for their survival.

ℓℓ ℓℓ ℓℓ ℓℓ ℓℓ ℓℓ ℓℓ ℓℓ ℓℓ ℓℓ

Cabomba caroliniana.
Cabomba produces delightful white flowers at the water's surface. Photo by H. Nash.

Ceratophyllum demersum
Free-floating *ceratophyllum* or hornwort provides cover for fish.
Photo by H. Nash.

Egeria densa.
Anacharis is visible submerged to the right in this pond.
Photo by H. Nash.

Eleocharis acicularis
Eleocharis acicularis forms a grassy carpet in earth ponds. It can choke out other submerged grasses. Photo by H. Nash.

Eleocharis acicularis. Hair grass.

A hardy, grassy species from North America, Europe, and Asia, submerged pale green, needlelike, leaves up to 8 in. (20 cm) long, and less than 0.02 in. (0.05 cm) thick grow from rapidly spreading rhizomatous roots. Egg-shaped brown spikes grow from a four-sided stem that is sheathed at the base. Quickly assuming nuisance proportions in a natural pond, the plant out-competes other, more desirable submerged plants. In the water garden without gravel or soil linings and with regular maintenance of potted plants, hair grass is an effective competitor for water nutrients.

Elodea canadensis
Elodea, on the left, is smaller-leaved than the commonly sold anacharis, on the right.
Photo by Ron Everhart.

Elodea canadensis. Canadian pondweed.

A native of North America that has spread to Europe, Asia, and Australia, this temperate species is one of the most efficient of submerged plants at removing nutrients from water. Multibranched, slightly brittle stems are covered with sessile curving whorls of medium-green pointed leaves up to 0.4 in. (1 cm) long and 0.1 in. (0.3 cm) wide. Like its similar-appearing cousin *Egeria densa*, the plant fares best in cooler waters. In temperatures above 70° F (21° C), it becomes rank in growth. It will grow in up to 8–10 ft. (2.5 to 3 m) of water and easily attain the surface of the typical water garden. If fish do not keep it under control, prune it back to prevent it from choking water lilies and depriving fish of swimming areas. Propagate from stem tip cuttings. It may be planted as anchored bunches dropped into the pond or in pots of gravel or sand. If only floated in the pond, excessive sunlight and air exposure may kill it.

Myriophyllum aquaticum
Parrot feather lends beautiful color, texture, and a feeling of lushness to the water garden.
Photo by Bob Romar.

Myriophyllum stricta
Myriophyllum stricta is easily collected from the wild. Not as efficient at removing nutrients from water, it sends up flowering spires to release prolific seeds on the water's surface.
Photo by H. Nash

Myriophyllum aquaticum Parrot feather

A slightly tender submerged species originally from South America and New Zealand, the plant is now naturalized across North America, often to nuisance proportions. The stems can grow 20–60 in. (50–150 cm) long with leaves 1–2 in. (2.5–5 cm) long in whorls of four to six, divided into four to eight bright green segments. Aerial parts of the stem develop a much deeper bluish green color with shorter, stiffer leaves that have a velvety sheen. While not among the most efficient of submerged plants at removing excess water nutrients, its foliage provides lush texture. Capable of rooting in wet soil above the water, the plant offers uses within waterfall crevices as well as around the pond edge. Supposedly prone to frost damage, it winters well beneath the ice in frozen ponds. Likewise, the plant seems to adapt to colder climates and is known to survive Zone 5 winters simply grown in mud.

The highly invasive *Myriophyllum stricta*, commonly found in lakes and ponds in North America, is not recommended for the water garden.

Of more restrained growth than *M. stricta*, *Myriophyllum heterophyllum* can be used in the water garden. It is more compact in growth and is a more attractive plant.

The reddish-tinged and crinkly leaves of *Potamogeton crispus* are an attractive underwater addition to the pond.

Potamogeton crispus.
Curled pondweed.
This hardy European species is now naturalized across northeastern and north central U.S. The stems can grow to 13 ft. (4 m) or more, bearing narrow sessile leaves about 3 in. (8 cm) long and 0.2–0.4 in. (0.5–1 cm) wide. The leaves are quite decorative—translucent and wavy-edged, varying from green to reddish brown. Not particularly invasive in the garden pond, it provides interest and texture to the submerged landscape.

Sagittaria natans (S. subulata).
Dwarf sagittaria may be difficult
to establish in some ponds, but
once it is growing healthily, you
may find it cropping up in every
submerged pot.
Photo by Ron Everhart.

Sagittaria natans (S. subulata) Dwarf *Sagittaria.*

A temperate species from North America, common along the Atlantic Coast from Maine to Florida, this grasslike plant gives a carpet effect to the water garden. Dark green, grassy foliage, often crooked, and obtuse at the tip, measures 2–12 in. (5–30 cm) long. Young plants grow from runners. Vigorous plants in shallow water can produce small egg-shaped floating leaves and sometimes linear aerial leaves with obtuse tips. White flowers float on the water surface. Very hard to establish in the pond with larger fish, it may require protection. Once established, it crops up in every pot in the pond.

Vallisneria

Vallisneria americana. Giant tape grass.

Narrow, ribbonlike leaves grow over 36 in. (90 cm) long and 0.75 in. (2 cm) wide. The female flower is borne on a spirally twisted stem at the water's surface. The plant grows in up to 8 ft. (2.4 m) of water and is usually too vigorous for the typical water garden.

Vallisneria spiralis. Spiral tape grass.

A tropical submerged species native to southern Europe and North Africa, it is now widespread in many tropical and subtropical areas. The specific name refers to the spiraling nature of the flower stalk, not to the leaves. Ribbonlike leaves grow from rosettes and are 8–32 in. (20–80 cm) long and 0.2–0.5 in. (0.5–1.3 cm) wide. These leaves can be mistaken for *Sagittaria*, but are distinguished by parallel leaf veins and a tiny jagged edge at the tips of the leaves. The species has separate male and female plants. Male flowers disconnect from the plant to float on the surface and release their pollen. Female plants grow their flower stalks to the surface, where they are pollinated by the free-floating male flowers. The stem then contracts in a spiral so that the seeds ripen below the surface.

Vallisneria.
Vallisneria is commonly called
tape grass. The shorter *spiralis*
form works better in the shal-
low waters of the water garden.

chapter five

FLOATING PLANTS
& Plants with Floating Leaves

Floating plants grow on or near the water's surface with no root system anchored in soil. The easiest of aquatics to "plant," you simply set them in the water.

Excessive coverage of the water's surface affects oxygen exchange in the water. Providing supplemental aeration may be necessary for your fish. Photo by H. Nash.

While providing interest to the water garden with texture, color, and blooms, these plants also help maintain water quality. Their roots remove dissolved mineral salts and other nutrients directly from the water, competing with the lower life form green water algae. This trait makes them excellent choices for natural filter systems.

Floating plants also shade the water and deprive algae of necessary sunlight. By the same token, an overabundance of these plants also shades submerged plants from sunlight. Some of these floaters are vigorous growers that require netting out their excess to allow other plants to grow below them. Remember, too, that coverage of the pond's surface lessens the amount of air-exchange available to the pond water that can affect fish. In ponds stocked with a maximum fish load, provide additional aeration if much of the surface is covered with floating plants or floating leaves.

Many floaters are also tropical plants. Zones 9 and 10 may still require plastic tenting over the pond to protect them during cold nights. Other zones can grow these plants as annuals or winter them over indoors or in greenhouses with minimum water temperatures of 60° F (15° C). Provide full-spectrum lighting for 10 to 14 hours to accommodate the light requirements of tropical plants. (See Chapter Two for more information on growing tropicals under lights indoors.)

Aeschynomene fluitans is a tropical floating plant new to the trade. It should be wintered indoors in a well-lighted aquarium or greenhouse pool.
Photo by Bob Romar.

Aponogeton distachyus.
Photo by Bob Romar.

Aponogeton distachyus. Water hawthorne.
Hardiness Zones: 6–9. Vanilla-scented white flowers with black speckles bloom in the cooler temperatures of autumn and early spring. Mottled, oblong, green and red leaves float on the water's surface. The plant usually goes dormant during the warm summer months. Grow in full sun to part shade. Propagate by division in spring or by sowing fresh seed. Dispensed seed sprouts spontaneously.

Azolla caroliniana. Fairy moss.
Fine roots trail below the lacy, bright green fronds that turn reddish in full sun and in the cooling temperatures of autumn. Pinnately branched, two-lobed, scalelike leaves reproduce rapidly and quickly cover the water's surface. Fish do not find them appetizing. Net out excess plants and add them to the compost pile, where their unique nitrogen-fixing nodules benefit the garden. Their capability of producing overwintering buds that sink to the pond's bottom has resulted in their gaining pest proportions as far north as New England and in Britain. However, this seldom seems to happen in the water garden. To assure a quantity for the following season, winter a portion over indoors in an aquarium or in a shallow pan of well-lighted water. They are usually sold in half-cup (0.12 l) portions.

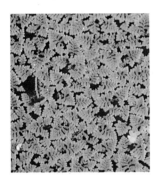

Azolla caroliniana.
Photo by Ron Everhart.

Ceratopteris pteridoides. Floating fern.
Native to South America, this rosette-growing plant is also found in Florida and along the Gulf Coast of Mississippi and Louisiana. An edible plant, taller, much-divided, larger fertile fronds stand erect in the middle of the pale green, floating, sterile fronds that are buoyed up with internal air pockets. Viviparous buds form in the notches of the leaf margins. Propagate by pegging the bulbils onto moist soil in temperatures of at least 74° F (24° C). Although a rapid spreader, it must be wintered indoors in a lighted aquarium.

Ceratopteris thalictroides. Water fern, water sprite, or water hornfern.
Native to eastern Asia and Madagascar, this species is cultivated in Japan as a spring vegetable. Sometimes rooting in mud, the species grows about 21–30 in. (52.5–75 cm) above the water with two types of leaves. Deeply segmented fertile fronds and parsleylike sterile fronds are a delicate pale green. Buds form in the notches of the fertile fronds to produce new plantlets. Propagate as with C. *pteridoides*. Winter indoors in zones below Zone 10.

Eichhornia azurea. Blue water hyacinth.

Pale blue, funnel-shaped flowers bear a dark blue throat with slightly hairy external surfaces that grow in pairs atop erect stems. Unlike *E. crassipes*, the plant does not have bulging air pockets to provide buoyancy nor is it a true floating plant. The leaves may be ribbonlike (4 in/19 cm) to rounded spoon shapes 3 in. (0.8 cm) in diameter. Plants root easily in shallowly submerged pots; their vigorous growth requires control. A tropical plant, winter indoors in lighted aquariums in Zones 4–9.

ⓦ ⓦ ⓦ ⓦ ⓦ ⓦ ⓦ ⓦ ⓦ ⓦ

Eichhornia crassipes.
Photo by Bob Romar.

Eichhornia crassipes. Water hyacinth.

Delicate flowers that last only one day grace this plant with bluish to lilac blooms marked with yellow peacock center eyes on 6 in. (15 cm) spikes at the center of a rosette of glossy green, bulbous leaves. Air pockets in the bulbous areas keep the plant afloat. Long, thick black roots trail to provide spawning and hiding areas for fish, as well as superb nutrient uptake from the water. Typical to its tropical nature, it requires heat and sunlight to flourish and bloom. Yellowing leaves indicate insufficient nutrition in the water; move "hungry" plants to separate containers and supply plant food in the water, rotating the sated plants with ones left in the pond. A vigorous reproducer by stolons, it can quickly take over the water garden. Remove excess plants. It is presently illegal to transport it across state lines, and in some states, it is illegal to sell it at all. Overwintering indoors is possible, but ample light, duration of light, and temperatures above 70° F (21° C) are required. A relatively inexpensive plant, most water gardeners simply replace it each year. Two cultivars may be available to the trade: 'Major,' a slightly larger plant with pinkish-lilac flowers, and 'Aurea', a yellow-flowered variety. The plant performs well in vegetative filters, but should not be used where its feathery roots may clog filter units.

ⓦ ⓦ ⓦ ⓦ ⓦ ⓦ ⓦ ⓦ ⓦ ⓦ

Euryale ferox.
Photo by Gail Perrone.

Euryale ferox. Prickly water lily, gorgon plant.

Hardiness Zones: 10–11. 4 to 5 ft. (1.2–1.5 m), deeply veined and flat leaves float on the water's surface. Sharp spines cover the surface of sepals, stems, and both sides of the leaves. Cup-shaped flowers of 23 or 24 petals are a deep violet with an outer row of white petals. Like the more beautiful *Victoria*, the plant propagates readily from seed. The seed must be stored moist. While not commonly advertised in all nursery catalogs, many nurseries do carry it. Just ask. A perennial in tropical climates, the gorgon plant is grown much like the *Victorias*.

ⓦ ⓦ ⓦ ⓦ ⓦ ⓦ ⓦ ⓦ ⓦ ⓦ

Hydrocleys nymphoides.
Photo by Bob Romar .

Hydrocleys nymphoides. Water poppy.

Thick, shiny, deep green, broadly heart-shaped oval leaves measure 2–4 in. (5–10 cm) on trailing stems up to 3 ft. (1 m) long. Flowers of light yellow with a red-and-brown center 2–2.5 in. (5–6 cm) across last but a day, but are produced in succession. Surviving in as much as 12–15 in. (30–38 cm) of water, it grows best in shallow waters of approximately 6 in. (15 cm). Plant it in rich topsoil. Propagate by disconnecting rooted plantlets. Winter over indoors in non-tropical climates in a shallow tub of water or pot up in a hanging basket and keep very moist. Provide at least 10 hours of full-spectrum light daily for healthy maintenance.

🌿 🌿 🌿 🌿 🌿 🌿 🌿 🌿 🌿 🌿

Hydrocharis morsus-ranae.
Photo by H. Nash.

Hydrocharis morsus-ranae. Frogbit.

Native to Europe and western Asia, this small plant resembles a miniature water lily. Long petioles are graced with kidney-shaped, green, shiny leaves about 1 in. (2.5 cm) across that grow in rosettes on the water. Stolons arise from leaf axils during the summer to produce new rosettes. An inconspicuous white flower with a yellow center may be tucked among the leaves. The undersides of the leaves are puffed with spongy, air-holding tissue. The plant does not grow as vigorously as other floating plants. Overwintering buds are produced in autumn that winter over on the pond bottom. Since this is not a reliable means of propagation, winter some plants indoors in an aquarium. (See also *Limnobium*)

🌿 🌿 🌿 🌿 🌿 🌿 🌿 🌿 🌿 🌿

Lemna minor; center;
Lemma trisulca, right.
Photo by H. Nash.

Lemna minor. Duckweed.

The most widespread of the duckweeds, this tiny floating plant can be found worldwide. Light green ovate leaves bear a single rootlet. It notoriously multiplies to nuisance proportions in the small pool. A favorite fish snack, it may not grow out of bounds in the well-stocked pond. The plant flourishes in the cooler temperatures of spring and fall. While it may disappear over the hot summer months, it often reappears when cooler temperatures return. A perennial, it appears again the following spring if the fish have not eaten it all. Many gardeners keep some growing in a fish-free container to ensure a constant supply. It can be wintered in a lighted aquarium, if desired. Encourage propagation from a small sample by keeping the portion confined together within a floating plastic hoop, or propagate it in a bucket.

🌿 🌿 🌿 🌿 🌿 🌿 🌿 🌿 🌿 🌿

Lemna trisulca. Star duckweed, ivy-leaved duckweed.

(See preceding photo. Note that ivy-leaved duckweed also roots in soil.)

This species tends to float just below the surface of the water. Its elliptical, nearly transparent, light green leaves form three branches that are all but inconspicuous. A slower propagator than its more aggressive cousins, the tiny plant is often lost among other floating plants. Wintered outside in Zone 5 tub gardens, it sinks and anchors itself to the mud in lily pots. The plants float to the surface for flowering.

Limnobium spongia. American frogbit.

Very similar in appearance to *Hydrocharus morsus-ranae,* this plant is hardy from Lake Ontario to the southern United States. Buoyant, spongy undersided leaves are glossy green and heart-shaped. A purplish tinge to the underside and its trailing roots distinguishes it from its look-alike. Inconspicuous tiny white flowers peek from the easily multiplied leaves that spread from stolons across the water.

Ludwigia sedioides. Photo by H. Nash.

Ludwigia sedioides. Mosaic plant.

Hardiness Zones: 9–10. This charming tropical plant adds interest and texture to the water's surface. Diamond-shaped red and green leaves grow in 4–6 in. (10–15 cm) rosettes and produce tiny buttercup-yellow flowers. The stems that grow from soil reach the surface, where considerable running growth spreads across the water's surface. Grow it in one-gallon (4 l) containers at a water depth of 12–24 in. (30–60 cm) in full sun. In colder zones, grow it as an annual or bring portions indoors to winter in a well-lighted aquarium. Provide adequate light. Propagate by stem cuttings. When rooted, pot in soil. Reduced light in fall leaves the plant susceptible to fatal fungal attack.

Neptunia aquatica (Neptunia oleracea, Neptunia plena). Sensitive plant.

Hardiness Zones: 9–11. Finely pinnate leaves are borne along white, spongy-tissued floating stems. Sparsely produced fringed female yellow flowers above inconspicuous male brown flowers in midsummer are ball-like. The leaves are touch-sensitive, like *Mimosa.* It can be anchored in one-gallon (4 l) pots of soil or pea gravel, but is usually floated in the pond. Grow it in sun to part shade. Highly invasive in tropical zones, it can be wintered indoors in a well-lighted aquarium. Propagate by stem cuttings.

Nuphar advena (N. lutea).
Photo by H. Nash.

Nuphar advena (N. lutea). Spatterdock, yellow pond lily, yellow cow lily, and brandy bottle.

Hardiness Zones: 3–9. The water lily–like *Nuphar* is not commonly used in the small water garden. Producing small and sparse blooms in relation to its large leaves and spread, it is more suited to the large, natural pond. There, even in conditions of slowly moving water and shade, the hardy perennial flourishes in depths up to several feet. The rhizome may grow to 6 in. (15 cm) thick and to lengths of 15 ft. (4.5 m). Leaves up to 14.5 × 10 in. (36 × 25 cm) spread 5–8 ft. (1.5–2.4 m). Thin, lightly ruffled submerged leaves are produced near the rhizome. 2–2.5 in. (5–6 cm) cup-shaped flowers of 20 deep yellow petals that never seem to fully open bloom from May into October. The flowers last four to five days, with an aroma on the first day like brandy. Propagate by division or seed.

Nymphoides cristatum.
Photo by Bob Romar.

Nymphoides aquatica. Banana lily.
Hardy in Zone 10. 4-inch leaves have rough undersides and combine with white flowers to make a surface-covering plant for tub gardens or aquariums. Leaves are viviparous. Plant in 1-gallon (4 l) containers and submerge in 6–20 in. (15–50 cm) of water in full sun. Winter in temperate zones in a heated greenhouse or indoor aquarium under bright light. Propagate by bananalike tubers or rooted plantlets produced at leaves.

Nymphoides cristatum. Variegated water snowflake.
Hardiness Zones: 7–10. Red-edged, round leaves sprawl across the water's surface with hundreds of small white flowers. Especially suited to growing in small pools and tub gardens, the plant may require some control as it continues to propagate by viviparous plantlets at the leaves. Grow as an annual in colder zones or try wintering plantlets in well-lighted aquariums or greenhouse tanks. Pot in one-gallon (4 l) containers and submerge in 1–24 in. (2.5–60 cm) of water in full sun. Propagate by viviparous plantlets.

Nymphoides geminata.
Photo by Bob Romar.

Nymphoides geminata. Yellow fringe.
Hardiness Zones: 7–10. Reddish brown and green lilylike leaves sprawl across the water in a rangy habit. One-inch (2.5 cm), fringed yellow blossoms add sparkle in summer. Pot in one-gallon (4 l) containers and submerge in 12–24 in. (30–60 cm) of water in full sun. Grow as an annual in colder zones or move into greenhouse or aquarium tanks in winter; supply adequate light. Propagate by rooted stem cuttings.

Nymphoides hydrocharioides. Orange snowflake.

Hardiness Zones: 7–10 . Wavy margined leaves spread across the water's surface in a sprawling and rangy habit. Fringed, orange flowers are produced on this Australian native. Like its *Nymphoides* cousins, the plant produces roots at junctions of the stems. Grow as an annual or winter indoors with adequate photo period. Pot in one-gallon (4 l) containers and submerge to a depth of 12–24 in. (30–60 cm) in full sun. Propagate by rooted stem sections.

🌿 🌿 🌿 🌿 🌿 🌿 🌿 🌿 🌿 🌿

Nymphoides indica 'Gigantea'. Giant water snowflake.

Hardiness Zones: 8–10. Originating in the East Indies, this tropical plant produces round, emerald-green, lilylike leaves and 1–1¼ paper-white, snowflake-shaped flowers. Plantlets are produced at the leaves and contribute to the plants' vigorous growth that requires management in the water garden. Grow as an annual in colder zones or try wintering indoors with adequate photo supplement. Pot in a 2–5 gallon (10 l) container and submerge in 12–24 in. (30–60 cm) of water in full sun. Propagate from rooted plantlets produced at leaves.

🌿 🌿 🌿 🌿 🌿 🌿 🌿 🌿 🌿 🌿

Nymphoides peltata. Photo by H. Nash.

Nymphoides peltata. Floating heart.

Hardiness Zones: 5–10. Known as the hardy floating heart, round, slightly dentate, glossy leaves with slightly overlapping lobes appear to be miniature water lily pads on the water. Short-lived, papery, nonfringed, golden yellow blooms are produced relatively shyly in comparison to the number of leaves. However, the plant is a vigorous grower, requiring control in the water garden, and seems to produce many flowers. Flower production is minimized in shade, although leaves still flourish. Pot in one-gallon (4 l) containers and submerge in up to 12–24 in. (30–60 cm) of water in full sun. Propagate from rooted plantlets produced along stems. Seed is viable, but more trouble than simply snipping the many plantlets.

🌿 🌿 🌿 🌿 🌿 🌿 🌿 🌿 🌿 🌿

Pistia stratiotes.
Photo by Bob Romar.

Salvinia
Photo by Bob Romar.

Victoria amazonica.
Photo by H. Nash.

Pistia stratiotes. Water lettuce.

Tropical. No, this plant is not edible, but it looks like lushly floating heads of lettuce or cabbage. Velvety, nearly lime-green, deeply veined leaves grow to 10 in. (25 cm) long and 4 in. (10 cm) wide. Arranged in spirals or rosettes, the leaves produce plantlets that stretch out from the mother plant on slender stems. Inconspicuous white flowers grow in the leaf axils. Feathery roots offer hiding places and spawning material for fish. Many water gardeners report goldfish and koi nibbling on both the roots and the leaves. Varying in its adaptability to the individual water garden, it does very well in some, while in others it yellows and malingers. Try rotating the yellowing plants in a separate container provided with fertilizer. The plant, too, seems to favor some shade in hot areas. Highly susceptible to frost, a brief exposure to such cold temperatures produces a white scalding on the leaves that quickly turns into rotted areas. Wintering efforts in a heated greenhouse may be successful, but most home wintering attempts are futile. A smaller, more compact, rosetted form from Asia is available to the trade, too. 🌿 🌿 🌿 🌿 🌿 🌿 🌿 🌿 🌿 🌿

Salvinia ssp. Water fern.

Native to Central and South America, Africa, India, and northern temperate Europe, this charming free-floating fern bears soft, silky-haired leaves formed in irregular branches of whorls of three leaves, two floating and one submerged. Sporocarps develop among the submerged leaves and sink to the bottom in autumn as the floating plant dies. Keep a portion in a well-lighted aquarium indoors to ensure a supply for the next year. The plant multiplies prodigiously and may require netting out to control it . 🌿 🌿 🌿 🌿 🌿 🌿 🌿 🌿 🌿 🌿

Stratiotes aloides. Water soldier, water aloe.

Primarily a plant of natural ponds in England and Europe, this unusual plant may become more commonly available in the U.S. as plants are imported. Resembling a floating aloe or floating pineapple plant, it rises to the water's surface to flower. After flowering, the plant descends below the surface where it develops many axillary shoots that develop into winter buds. The plant resurfaces again later in the summer. Separate male and female flowers are produced on separate plants. 🌿 🌿 🌿 🌿 🌿 🌿 🌿 🌿

Victoria amazonica. Amazon water lily.

Tropical. Yellowish green leaves are round, beginning flat and then developing a rim 3–6 in. (7.5–15 cm) high. The undersides of the leaves and the exterior of the rim are sharply spined. They grow 4–6 ft. (1.2–2 m) across and spread 15–20 ft. (4.5–6 m). Double, night-blooming flowers of 9–12 in. (23–30 cm) open a creamy white and then turn pink. Requires water temperature of 85–90° F (29–32° C). Propagate by seed. 🌿 🌿 🌿 🌿 🌿 🌿 🌿 🌿 🌿 🌿

Victoria cruziana.
Photo by H. Nash.

Victoria cruziana. Santa Cruz water lily.

Very similar in appearance and habit to the Amazon species, the rim develops with a green exterior, veined red. The underside is a violet-purple, while the *amazonica* is a reddish-purple. Rims on the Santa Cruz grow 5–8 in. (13–20 cm); leaves are 4–5.5 ft. (1.2–1.7 m) across. The plant spreads 15–18 ft. (4.5–5.5 m). Slightly more double flowers of creamy white turning pink open at night for two consecutive nights. The major difference between the two species is that the *cruziana* will grow in water of at least 65–70° F (18–21° C). Propagate by seed.

🌿 🌿 🌿 🌿 🌿 🌿 🌿 🌿 🌿 🌿

Victoria 'Longwood Hybrid'
Photo by H. Nash.

Victoria 'Longwood Hybrid'.

Developed by Patrick Nutt at Longwood Gardens in Pennsylvania in 1961 by crossing *V. cruziana* with *V. amazonica*. An acknowledged improvement on either parent, the 'Longwood' *Victoria* grows yellowish-green leaves of 4–8 ft. (1.2–2.5 m) across and spreading 12–40 ft. (3.5–12 m). Spines grow on the underside of leaves, on the outside of the rim, and on the outside of the flower sepals. Its 73 to 75 petals number more than either parent with the nightblooming flowers measuring 10–16 in. (25–40 cm) across. Flowering 3 to 11 days earlier than its parents, 'Longwood' produces more flowers in a season, with the blooms opening earlier in the evening, as well. Propagate by seed. (See Chapter 2.)

🌿 🌿 🌿 🌿 🌿 🌿 🌿 🌿 🌿 🌿

Wolffia. Water meal.

Known as the smallest flowering plant in the world, this tiny plant actually resembles a green, floating grain in the water. Although there are eight species throughout the world, the one most commonly encountered is *W. arrhiza*, also known as rootless duckweed. Native to eastern Brazil, Africa, Europe, and western Asia, another hardy form has often been mistaken in the U.S. for algae. The plant is not deliberately planted in the water garden, but may be found in portions of other small surface floaters. In the natural pond, the plant can become a nuisance, fully carpeting the water in a glowing green.

🌿 🌿 🌿 🌿 🌿 🌿 🌿 🌿 🌿 🌿

chapter six

WATER LILIES—
Hardies and Tropicals

TROPICAL WATER LILIES

Tropical water lilies are considered the largest and showiest of all water lilies.

Flowers of day bloomers open in midmorning and close in late afternoon. Flowers of night bloomers open in late afternoon and close the following midmorning. Cool fall days may allow them to remain open for longer periods. Blooms open for three to four consecutive days, while new blooms continue in succession. Tropicals often hold their flowers well above the water.

In nontropical climate zones, place them in the pond once the water temperature has warmed to more than 70° F (21° C). Established plants often tolerate cooler temperatures and even withstand light frost before dying.

To plant a tropical water lily, separate the plant from the sprouted tuber and spread the roots out in a depression in the middle of the planter. Firm the soil down and top with 1 in. (2.5 cm) of fine gravel or coarse sand. Place the planting immediately under 6–12 in. (15-30 cm) of water. Planting before the water temperature averages above 70° F (21° C) may cause plants to go dormant and/or die.

Although all tropicals are planted in the same range of water depths, the various species and cultivars vary in their range of spread, or amount of surface area covered by the leaves. While you can control the spread to a small degree by pruning leaves, select varieties that will have ample room to grow in your garden. For information on potting, seasonal care, and wintering tropical water lilies, see Chapter Two. For information on propagation, see Chapter Three.

Note: Names of cultivars are followed by any synonyms, the hybridizer or introducer, and the date of introduction, if known. Sizes of flowers, leaves, and plant spread refer to mature plants grown under optimal conditions. The number of petals is given to provide guidance in the amount of "singleness" or "doubleness" of the blossom. Codes are given for lilies suitable for small pond or tub culture (ST) and for large gardens or natural, earth ponds (LN). Additional information about distinctive fragrance, viviparity, type of rhizome, and special growing notes is provided when applicable. Lilies known to be very free blooming, usually providing a succession of multiple blooms at a time, are denoted as "Excellent" bloomers, while those of lesser proclivity are noted as merely "Good" or "Sparse."

N. gigantea, a species of tropical water lily, can usually be found in the marketplace.
Photo by Perry D. Slocum.

Nymphaea 'August Koch'
Photo by Perry D. Slocum.

Nymphaea 'Bagdad'
Photo by Perry D. Slocum.

Nymphaea 'Blue Beauty'
Photo by Perry D. Slocum.

TROPICAL DAY-BLOOMING WATER LILIES

BLUE/PURPLE

Nymphaea 'August Koch' (August Koch and George H. Pring 1922)
Probably *N.* 'Blue Beauty' × *N.* 'Mrs. Woodrow Wilson'. Highly viviparous. Fragrant. Excellent bloomer. 22–25 petals. Rich blue petals and lilac-purple sepals form cup-shaped flowers that measure 4.5–5.5 in. (11–14 cm). Leaves are olive-green, nearly round, and unevenly serrated with some wavy edges. Leaves measure 12.5 × 12 in. (31.5 × 30 cm) and spread 4–6 ft. (1.2–2 m).

Nymphaea 'Bagdad' (George H. Pring 1941)
N. 'Pink Platter' × unnamed hybrid. Viviparous. Fragrant. Excellent bloomer. 30–32 petals. Withstands more cold than other tropicals. Light blue petals and lavender sepals form full, stellate blossoms measuring 8 in. (20 cm). Green leaves are heavily mottled and blotched with purple and red, are nearly round, and measure 10–12 in. (25–30 cm). Spreads 6–7 ft. (2–2.1 m).

Nymphaea 'Blue Beauty' (syn. 'Pennsylvania') (Henry Conard and William Tricker 1897)
N. caerulea × *N. capensis* var. *zanzibariensis*. Fragrant. 21–23 petals. Excellent bloomer. Deep, rich blue petals with pale blue sepals that are heavily streaked, greenish, form 8–11 in. (20–28 cm) stellate flowers. 14 × 13 in. (35 × 33 cm) leaves are serrated and wavy-edged with purple specks on young leaves. Spreads 4–7 ft. (1.2–2.2 m).

Nymphaea 'Charles Thomas'
Photo by Perry D. Slocum.

Nymphaea 'Charles Thomas' (John Wood 1985)
Unknown parents. Viviparous. 24–25 petals. Excellent bloomer.
Sky blue, stellate flowers of 5–6 in. (13–15 cm). Leaves, heavily
mottled and blotched purple, measure 10–11 in. (25–28 cm) and
spread 4–6 ft. (1.2–2 m).

Nymphaea 'Daubeniana'
Photo by Perry D. Slocum.

Nymphaea 'Daubeniana' (syn. 'Dauben') (Daubeny 1863)
Probably *N. micrantha* and *N. caerulea*. Highly viviparous.
Fragrant. 21 petals. Excellent bloomer. Tolerates more cold than
most other tropicals. ST. Light blue petals with slightly darker tips
often fade to near-white in full sunlight, with green striped sepals.
4–6 in. (10–15 cm) cup-shaped flowers. Egg-shaped, green leaves
have wavy edges. Leaves measure up to 12 × 10 in. (30 × 25 cm)
and spread 3–7 ft. (1–2.2 m).

Nymphaea 'Director George T. Moore'
Photo by Perry D. Slocum.

Nymphaea 'Director George T. Moore' (George H. Pring 1941)
N. 'Judge Hitchcock' × *N. colorata*. Nonviviparous. Fragrant.
13–26 petals. Excellent bloomer. Deep violet-blue petals and sepals
combine to form a wide-open 7–10 in. (18–25 cm) bloom.
Lightly blotched with purple, round leaves measure 10–12 in.
(25–30 cm) and spread 5–8 ft. (1.5–2.5 m).

Nymphaea 'King of Blues'
Photo by Perry D. Slocum.

Nymphaea 'King of Blues' (Perry D. Slocum 1955)
26–28 petals. Excellent bloomer. Readily produces fertile seeds. Deep violet-blue, full stellate blossoms measure 7–9 in. (18–23 cm). Leaves up to 13 × 11 in. (33 × 28 cm) are yellowish green and ovate with jagged and wavy edges that spread 6–8 ft. (2–2.5 m).

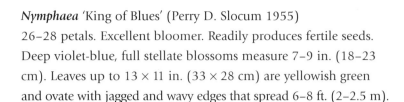

Nymphaea 'Leopardess'
Photo by Perry D. Slocum.

Nymphaea 'Leopardess' (Martin E. Randig 1931)
Unknown parentage. Slightly fragrant. 30 petals, 4 sepals. Good bloomer. Incredible leaves! Clear blue petals are tipped with purple and form 4–5 in. (10–13 cm) cup-shaped flowers. Nearly round purple leaves are blotched with green and measure 10–12 in. (25–30 cm) with a spread of 4–5 ft. (1.2–1.5 m).

Nymphaea 'Midnight'
Photo by H. Nash.

Nymphaea 'Midnight' (George H. Pring 1941)
N. colorata × N. capensis var *. zanzibariensis.* Slightly fragrant. 95–123 petals. Excellent bloomer. Unique anthers develop as small petals to lend fringe effect in center of blooms. Deep violet-blue, star-shaped flowers measure 6–8 in. (15–20 cm). Bright green, nearly round, and quite dentate leaves measure 9–10 in. (23–25 cm). Leaves spread 4–6 ft. (1.2–2 m).

Nymphaea 'Mrs. Edwards Whitaker'
Photo by Perry D. Slocum.

Nymphaea 'Mrs. Edwards Whitaker' (George H. Pring 1917) *N. ovalifolia* × *N.* 'Castaliflora'. Very fragrant. 21 petals. Excellent bloomer. Light blue petals and green-tipped sepals form large, stellate blooms of 9–12 in. (23–30 cm). Up to 13 × 12 in. (33 × 30 cm) green leaves show small purple mottlings. Spreads 6–7 ft. (2–2.1 m).

🌿 🌿 🌿 🌿 🌿 🌿 🌿 🌿 🌿 🌿

Nymphaea 'Mrs. Martin E. Randig'
Photo by Perry D. Slocum.

Nymphaea 'Mrs. Martin E. Randig' (Martin E. Randig 1938) Perry D. Slocum notes parentage includes *N.* 'Panama Pacific', *N.* 'Daubeniana' *N.* 'Lilac Queen, *N.* 'Royal Zanzibar', *N.* 'Indigo Zanzibar' and *N.* 'Amethyst'. Viviparous. Fragrant. 23–24 petals. Excellent bloomer. Deep violet-blue flowers are somewhat cup-shaped and 4.5–6 in. (11–15 cm) across. Nearly round green leaves measure 10 × 8 in. (25 × 20 cm) and spread 3–5 ft. (1–1.5 m).

🌿 🌿 🌿 🌿 🌿 🌿 🌿 🌿 🌿 🌿

Nymphaea 'Pamela'
Photo by Perry D. Slocum.

Nymphaea 'Pamela' (August Koch 1931) Unknown parentage. Fragrant. 21–27 petals. Excellent bloomer. Rich sky-blue, stellate and then flat flowers are 8–13 in. (20–33 cm) across. New leaves are heavily blotched purple but mature to green with the lobes often rising up at the overlap. Measuring up to 15 × 13.5 in. (38 × 33.5 cm), the leaves spread 5–8 ft. (1.5–2.5 m).

🌿 🌿 🌿 🌿 🌿 🌿 🌿 🌿 🌿 🌿

Nymphaea 'Panama Pacific'
Photo by Perry D. Slocum.

Nymphaea 'Panama Pacific' (William Tricker 1914)
Unknown parentage. Highly viviparous. Highly fragrant. 21–22 petals. Excellent bloomer. Hardier than many other tropicals. Deep violet-purple flowers open cup-shaped and then evolve stellate to measure 4.5–6 in. (11–15 cm) across. Nearly round green leaves with purple mottlings measure 9–11 in. (23–28 cm) and spread 4–6 ft. (1.2–2 m).

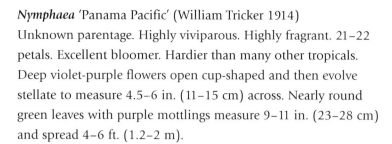

Nymphaea 'Paul Stetson'
Photo by Perry D. Slocum.

Nymphaea 'Paul Stetson' (John Wood 1984)
Unknown parentage. Viviparous. Fragrant. 18 petals. Excellent bloomer. ST. Sky-blue petals and lighter sepals with darker blue veins measure 4–6 in. (10–15 cm) in stellate form. Nearly round leaves with pointed lobe tips are bright green with maroon spots. Measuring 6–9 in. (15–23 cm), they spread 3–4 ft. (1–1.2 m).

Nymphaea 'Perry's Blue Heaven' (Perry D. Slocum 1997)
Nymphaea caerulea × *Nymphaea capensis* var. *zanzibariensis* 'Rosea.' With flowers like *N.* 'Blue Beauty' and leaves like *N.* 'Pamela', this is a new, very free-blooming beauty.

Nymphaea 'Perry's Blue Heaven'
Photo by Perry D. Slocum.

Nymphaea 'Persian Lilac'
Photo by H. Nash.

Nymphaea 'Persian Lilac' (George H. Pring 1941)
Unknown parentage. Fragrant. 41–42 petals. Excellent bloomer. Pinkish lilac, peony-shaped flowers measure 8–10 in. (20–25 cm). Jagged light green leaves with brownish flecks in new leaves are up to 10 in. (25 cm) across with a spread of 5–6 ft. (1.5–2 m).

Nymphaea 'Tina'
Photo by Bob Romar.

Nymphaea 'Tina' (Van Ness Water Gardens 1974)
Unknown parentage. Viviparous. Fragrant. 15–16 petals. Excellent bloomer. ST. Deep violet-purple, cup-shaped flowers measure 4.5–6 in. (11–15 cm). Green leaves are slightly longer than they are wide with smooth, wavy edges, and measure 10.5 × 9.5 (26 × 24 cm), and spread 3–5 ft. (1–1.5 m).

N. 'Wood's Blue Goddess'
Photo by Perry D. Slocum.

N. 'Wood's Blue Goddess' (John Wood 1989)
N. ampla is one parent. Good flowering. Forms bulblets around the main tuber. Nearly black stamens provide unique contrast. Deep sky-blue petals that fade to lighter shade in warmth of summer. Stellate flowers of 10–12 in. (25–30 cm). Leaves measure 12–13 in. (30–33 cm) and spread 8 ft. (2.5 m).

Nymphaea 'Evelyn Randig'
Photo by Gail Perrone.

PINK

Nymphaea 'Evelyn Randig' (Martin E. Randig 1931)
Unknown parentage. 25 petals. Excellent bloomer. Deep raspberry-pink petals and greenish-based sepals with tiny purple veins form cup-shaped blossoms that evolve into stellate form and measure 7–9 in. (18–23 cm). Purple-blotched, round, green leaves measure 14–15 in. (35–38 cm) and spread 5–7 ft. (1.5–2.1 m).

Nymphaea 'General Pershing'
Photo by Perry D. Slocum.

Nymphaea 'General Pershing' (George H. Pring 1920)
N. 'Mrs. Edwards Whitaker' and *N.* 'Castaliflora.' Fragrant. 25–27 petals. Excellent bloomer. Lavender-pink petals and sepals form 8–11 in. (20–28 cm) cup-shaped flowers that evolve into flat, open form. Olive-green, nearly round and wavy-edged leaves measure 9.5–10.5 in. (24–27 cm) and spread 5–6 ft. (1.5–2 m).

Nymphaea 'Enchantment'
Photo by Perry D. Slocum.

Nymphaea 'Enchantment' (Martin E. Randig 1963)
Unknown parentage. Fragrant. 24–25 petals. Good bloomer. Rich medium-pink petals and sepals form 7–10 in. (18–25 cm) flat blooms. Slightly serrated with wavy edges, the bright green, oval leaves measure up to 15×13.5 in. (38×34 cm) and spread 5–9 ft. (1.5–2.7 m).

Nymphaea 'Noelene'
Photo by Bob Romar.

Nymphaea 'Noelene' (Charles Winch 1972)
Unknown parentage. Highly fragrant. 16 petals. Good bloomer.
Lavender-pink, stellate flowers measure 6–9 in. (15–23 cm)
across. Maroon mottling marks the bright green, nearly round,
wavy-edged leaves. They measure 8–10 in. (20–25 cm) and
spread 5–7 ft. (1.5–2.1 m).

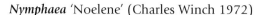

Nymphaea 'Texas Shell Pink' (Rolf Nelson 1979)
Unknown parentage. Cinnamon fragrance. 16–20 petals. Good
bloomer. Creamy white petals and sepals bear reddish-purple
tips. Flat, platelike flowers measure up to 8 in. (20 cm). Dark yellow-green leaves measure 13–15 in. (33–38 cm) and spread 5–6
ft. (1.5–2 m).

Nymphaea 'Texas Shell Pink'
Photo by Bob Romar.

SUNSET/ORANGE SHADES

Nymphaea 'Albert Greenberg' (Monroe Birdsey 1969)
Chance seedling. Fragrant. Excellent bloomer. 20 petals. Yellow
flowers have orange-pink tips on petals. Cup-shaped blooms
measure 6–7 in. (15–18 cm). Green leaves, heavily blotched purple, are large and nearly round with rounded notches and wavy
edges. Leaves measure up to 19 × 18 (48 × 45 cm) and spread
5–8 ft. (1.5–2.5 m).

Nymphaea 'Albert Greenberg'
Photo by Bob Romar.

Nymphaea **'Mrs. George H. Pring'**
Photo by H. Nash.

Nymphaea 'Mrs. George H. Pring' (George H. Pring 1922)
N. ovalifolia × *N.* 'Mrs. Edwards Whitaker.' Lightly fragrant. 21 petals. Excellent bloomer. Creamy white flowers with greenish gray stripes in outer petals and sepals are stellate and measure 7–8 in. (18–20 cm). Ovate leaves are green with new leaves blotched purple. Measuring up to 16.5 × 13 in. (41 × 33 cm), they spread 6–9 ft. (2–2.7 m).

Nymphaea 'White Delight' (Charles Winch 1984)
Unknown parents. Excellent bloomer. 26–29 petals. Pale yellow to creamy white stellate flowers of 10–12 in. (25–30 cm). Leaves measure up to 13 × 12 in. (33 × 30 cm) and spread 6–7 ft. (2–2.2 m).

Nymphaea **'White Delight'**
Photo by Perry D. Slocum.

Nymphaea 'Wood's White Knight' (John Wood 1977)
N. 'Sir Galahad' and *N.* 'Missouri' included in parentage. 28–30 petals. Excellent bloomer. Very full, peony-type white flowers measure 10–12 in. (25–30 cm). Nearly round, green leaves have scalloped and slightly wavy edges, measure 12–15 in. (30–38 cm) and spread 8–10 ft. (2.5–3 m).

Nymphaea **'Wood's White Knight'**
Photo by Bob Romar.

***Nymphaea* 'Eldorado'**
Photo by Perry D. Slocum.

***Nymphaea* 'St. Louis'**
Photo by Perry D. Slocum.

***Nymphaea* 'St. Louis Gold'**
Photo by Perry D. Slocum.

***Nymphaea* 'Yellow Dazzler'**
Photo by Bob Romar.

YELLOW

Nymphaea 'Eldorado' (Martin E. Randig 1963)
Unknown parentage. Fragrant. 20–22 petals. Excellent bloomer. Lemon-yellow petals and sepals frequently edged with pinkish orange form large 9–11 in. (23–28 cm) stellate blossoms. Bronze-colored new leaves turn green with many purple blotches. Ovate and smooth-edged, they measure up to 12 × 10 (30 × 25 cm) and spread 6 ft. (2 m).

🌿 🌿 🌿 🌿 🌿 🌿 🌿 🌿 🌿 🌿

Nymphaea 'St. Louis' (George H. Pring 1932)
N. stuhlmannii × *N.* 'Mrs. George H. Pring.' Fragrant. 29–31 petals. Excellent bloomer. Lemon-yellow stellate blooms measure 8–11 in. (20–28 cm). Smooth and nearly round green leaves have somewhat wavy edges and measure up to 20 × 19 (50 × 48 cm). They spread 8–10 ft. (2.5–3 m).

🌿 🌿 🌿 🌿 🌿 🌿 🌿 🌿 🌿 🌿

Nymphaea 'St. Louis Gold' (George H. Pring 1956)
N. 'Sulfurea' × *N.* 'African Gold.' 20–22 petals. Good bloomer. Opens and closes later in day than other day-bloomers. Deep yellow stellate blossoms measure 5–6 in. (12.5–15 cm). Bronze and purple-blotched, ovate, new leaves turn olive-green and measure 8–10 in. (20–25 cm). They spread 4–5 ft. (1.2–1.5 m).

🌿 🌿 🌿 🌿 🌿 🌿 🌿 🌿 🌿 🌿

Nymphaea 'Yellow Dazzler' (Martin E. Randig 1938)
Unknown parentage. Very fragrant. 23 petals. Good bloomer. Lemon-yellow petals with veined yellowish green sepals form stellate blooms of 8–10 in. (20–25 cm). Ovate, smooth-edged with some waviness, slightly blotched purple leaves measure up to 17 × 14.5 (43 × 36 cm) and spread 6–8 ft. (2–2.5 m).

🌿 🌿 🌿 🌿 🌿 🌿 🌿 🌿 🌿 🌿

***Nymphaea* 'Emily Grant Hutchings'**
Photo by Perry D. Slocum.

***Nymphaea* 'Antares'**
Photo by Perry D. Slocum.

Tropical Night-Blooming Water Lilies

Cultivars of night-blooming tropical water lilies usually open about dusk and close between 11 AM and noon the following day. Cold fall days can cause them to remain open for longer periods, as can periods of cloudy days. A single blossom lasts three or four successive days. At this time there are no blue, yellow, or orange/sunset-colored, or viviparous night-blooming tropical cultivars. Most night-bloomers exude a pungent, light fragrance that helps pollinating insects locate the flowers in the dark.

PINK

Nymphaea 'Emily Grant Hutchings' (George H. Pring 1922)
N. 'C.E. Hutchings' × unknown. Excellent bloomer. Tubers send out short runners that develop new plants at the tips. Blooms earlier in the season that most other night-blooming varieties. Dark pink, cup-shaped blossoms measure 6–8 in. (15–20 cm). Leaves spread 6–7 ft. (2–2.2 m).

🌿 🌿 🌿 🌿 🌿 🌿 🌿 🌿 🌿 🌿

RED

Nymphaea 'Antares' (Longwood Gardens 1962)
Hybridized by Patrick Nutt. *N* 'H.C. Haarstick' × *N.* 'Emily Grant Hutchings.' 30–36 petals. Good bloomer. Dark rosy-red petals and sepals combine with orange stamens in a strikingly beautiful cup-shaped blossom measuring 6–10 in. (15–25 cm). 10–12 in. (25–30 cm) green leaves bear undulating edges and pointed projections. New leaves are bronze with green veins. Spreads 5–7 ft. (1.5–2.2 m).

🌿 🌿 🌿 🌿 🌿 🌿 🌿 🌿 🌿 🌿

Nymphaea 'Maroon Beauty'
Photo by Perry D. Slocum.

Nymphaea 'Maroon Beauty' (Perry D. Slocum 1950)
Seedling of *N.* 'H.C. Haarstick'. 24–26 petals. Good bloomer.
Deep red, 10–12 in. (25–30 cm), round and flat blossoms are
accented with red-tipped chocolate-brown anthers. Reddish
brown color, round form, and jagged and wavy edges describe
the 16 in. (40 cm) leaves that spread 6–12 ft. (2–3.5 m).

Nymphaea 'Red Beauty'
Photo by Perry D. Slocum.

Nymphaea 'H.C. Haarstick' (James Gurney 1922)
N. 'Mrs. D.R. Francis' × unknown. Tropical night bloomer. 22–24
petals. Excellent bloomer. Red, round, flat blossoms are graced by
orange-red anthers and stamens and measure 10–12 in. (25–30 cm)
across. Reddish brown leaves measure up to 16 in. (40 cm) and spread
6–12 ft. (2–3.5 m).

Nymphaea 'Red Flare'
Photo by Perry D. Slocum.

Nymphaea 'Red Flare' (Martin E. Randig 1938)
Unknown parentage. 19–20 petals. Excellent bloomer. Blooms
held 12 in. (30 cm) above water Deep red, round, flat flowers
measure 7–10 in. (18–25 cm). Reddish bronze leaves bear a few
small purple blotches and grow more round with age. Heavily
serrated and wavy leaves measure 10–12 in. (25–30 cm). The
leaves spread 5–6 ft. (1.5–2 m).

Nymphaea 'Bali Night'
Photo by Don Bryne.

Nymphaea 'Missouri'
Photo by Perry D. Slocum.

Nymphaea 'Sir Galahad'
Photo by Perry D. Slocum.

Nymphaea 'Trudy Slocum'
Photo by Perry D. Slocum.

WHITE

Nymphaea 'Bali Night' (Don Bryne & Peter Slocum 1997)
Discovered in Bali by Don Bryne and Peter Slocum, flushed pink outer petals surround radiant white.

Nymphaea 'Missouri' (George H. Pring 1932)
Parents probably *N.* 'Mrs. George C. Hitchcock' × *N.* 'Sturtevantii'. 31 petals. Good bloomer. Flowers wilt in excessive heat. 10–14 in. (25–35 cm) white, flat, platelike blossoms bear yellow anthers and stamens. Large, green leaves are very dentate with wavy margins. Measuring up to 14 × 12 (35 × 30 cm), the leaves spread 6–10 ft. (2–3 m).

Nymphaea 'Sir Galahad' (Martin E. Randig 1965)
Unknown parentage. 28 petals. Good bloomer. Flowers held 10–11 in. (25–28 cm) above water. White flowers, round and flat in form, measure 9–12 in. (23–30 cm). Nearly round, serrated green leaves are 13–15 in. (33–38 cm) and spread 6–9 ft. (2–2.7 m).

Nymphaea 'Trudy Slocum' (Perry D. Slocum 1948)
Seedling of *N.* 'Juno.' 19–29 petals. Excellent bloomer. Readily produces seed. Nearly flat, white flowers measure 6–8 in. (15–20 cm). Nearly round, green leaves are lightly blotched purple and measure 13.5 × 12.5 (34 × 32 cm) with a 5–6 ft. (1.5–2 m) spread.

Hardy Water Lily Cultivars

Hardy water lilies usually float upon the water's surface, although a few varieties hold their blooms above the water.
Photo by Perry D. Slocum.

Some water lilies do not tolerate high summer temperatures. Their petals crispen and seem to burn or melt. Photo by H. Nash.

Between 1880 and 1910 at Temple-sur-Lot, Joseph Bory Latour-Marliac hybridized over 100 varieties of hardy water lilies, many of which are still cherished today. After Marliac's death, two generations of his in-laws, the Laydeker family, continued to operate his nursery until it was sold to Stapeley Water Gardens of Nantwich, Cheshire, England, in 1991. Marliac's contribution to our world of colored hardy water lily cultivars is so significant that the characteristic rhizome form of many of his cultivars bears his name.

Hardy water lilies are true perennial plants. So long as the rhizome does not freeze, the plant survives winter dormancy. They are now available in red to near-black, pink, white, yellow, orange or peach shades, and "changeable" or "sunset" shades that change color over the three to four day bloom period of the flower. While there are no blue hardies, hybridizing efforts in recent years have produced the very deep red shades that approach nearly black and the delightful peachy orange shades seen before only in one phase of a sunset lily's life span. The efforts of Perry D. Slocum and Dr. Kirk Strawn are particularly noteworthy in this area.

Typically, hardy water lilies do not bloom as profusely as their tropical cousins, nor do they hold their blossoms so highly out of water. Often, hardy blossoms float upon the water's surface. Because many of the hardy cultivars are sterile and do not reproduce by seed, their availability to the trade is a testimony to the efforts to reproduce them vegetatively, by division and by growing on of the "eyes" often found along the rhizomes. With the exception of *Nymphaea* 'Colonel A.J. Welch,' *N.* 'Cherokee,' and *N.* 'Perry's Viviparous Pink,' hardies do not reproduce viviparously.

Hardy water lilies do not bloom at night either. In most cases, they open by midmorning and close by mid to late afternoon. As days lengthen in the autumn, many varieties stay open until very late afternoon or early evening.

As hardy perennials, these cultivars fare well in the temperate-zone pond. Early spring finds their fresh pads making their way to the water's surface. By mid to late spring, many will be in bloom. Interestingly, some varieties prove susceptible to extended periods of heat. These particular lilies have limited success in Zones 8 through 10. They may not bloom as much or at all, or they may display burning, melting, or wilting, with the petals collapsing or blackening. Cultivars susceptible to these conditions are generally in the red-to-pink color range, although some changeables, particularly *N.* 'Sioux', burn with temperatures in the high 90s F (above 35° C).

Nymphaea **'Carolina Sunset'**
Photo by Perry D. Slocum.

Nymphaea **'Florida Sunset'**
Photo by Perry D. Slocum.

Varieties Especially Subject to Burning or Wilting in Hot Temperatures

N. 'Attraction'

N. 'Atropurpurea'

N. 'Conqueror'

N. 'Perry's Red Beauty"

N. 'Sioux'

N. 'Perry's Wildfire'

N. 'Almost Black'

N. 'Pink Sunrise'

N. 'William Falconer'

Red Hardy Water Lilies That Do Not Wilt in Heat

N. 'Charles de Meurville'

N. 'Escarboucle'

N. 'Froebeli'

N. 'James Brydon'

N. x*laydeckeri* 'Fulgens'

N. 'Perry's Black Opal'

N. 'Perry's Baby Red'

N. 'Perry's Red Wonder'

N. 'Rembrandt'

N. 'Splendida'

ORANGE/PEACH SHADES

Nymphaea 'Carolina Sunset' (Perry D. Slocum 1991)
Seedling of *N.* 'Texas Dawn.' Marliac rhizome. 29–33 petals.
Good bloomer. Inner petals are a deep yellow with the middle
petals a light yellow blushed peach. By third day, flowers are a
pastel yellow suffused with a peachy glow. Cup-shaped flowers
bear turned-down sepals, 7–8 in. (18–20 cm). Nearly round
leaves, 11 × 11.5 (28 × 29 cm), are green with chartreuse; new
leaves are heavily mottled purple and/or green. Spreads 4–5 ft.
(1.2–1.5 m).

❦ ❦ ❦ ❦ ❦ ❦ ❦ ❦ ❦ ❦

Nymphaea 'Florida Sunset' (Perry D. Slocum 1995)
Seedling of *N.* 'Texas Dawn.' 31–33 petals. Excellent bloom. A
glowing yellow flushed with a peachy glow characterizes the cup-
shaped flowers of 7–8 in. (18–20 cm). Nearly round leaves, 11 ×
11.5 (28 × 29 cm) spread 4–5 ft. (1.2–1.5 m).

❦ ❦ ❦ ❦ ❦ ❦ ❦ ❦ ❦ ❦

Nymphaea 'Peaches and Cream'
Photo by Perry D. Slocum.

Nymphaea 'Peaches and Cream' (Perry D. Slocum 1997)
U.S. Plant Patent No. 9,676, October 29, 1996.
N. 'Texas Dawn' × N. 'Perry's Viviparous Pink.' 32–37 petals. Pink outer petals and yellow inner petals curl inwardly. Delightful fragrance. Round leaves have convolutions along the edges and are flecked purple when young .

PINK

Nymphaea 'American Star' (Perry D. Slocum 1985)
Chance seedling of N. 'Rose Arey.' 30–31 petals. Good bloomer. Rich salmon-pink with lighter-hued petal tips. Stellate flower shape measures up to 6–7 in. (15–18 cm) across. Round, green leaves begin a purple-green and grow to 10–11 in. (25–28 cm) with a spread of 4–5 ft. (1.2–1.5 m).

Nymphaea 'American Star'
Photo by Bob Romar.

Nymphaea 'Arc-en-Ciel' (Joseph B.L. Marliac 1901)
18–24 petals. Good bloomer, but often grown for incredibly variegated leaves. Fragrant. Stellate-shaped flowers, 5–6 in. (13–15 cm), with long, narrow petals open shell-pink and fade to white by the second day. Round leaves, 9.5 in. (24 cm) open predominantly pink with cream and pale green splotches, and age into green and cream with pink and maroon splashes of color.

Nymphaea 'Arc-en-Ciel'
Photo by H. Nash.

Nymphaea 'Colossea'
Photo by H. Nash.

Nymphaea 'Colossea' (Joseph B.L. Marliac 1901)
23–25 petals. Prolific bloomer. Pale pink, cup-shaped flowers fade to near-white as the 6–8 in. (15–20 cm) blooms become stellate. New leaves are bronze and turn green, 10–12 in. (25–30 cm), and spread 5–6 ft. (1.5–2 m).

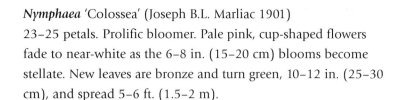

Nymphaea 'Darwin'
Photo by Perry D. Slocum.

Nymphaea 'Darwin' (aka 'Hollandia') (Joseph B. L. Marliac 1909)
36–37 petals. Good bloomer. Inner petals are light pink and then deepen in hue with age; outer petals are white and pinkish by third day. With deeper inner coloration, a sense of glowing color emanates from the flowers. Double, peony-shaped flower is 6–7.5 in. (15–19 cm). Leaves, 10–11 in. (25–28 cm), are green and spread 4–5 ft. (1.2–1.5 m).

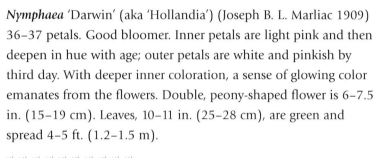

Nymphaea 'Fabiola'
Photo by Perry D. Slocum.

Nymphaea 'Fabiola' (formerly 'Mrs. Richmond') (Latour-Marliac Nursery 1913)
24–25 petals. Profuse bloomer. Peony-shaped flowers bear inner petals of highly flecked pinkish red with outer petals a lighter hue, also highly flecked and with white tips. They measure 6–7 in. (15–18 cm). Bronze-purple new leaves turn green and measure 12 × 11 in. (30 × 28 cm) and spread to 5 ft. (1.5 m).

***Nymphaea* 'Firecrest'**
Photo by Perry D. Slocum.

Nymphaea 'Firecrest'

29 petals. Good bloomer. Does well in earth ponds. Lavender pink petals form stellate flowers of 5.5–6 in. (14–15 cm). Startling orange stamens on flowers held high above the water make for special attraction. Very deep purple new leaves turn green, measure 9 in. (23 cm), and spread 4 ft. (1.2 m). An "improved" version is available.

❧ ❧ ❧ ❧ ❧ ❧ ❧ ❧ ❧

***Nymphaea xlaydekeri* 'Rosea'**
Photo by Perry D. Slocum.

Nymphaea xlaydekeri 'Rosea' (Joseph B.L. Marliac 1893)

25–26 petals. Good bloomer. Cup-shaped flowers of pink petals that deepen towards the center measure 4–5 in. (10–13 cm). Leaves are mottled purple when new and then turn wholly green. Measuring 9 × 7.5 (23 × 19 cm), they spread 4–5 ft. (1.2–1.5 m).

❧ ❧ ❧ ❧ ❧ ❧ ❧ ❧ ❧ ❧

***Nymphaea* 'Lily Pons'**
Photo by Perry D. Slocum.

Nymphaea 'Lily Pons' (Perry D. Slocum 1996)

N. 'Perry's Fire Opal' × *N.* 'Gloire du Temple-sur-Lot.' Tuberosa/odorata rhizome. Nearly 100 petals per flower. Excellent bloomer. Double blooms open a medium pink and delicately turn a shell pink by the fourth day. Spreads 4–5 ft. (1.2–1.5 m)

❧ ❧ ❧ ❧ ❧ ❧ ❧ ❧ ❧ ❧

***Nymphaea* 'Madame Wilfron Gonnere'**
Photo by Perry D. Slocum.

Nymphaea 'Madame Wilfron Gonnere' (syn. 'Pink Gonnere')
(Latour-Marliac Nursery after 1912)
33 petals. Excellent bloomer. ST. Peony-shaped flowers, 5 in. (13 cm), with inner petals of rich pink and lighter outer petals that glow with vibrancy. Leaves measure 9.5–10 in. (24–25 cm) and spread to 4 ft. (1.2 m).

🌿 🌿 🌿 🌿 🌿 🌿 🌿 🌿 🌿 🌿

***Nymphaea xmarliacea* 'Carnea'**
Photo by Bob Romar, © Maryland Aquatic Nurseries.

Nymphaea xmarliacea 'Carnea' (syn. 'Marliac Flesh,' 'Morning Glory') (Joseph B.L. Marliac 1887)
23 petals. Excellent bloomer. Light pink, cup-shaped flowers measure 4.5–5 in. (11–13 cm). Green leaves measure 7.5–8 in. (19–20 cm) and spread 4–5 ft. (1.2–1.5 m).

🌿 🌿 🌿 🌿 🌿 🌿 🌿 🌿 🌿 🌿

***Nymphaea* 'Masaniello'**
Photo by Ron Everhart.

Nymphaea 'Masaniello' (Joseph B.L. Marliac 1908)
25 petals. Excellent bloomer. One of the better bloomers in part shade. Slightly subject to crown rot. Cup-shaped flowers with raspberry-pink inner petals and lighter outer petals measure 5–6 in. (13–15 cm). Leaves measure up to 10 × 9 in. (25 × 23 cm) and spread to 4 ft. (1.2 m).

🌿 🌿 🌿 🌿 🌿 🌿 🌿 🌿 🌿 🌿

Nymphaea 'Mrs. C.W. Thomas'
Photo by H. Nash.

Nymphaea 'Mrs. C.W. Thomas' (George L. Thomas)
36 petals. Good bloomer. Good cultivar for earth ponds. Stays open later than many others. With inner petals of a pale pink and outer petals a shell pink, the 6–7 in. (15–18 cm) peony-shaped flowers appear to glow as they age to a paler pink. Leaves measure 9–10 in. (23–25 cm) and spread 4–6 ft. (1.2–2 m).

🌿 🌿 🌿 🌿 🌿 🌿 🌿 🌿 🌿

Nymphaea 'Norma Gedye'
Photo by Perry D. Slocum.

Nymphaea 'Norma Gedye' (Laurence Gedye 1973)
19–20 petals. Good bloomer. Stellate-shaped flowers, 6.5–7.5 in. (16–19 cm), of medium pink deepen in hue toward the petal bases. Leaves measure up to 11 in. (28 cm) with a 4–5 ft. (1.2–1.5 m) spread.

🌿 🌿 🌿 🌿 🌿 🌿 🌿 🌿 🌿

Nymphaea 'Pearl of the Pool'
Photo by Perry D. Slocum.

Nymphaea 'Pearl of the Pool' (Perry D. Slocum 1946)
N. 'Pink Opal' × *N.* x*marliacea* 'Rosea.' 40–48 petals. Good bloomer. Medium pink, cup-shaped blossoms turn stellate and measure 5–6 in. (13–15 cm). Leaves measure up to 10 in. (25 cm) and spread 4–5 ft. (1.2–1.5 m).

🌿 🌿 🌿 🌿 🌿 🌿 🌿 🌿 🌿

Nymphaea 'Perry's Cactus Pink'
Photo by Perry D. Slocum.

Nymphaea 'Perry's Cactus Pink' (Perry D. Slocum 1990)
Probably *N.* 'Perry's Pink' × *N.* 'American Star.' 28 petals. Fragrant.
Good bloomer. Uniquely rolled and narrow shell-pink petals
with deeper-hued bases form a stellate flower of 5–6 in. (13–15
cm). Leaves measure 7–8 in. (18–20 cm) and spread about 4 ft.
(1.2 m).

🌿 🌿 🌿 🌿 🌿 🌿 🌿 🌿 🌿 🌿

Nymphaea 'Perry's Crinkled Pink'
Photo by Perry D. Slocum.

Nymphaea 'Perry's Crinkled Pink' (Perry D. Slocum 1989)
N. 'Gloire du Temple-sur-Lot' × *N.* 'Vesuve.' 27–33 petals. Good
bloomer. Deep shell-pink, crinkled petals form a full stellate
flower of 4.5–5.5 in. (11–14 cm). Leaves measure 8–9 in. (20–
23 cm) and spread 4 ft. (1.2 m).

🌿 🌿 🌿 🌿 🌿 🌿 🌿 🌿 🌿 🌿

Nymphaea 'Perry's Fire Opal'
Photo by Perry D. Slocum.

Nymphaea 'Perry's Fire Opal' (Perry D. Slocum 1987)
40–50 petals. Good bloomer. ST. Peony-shaped flower of very
rich pink petals, each marked with a lengthwise stripe, measures
5–6 in. (13–15 cm). Leaves, with unusual vein patterns radiating
from centers, measure 7–10 in. (18–25 cm) and spread 3–4 ft.
(1–1.2 m).

🌿 🌿 🌿 🌿 🌿 🌿 🌿 🌿 🌿 🌿

Nymphaea 'Perry's Magnificent'
Photo by Perry D. Slocum.

Nymphaea 'Perry's Magnificent' (Perry D. Slocum 1990)
N. 'Perry's Pink' × *N.* 'Director George T. Moore'. 33–38 petals. Good bloomer. Very deep dusty rose petals form a stellate flower 6–7 in. (15–18 cm) with a yellow-edged center. A prominent red center dot marks the stigmal area. Leaves of 10 in. (25 cm) spread to 4–5 ft. (1.2–1.5 m).

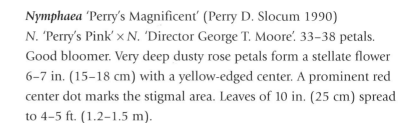

Nymphaea 'Perry's Pink'
Photo by Perry D. Slocum.

Nymnphaea 'Perry's Pink' (Perry D. Slocum 1984)
Chance seedling of *N.* 'Rose Arey'. 35–39 petals. Good bloomer. Rich pink petals combine in a 6–7 in. (15–18 cm) stellate flower. A red dot marks the stigma. Leaves, up to 11 in. (28 cm), spread 4–5 ft. (1.2–1.5 m).

Nymphaea 'Perry's Pink Delight'
Photo by Perry D. Slocum.

Nymphaea 'Perry's Pink Delight' (Perry D. Slocum 1990)
Probably *N.* 'Colonel A.J. Welch' × *N.* 'Splendida'. Mildly viviparous from flowers. 28 petals. Excellent bloomer. Evenly pink petals pale with age on the stellate flowers that measure 5.5–7 in. (14–18 cm). Leaves measure up to 10 in. (25 cm) and spread 4–5 ft. (1.2–1.5 m).

Nymphaea 'Perry's Pink Heaven'
Photo by Perry D. Slocum.

Nymphaea 'Perry's Pink Heaven' (Perry D. Slocum 1990)
Probably *N.* 'Perry's Fire Opal' × *N.* 'Pearl of the Pool.' 44–45 petals. Good bloomer. Leaves and flowers nearly same in size. A darker pink base and center vein on pink petals form a stellate flower that measures 6–8 in. (15–20 cm). Leaves measure 7.5 × 8 in. (19 × 20 cm) and spread 4–5 ft. (1.2–1.5 m).

🌿 🌿 🌿 🌿 🌿 🌿 🌿 🌿 🌿 🌿

Nymphaea 'Perry's Rich Rose'
Photo by Perry D. Slocum.

Nymphaea 'Perry's Rich Rose' (Perry D. Slocum)
N. 'Perry's Pink' × *N.* 'Mrs. Martin E. Randig. 29–30 petals. Good bloomer. Stays open later than other hardies. Rich, old-rose petals form a stellate-shaped flower 6–8 in. (15–20 cm). Marked with a pink dot in the middle of the stigmal area. Leaves measure 9 in. (23 cm) and spread 4–4.5 ft. (1.2–1.4 m).

🌿 🌿 🌿 🌿 🌿 🌿 🌿 🌿 🌿 🌿

Nymphaea 'Perry's Strawberry Pink'
Photo by Perry D. Slocum.

Nymphaea 'Perry's Strawberry Pink' (Perry D. Slocum 1989)
Probably *N. alba* plant from New Zealand and *N.* 'Vesuve.' 29–30 petals. Good bloomer. Adapts to small pond. Inner petals are a deep strawberry-pink with even darker outer petals. Cup-shaped flower with stellate petals measures 5–5.5 in. (13–14 cm). Leaves measure 7 in. (18 cm) and spread 4–5 ft. (1.2–1.5 m).

🌿 🌿 🌿 🌿 🌿 🌿 🌿 🌿 🌿 🌿

Nymphaea 'Perry's Super Rose' (Perry D. Slocum 1990)
Probably *N.* 'Perry's Pink' × *N.* 'Sirius.' 37–38 petals. Good
bloomer. Rich, deep rose-pink petals form stellate-shaped flowers
6.5–7.5 in. (16–19 cm). Inner petals are beautifully rolled. Leaves
measure up to 10.5 × 11 in. (27 × 28 cm) and spread 4–5 ft.
(1.2–1.5 m).

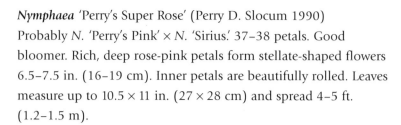

Nymphaea 'Perry's Super Rose'
Photo by Perry D. Slocum.

Nymphaea 'Perry's Vivid Rose' (Perry D. Slocum 1990)
N. 'Perry's Pink' × *N.* 'Pamela.' 38–39 petals. Good bloomer.
Pinkish red petals bear a yellow edging on inner petals. Cup-
shaped blossoms measure 5.5–6 in. (14–15 cm). Leaves measure
8–8.5 in. (20–22 cm) and spread 4–5 ft. (1.2–1.5 m).

Nymphaea 'Perry's Vivid Rose'
Photo by Perry D. Slocum.

Nymphaea 'Perry's Viviparous Pink' (Perry D. Slocum 1990)
N. 'Perry's Pink' × *N.* 'Colonel A.J. Welch.' 44–47 petals. Slightly
viviparous from flowers. Good bloomer. Long bloom season.
Deep pink petals in stellate form measure 6–7.5 in. (15–19 cm).
Red spot in stigma. Leaves up to 10.5 in. (26 cm) spread about
5 ft. (1.5 m).

Nymphaea 'Perry's Viviparous Pink'
Photo by Perry D. Slocum.

Nymphaea 'Perry's Wildfire'
Photo by Perry D. Slocum.

Nymphaea 'Perry's Wildfire' (Perry D. Slocum 1990)
N. 'Perry's Pink' × *N.* 'Mrs. Martin E. Randig.' Fragrant. 28–29 petals. Good bloomer. Stays open later in the day than others. Glowing purplish red stellate-shaped flowers with orange-red stamens measure up to 6–7 in. (15–18 cm). Heart-shaped leaves measure up to 10 × 9 in. (25 × 23 cm) and spread 4–5 ft. (1.2–1.5 m).

Nymphaea 'Peter Slocum'
Photo by Perry D. Slocum.

Nymphaea 'Peter Slocum' (Perry D. Slocum 1984)
A chance seedling of *N.* 'Pearl of the Pool.' 40–41 petals. Fragrant. Good bloomer. Medium pink, concave petals fade slightly with age in this peony-style flower of 6–7.5 in. (15–19 cm). Leaves measure up to 11 in. (28 cm) and spread 5–6 ft. (1.5–2 m).

Nymphaea 'Pink Beauty'
Photo by Perry D. Slocum.

Nymphaea 'Pink Beauty' (formerly 'Fabiola'; syn. 'Luciana') (Henry A. Dreer 1899)
24–25 petals. Excellent bloomer. Cup-shaped, medium pink flowers measure 6–7 in. (15–18 cm). Purplish leaves turn green and measure 8–9 in. (20–23 cm) with a spread of 3–4 ft. (1–1.2 m).

Nymphaea 'Pink Opal'
Photo by Bob Romar.

Nymphaea 'Pink Opal' (Helen Fowler 1915)
26 petals. Fragrant. Good bloomer. Holds blooms 3–5 in. (8–13 cm) above the water. Coral-pink petals form a cup-shaped flower of 3–4 in. (8–10 cm). Leaves measure 8–9 in. (20–23 cm) and spread up to 3 ft. (1 m).

Nymphaea 'Pink Sensation'
Photo by Perry D. Slocum.

Nymphaea 'Pink Sensation' (Perry D. Slocum 1947)
Chance seedling or mutation of *N.* 'Lustrous.' 20 petals. Excellent bloomer. Stays open later in day than many others. Cup-shaped flowers that become stellate measure 5–6 in. (13–15 cm). The gradation of rich pink color tones makes the blossoms glow with an inner life. Leaves measure up to 10 in. (25 cm) and spread to 4 ft. (1.2 m).

Nymphaea 'Pink Starlet'
Photo by Perry D. Slocum.

Nymphaea 'Pink Starlet' (Kenneth Landon 1970)
Natural hybrid involving *N. tuberosa.* Fragrant. 29–30 petals. Good bloomer. Light pink stellate flowers measure 5–7 in. (13–18 cm.). Leaves measure 6–10 in. (15–25 cm) and spread 3–6 ft. (1–2 m).

Nymphaea 'Ray Davies'
Photo by Perry D. Slocum.

Nymphaea 'Ray Davies' (Perry D. Slocum 1985)
Seedling of *N*. 'Rosanna'. 53–55 petals. Good bloomer. Peony-shaped flowers measure 6–7 in. (15–18 cm). Yellow inner petals and light pink outer petals deepen in shade toward their base. Leaves measure up to 10–11 in. (25–28 cm) and spread 5 ft. (1.5 m) .

Nymphaea 'Rene Gerard'
Photo by H. Nash.

Nymphaea 'Rene Gerard' (syn. 'La Beaugere') (Latour-Marliac Nursery 1914)
20–24 petals. Good bloomer. Inner petals are a deep rosy red, paling toward outer petals that bear much flecking. Stellate-shaped flowers grow to 6–9 in. (15–23 cm). Leaves measure up to 10–11 in. (25–28 cm) and spread 5 ft. (1.5 m).

Nymphaea 'Rosy Morn'
Photo by Perry D. Slocum.

Nymphaea 'Rosy Morn' (Harry Johnson 1932)
N. 'Rose Arey' × *N*. 'Escarboucle'. 24 petals. Excellent bloomer. Inner petals are a rich strawberry-pink and outer petals a very pale pink that fades with age on a star-shaped flower measuring 6–7 in. (15–18 cm). Leaves measure 8–9 in. (20–23 cm) and spread 3–4 ft. (1–1.2 m).

Nymphaea **'Splendida'**
Photo by Perry D. Slocum.

Nymphaea 'Splendida' (Joseph B.L. Marliac 1909)
Fragrant. 30 petals. Excellent bloomer. Inner petals are a reddish pink that deepen with age as the outer petals also deepen from their initial light pink. Globular-shaped flowers measure 5–6 in. (13–15 cm). Leaves measure 9 in. (23 cm) and spread 4–5 ft. (1.2–1.5 m).

🌿 🌿 🌿 🌿 🌿 🌿 🌿 🌿 🌿

RED

Nymphaea 'Almost Black' (Perry D. Slocum 1996)
N. 'Perry's Fire Opal' × N. 'Blue Beauty.' 36 petals. Excellent bloomer. Very dark red bloom approaches black at its center. Flowers measure 8–9 in. (20–22.5 cm) across. Large spread is suited to the medium to large pool.

🌿 🌿 🌿 🌿 🌿 🌿 🌿 🌿 🌿

Nymphaea **'Almost Black'**
Photo by Perry D. Slocum.

Nymphaea 'Black Princess' (Perry D. Slocum 1998)
U.S. Plant Patent No. 09, 662.

🌿 🌿 🌿 🌿 🌿 🌿 🌿 🌿 🌿

Nymphaea **'Black Princess'**
Photo by Perry D. Slocum.

Nymphaea 'Atropurpurea'
Photo by Perry D. Slocum.

Nymphaea 'Atropurpurea' (Joseph B.L. Marliac 1901)
39–33 petals. Good bloomer except in Zones 8–10, where blossoms wilt with heat. Deep red petals on the round, flat blooms evolve into 7–8 in. (18–20 cm) stellate form as they grow darker with each day. Stamens are burnt orange. Round green leaves, 9–10 in. (23–25 cm), are purple when new.

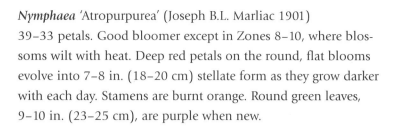

Nymphaea 'Attraction'
Photo by Perry D. Slocum.

Nymphaea 'Attraction' (Joseph B.L. Marliac 1910)
26–28 petals. Good bloomer. May burn or wilt in hot climates. Subject to crown rot. Inner petals of the cup-shaped, then stellate-shaped flowers are a deep garnet-red with lighter outer petals. Flowers measure up to 6–8 in. (15–20 cm) across. Oval-shaped, 10–12 in. (25–30 cm) leaves are green, but new leaves are a light bronze. Spreads 4–5 ft. (1.2–1.5 m).

Nymphaea 'Charles de Meurville'
Photo by Perry D. Slocum.

Nymphaea 'Charles de Meurville' (Latour-Marliac Nursery 1931)
22 petals. Excellent bloomer. Subject to crown rot. Inner petals are a dark pinkish red, with outer petals pink. Stellate flower shape, 6–7 in. (15–18 cm). Leaves, 10 × 8 in. (25 × 20 cm) are dark green and spread 4–5 ft. (1.2–1.5 m).

Nymphaea 'Conqueror'
Photo by Perry D. Slocum.

Nymphaea 'Conqueror' (Joseph B.L. Marliac 1910)

28 petals. Excellent bloomer. Wilts in hot weather. Inner petals are a deep red that darken with age, while outer petals begin white and turn pink. Star-shaped flower is 7–8 in. (18–20 cm). New leaves are slightly bronze, turn deep green, and measure up to 10–11 in. (25–28 cm) with a spread of 5 ft. (1.5 m).

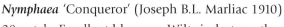

Nymphaea 'Ellisiana'
Photo by Perry D. Slocum.

Nymphaea 'Ellisiana' (Joseph B.L. Marliac 1896)

21–22 petals. Excellent bloomer. Tends to stop blooming in very hot weather and does better in the more northern climates. ST. Brilliant red petals form a full stellate flower 4–5 in. (10–13 cm). Leaves are green, 7–8 in. (18–20 cm), and spread to 3 ft. (1 m).

Nymphaea 'Escarboucle'
Photo by Perry D. Slocum.

Nymphaea 'Escarboucle' (syn. 'Aflame') (Joseph B.L. Marliac 1909)

25 petals. Excellent bloomer. Stays open longer than most others. Very bright vermilion red with the outer petal row tipped in white. Cup-shaped flowers evolve into stellate form, 6–7 in. (15–18 cm). New brownish leaves turn green, measure 10–11 in. (25–28 cm), and spread to 4–5 ft. (1.2–1.5 m).

Nymphaea 'Froebeli'
Photo by Perry D. Slocum.

Nymphaea 'Froebeli' (Otto Froebel 1898)
18 petals. Good bloomer. Does well in part shade. Wilts in hot climates. Deep burgundy-red petals form cup-shaped and then stellate flowers, measuring 4.5–5 in. (11–13 cm). Green leaves measure 6 in. (15 cm) and spread 3 ft. (1 m).

Nymphaea 'Gloriosa'
Photo by Perry D. Slocum.

Nymphaea 'Gloriosa' (Joseph B.L. Marliac 1896)
27–30 petals. Excellent bloomer. Very subject to crown rot. Lightly flecked bright red petals begin cup-shaped and turn stellate-formed in flowers of 5 in. (13 cm). Leaves measure 8–9 in. (20–23 cm) and spread to 5 ft. (1.5 m).

Nymphaea xlaydekeri 'Fulgens'
Photo by H. Nash.

Nymphaea xlaydekeri 'Fulgens' (syn. 'Red Laydeker') (Joseph B.L. Marliac 1895)
20 petals. Profuse bloomer. Long bloom season. Typical of *laydekeri* group, produces long stems. Cup-shaped flowers of vivid burgundy-red deepen in color with age and measure 5–6 in. (13–15 cm). New leaves blotched purple, turn green, measure 8.5 × 7.5 in. (22 × 19 cm), and spread 4–5 ft. (1.2–1.5 m).

Nymphaea 'James Brydon'
Photo by Perry D. Slocum.

Nymphaea 'James Brydon' (Dreer Nurseries 1900)
27 petals. Not subject to crown rot and does well in only 2–3 hours of sunlight. Tends to stop blooming in very hot weather. Bloom tends to come in spurts. Adapts well to small pool culture. Very vivid rose-red, cuplike flowers measure 4–5 in. (10–13 cm). Fragrant. New leaves are purplish and mottled. Round leaves measure 7 in. (18 cm) and spread 3–4 ft. (1–1.2 m).

Nymphaea 'Little Champion'
Photo by Perry D. Slocum.

Nymphaea 'Little Champion' (Perry D. Slocum 1997)
Crossing *N. odorata* var. *gigantea* × *N.* 'William Falconer' produced a vivid red water lily suited to the small-pond and tub-garden culture. Excellent bloomer, too.

Nymphaea 'Lucida'
Photo by H. Nash.

Nymphaea 'Lucida' (Joseph B.L. Marliac 1894)
18–20 petals. Good bloomer. Tolerates part shade. Subject to crown rot. Stellate-shaped flowers of red inner petals and outer whitish pink petals with pink veins measure 5–6 in. (13–15 cm). Green leaves, mottled and blotched with purple, measure up to 10 × 9 in. (25 × 23 cm) and spread 4–5 ft. (1.2–1.5 m).

Nymphaea 'Perry's Baby Red'
Photo by Perry D. Slocum.

Nymphaea 'Perry's Baby Red' (Perry D. Slocum 1989)
Probably *N.* 'Alba Plenissima' × *N.* 'Atropurpurea.' 24–31 petals.
Excellent bloomer. ST. Deep red, cup-shaped flowers measure
3–3.5 in. (8–9 cm). Leaves measure 4.5–6 in. (11–15 cm) and
spread to 30 in. (75 cm).

Nymphaea 'Perry's Black Opal'
Photo by Perry D. Slocum.

Nymphaea 'Perry's Black Opal' (Perry D. Slocum 1990)
Probably *N.* 'Vesuve' × *N.* 'Splendida.' 24 petals. Good bloomer.
Blooms well in heat. Very dark red petals form a stellate flower
measuring 6–7 in. (15–18 cm). Leaves measure 10 × 9.5 (25 ×
24 cm) and spread 3.5–5 ft. (1.1–1.5 m).

Nymphaea 'Perry's Dwarf Red'
Photo by Perry D. Slocum.

Nymphaea 'Perry's Dwarf Red' (syn. 'Perry's Red Dwarf') (Perry D.
Slocum 1989)
Probably *N.* 'Alba Plenissima' and *N.* 'Atropurpurea.' 30 petals.
Good bloomer. ST. Brilliant red, peony-shaped flowers range
4–4.5 in. (10–11 cm). Leaves measure 6 in. (15 cm) and spread
3 ft. (1 m).

Nymphaea 'Perry's Red Beauty'
Photo by Perry D. Slocum.

Nymphaea 'Perry's Red Beauty' (Perry D. Slocum 1989)
N. 'Vesuve' is one parent. 24–30 petals. Good bloomer. Very deep red petals deepen in color with age on stellate-shaped bloom of 6.5–7 in. (16–18 cm). Many of the petals curl inward. Leaves measure up to 10 × 8.5 in. (25 × 22 cm) and spread 4 ft. (1.2 m).

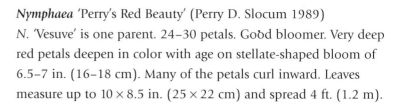

Nymphaea 'Perry's Red Bicolor'
Photo by Perry D. Slocum.

Nymphaea 'Perry's Red Bicolor' (Perry D. Slocum 1989)
N. 'Vesuve' is a probable parent. 16–19 petals. Good bloomer. Deep, rich red inner petals combine with outer petals of pinkish red in a stellate-shaped flower of 5.5–6 in. (14–15 cm). Leaves, marked with a small, ragged purple circle in the middle at the stem, measure 7.5 × 7 in. (19 × 18 cm) and spread 4 ft. (1.2 m).

Nymphaea 'Perry's Red Blaze'
Photo by Perry D. Slocum.

Nymphaea 'Perry's Red Blaze' (Perry D. Slocum 1989)
N. 'Pearl of the Pool' × *N.* 'Charles de Meurville.' 33 petals. Good bloomer. Cherry-red petals form a full, stellate bloom with downward-turning outer petals and sepals to measure 6 in. (15 cm) across. Leaves measure 9.5 × 8.5 (24 × 22 cm) and spread 4–5 ft. (1.2–1.5 m).

Nymphaea **'Perry's Red Wonder'**
Photo by Perry D. Slocum.

Nymphaea 'Perry's Red Wonder' (syn. 'Perry's Red Volunteer')
(Perry D. Slocum 1989)
N. 'Splendida' is a probable parent. 21–22 petals. Excellent
bloomer. Flowers and leaves nearly same size. Stellate flowers,
5.5–6.5 in. (14–16 cm), of bright red petals with lighter veins
and green flushed sepals. Leaves measure 5.5–7 in. (14–18 cm)
and spread 30–36 in. (75–91 cm).

🌿 🌿 🌿 🌿 🌿 🌿 🌿 🌿 🌿 🌿

Nymphaea **'Perry's Super Red'**
Photo by Perry D. Slocum.

Nymphaea 'Perry's Super Red' (Perry D. Slocum 1989)
N. 'Charles de Meurville' × *N.* 'Gloire du Temple-sur-Lot'
Marliac rhizome. 38–43 petals. Good bloomer. Stays open later
in day than many others. LN. Inner petals are a brilliant vermilion red with pinkish outer petals on peony-shaped flower measuring 5.5–7.5 in. (14–19 cm). Leaves measure up to 10 in.
(25 cm) and spread 5 ft. (1.5 m).

🌿 🌿 🌿 🌿 🌿 🌿 🌿 🌿 🌿 🌿

Nymphaea **'Red Sensation'**
Photo by Perry D. Slocum.

Nymphaea 'Red Sensation' (Perry D. Slocum 1991)
Probably *N.* 'Alba Plenissima ' × *N.* 'Atropurpurea.' 37–38 petals.
Good bloomer. Deep red with some flecking on petals that form
a peony-shaped flower measuring 6–7.5 in. (15–19 cm). Leaves
measure up to 10 in. (25 cm) and spread 4–5 ft. (1.2–1.5 m).

🌿 🌿 🌿 🌿 🌿 🌿 🌿 🌿 🌿 🌿

Nymphaea 'Sirius'
Photo by H. Nash.

Nymphaea 'Sirius' (Latour-Marliac Nursery 1913)
27 petals. Excellent bloomer. Inner petals are a deep purple-red with some flecking, and outer petals a lighter hue with flecking and white tips. Deep glowing red stamens mark the 6–7 in. (15–18 cm) stellate flowers. Leaves measure up to 11 in. (28 cm) and spread 5–6 ft. (1.5–2 m).

Nymphaea 'Sultan'
Photo by Perry D. Slocum.

Nymphaea 'Sultan' (Latour-Marliac Nursery)
24–25 petals. Excellent bloomer. One of few reds to fare well in hot southern climates. Renamed *N.* 'Gresille' by the Marliac Nursery. Inner petals open a deep pink but turn a deep red by the second day. Outer petals open a pale pink, but are also a rich red by the second day. Flecking develops on the petals of the cup-shaped blooms that evolve into stellate form and measure 6–7 in. (15–18 cm). Leaves measure 10–11 in. (25–28 cm) and spread 4–5 ft. (1.2–1.5 m).

Nymphaea 'Vesuve'
Photo by H. Nash.

Nymphaea 'Vesuve' (Joseph B.L. Marliac 1906)
22–23 petals. Excellent bloomer. Long bloom season; stays open later in day than most other hardies. Brilliant, glowing red deepens with age in the star-shaped flowers that measure 7 in. (18 cm). Concave petals may have two lengthwise creases. Leaves measure 9–10 in. (23–25 cm) and spread to 4 ft. (1.2 m).

Nymphaea **'Chrysantha'**
Photo by Perry D. Slocum.

Nymphaea **'Comanche'**
Photo by Perry D. Slocum.

Nymphaea **'Indiana'**
Photo by Perry D. Slocum.

SUNSET/CHANGEABLES

Nymphaea 'Chrysantha' (formerly 'Graziella') (Joseph B.L. Marliac 1905)

Upright rhizome. 16–19 petals. Excellent bloomer except in very hot regions. Often mislabeled as 'Graziella' or 'Paul Hariot' (which has larger blooms and is subject to crown rot). Cup-shaped flower, 3–4 in. (8–10 cm), bears outer petals of a cream-yellow with a large green patch on the outside, inner petals of a deeper cream-yellow. All petals are flushed with orange that deepens in color each day. New leaves are blotched purple, then turn green, and measure 6.5 × 5.5 in. (16 × 14 cm) with a spread of 2–3 ft. (0.6–1 m).

🌿 🌿 🌿 🌿 🌿 🌿 🌿 🌿 🌿 🌿

Nymphaea 'Comanche' (formerly 'J.C.N. Forestier') (Joseph B.L. Marliac 1908)

22–26 petals. Excellent bloomer. Highly subject to crown rot. First-day flowers are yellow-apricot with deeper hues toward the center; second day, gold-orange flushed pink; third day, deep orange, with the center petals flushed red and with pale yellow tips. Flowers are cup-shaped and then stellate, 5–6 in. (13–15 cm). New leaves grow up to 12 × 11 in. (30 × 28 cm), begin bronze and turn green. Spread 4–5 ft. (1.2–1.5 m).

🌿 🌿 🌿 🌿 🌿 🌿 🌿 🌿 🌿 🌿

Nymphaea 'Indiana' (Latour-Marliac Nursery 1912)

15–19 petals. Excellent bloomer. Subject to crown rot. ST. Cup-shaped flowers open apricot, change to apricot-orange, and then to a deep orange-red, and measure 3.5–4 in. (9–10 cm). Leaves blotched purple measure 5 × 4.5 in. (13 × 11 cm) and spread to 30 in. (75 cm).

🌿 🌿 🌿 🌿 🌿 🌿 🌿 🌿 🌿 🌿

Nymphaea 'Sioux'
Photo by H. Nash.

Nymphaea 'Sioux' (Joseph B.L. Marliac 1908)
19–20 petals. Excellent bloomer. Flowers stay open very late in the day. May burn or wilt in hot temperatures. Petal colors deepen each day and progress from lightest in the center to deepest in outer rows. Color ranges from yellowish apricot to orange-red in lanceolate petals that form a star-shaped bloom measuring 5–6 in. (13–15 cm). Leaves measure 8–9 in. (20–23 cm) and spread to 4 ft. (1.2 m).

Nymphaea 'Solfatare'
Photo by Ron Everhart.

Nymphaea 'Solfatare' (Joseph B.L. Marliac 1906)
29 petals. Good bloomer. Subject to crown rot. Inner petals begin a yellowish apricot, turn a creamy peach, and then peach. Outer petals are darker shades in cup-shaped flowers that measure 3–4 in. (8–10 cm). Leaves measure 6 × 5 in. (15 × 13 cm) and spread 30–40 in. (75–100 cm) .

WHITE

Nymphaea 'Gladstoniana'
Photo by Perry D. Slocum.

Nymphaea 'Gladstoniana' (syn. 'Gladstone') (George Richardson 1897)
22–25 petals. Good bloomer. Not recommended for small gardens. LN. White stellate flowers measure 5.5–7 in. (14–18 cm). Round green leaves measure 11–12 in. (28–30 cm) and spread 5–8 ft. (1.5–2.5 m).

Nymphaea 'Gonnere'
Photo by Michael Duff.

Nymphaea 'Gonnere' (syn. 'Snowball,' 'Crystal White') (Latour-Marliac Nursery 1914)
Fragrant. 57–62 petals. Good bloomer. Performs best in cooler climates. Stays open later in day than most others. White, ball-shaped flowers measure 4–6 in. (10–15 cm). Round leaves measure 6–8 in. (15–20 cm) and spread 3–4 ft. (1–1.2 m).

Nymphaea 'Hal Miller'
Photo by Perry D. Slocum.

Nymphaea 'Hal Miller'
One parent is *N. mexicana.* Excellent bloomer. May wilt in hotter climates. Somewhat subject to crown rot. Blooms in partial shade. Provide adequate winter protection in zones colder than 5. Stellate-shaped flowers of creamy white outer petals often bear innermost petals of yellow. Flowers measure 7–10 in. (18–25 cm). Leaves vary from green to olive-green with some blotching marks, measure 9–12 in. (23–30 cm), and spread 4–6 ft. (1.2–2 m).

Nymphaea 'Hermine'
Photo by Perry D. Slocum.

Nymphaea 'Hermine' (Joseph B.L. Marliac 1910)
17–20 petals. Excellent bloomer. ST. Star-shaped, white flowers measure 5–5.5 in. (13–14 cm). Olive-green leaves measure 7 × 6 in. (18 × 15 cm) and spread 30 in. (75 cm).

Nymphaea xlaydekeri 'Alba'
Photo by Perry D. Slocum.

Nymphaea xlaydekeri 'Alba' (syn. 'White Laydeker') (Latour-Marliac Nursery)
17–19 petals. Excellent bloomer. Dies back in hotter climates; protect from rotting. Subject to crown rot. Waxy white, cup-shaped flowers measure 3–4 in. (8–10 cm). Deep green leaves with prominent yellow veins measure 8 in. (20 cm) and spread 3–4 ft. (1–1.2 m).

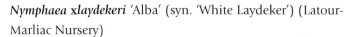

Nymphaea xmarliacea 'Albida'
Photo by Bob Romar.

Nymphaea xmarliacea 'Albida' (syn. 'Marliac White') (Joseph B.L. Marliac 1880)
23–26 petals. ST. Excellent bloomer. White, cup-shaped flowers measure 5–6 in. (13–15 cm). Leaves measure 9 in. (23 cm) and spread 3–4 ft. (1–1.2 m).

Nymphaea 'Gloire du Temple-sur-Lot'
Photo by Perry D. Slocum.

Nymphaea 'Gloire du Temple-sur-Lot' (Latour-Marliac Nursery 1913)
128–129 petals. Sparse bloomer. Flowers are worth waiting for! LN. Incredible double flowers of shell pink fade to white and measure 5–6 in. (13–15 cm). Leaves measure 10 in. (25 cm) and spread 4–5 ft. (1.2–1.5 m).

Nymphaea 'Mt. Shasta'
Photo by Perry D. Slocum.

Nymphaea 'Mt. Shasta' (Perry D. Slocum 1996)
Unknown parents. 36 petals. Excellent bloomer. Huge, 8 to 9 in. (20–23 cm) blossoms of pristine white grace this new hybrid that spreads 4–5 ft. (1.2–1.5 m) in the medium-to-large water garden.

🌿🌿🌿🌿🌿🌿🌿🌿🌿🌿

Nymphaea 'Perry's Double White'
Photo by Perry D. Slocum.

Nymphaea 'Perry's Double White' (Perry D. Slocum 1990)
Seedling of *N. tuberosa* 'Richardsonii' No. 2 and probably *N.* 'Perry's Super Red.' 44 petals. Good bloomer. Long bloom season. Pure white, stellate-formed flowers 6–7 in. (15–18 cm). Leaves, with slightly ruffled edges, measure 9–10 in. (23–25 cm) and spread 4–5 ft. (1.2–1.5 m).

🌿🌿🌿🌿🌿🌿🌿🌿🌿🌿

Nymphaea 'Perry's White Star'
Photo by Perry D. Slocum.

Nymphaea 'Perry's White Star' (Perry D. Slocum 1990)
N. 'Pink Starlet' × *N.* 'Pamela' 32–34 petals. Good bloomer. Blooms are held 2–4 in. (5–10 cm) above the water. Stellate-shaped blossoms of long, narrow white petals, measure 5.5–7 in. (14–18 cm). Leaves measure 8–9.5 × 7.5–9 in. (20–24 × 19–23 cm) and spread 4–5 ft. (1.2–1.5 m).

🌿🌿🌿🌿🌿🌿🌿🌿🌿🌿

Nymphaea 'Perry's White Wonder'
Photo by Perry D. Slocum.

Nymphaea 'Perry's White Wonder' (Perry D. Slocum 1990)
N. tetragona and *N. alba* plant from New Zealand. 27–31 petals.
Excellent bloomer. Adapts to small pools. White cup-shaped
blooms turn stellate and measure 3.5–6 in. (9–15cm). Leaves
measure up to 9 × 8 in. (23 × 20 cm) and spread 3.5–4.5 ft.
(1.1–1.4 m).

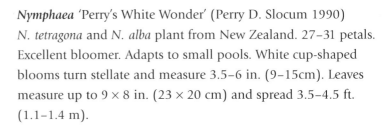

Nymphaea tetragona
Photo by Perry D. Slocum.

Nymphaea tetragona

Nymphaea tetragona is a dwarf species water lily that prefers more
cold than many others. It reproduces by seed and cannot be
divided vegetatively. Often not opening until afternoon, it does
stay open late. The variety *N. tetragona* var. *angusta*, native to
China and Japan, fares better in warm-weather climates. *(*Water
gardeners in climate zones warmer than Zone 6 should look for
the variety marketed as 'Japanese *tetragona.'*)

Nymphaea 'Venus'
Photo by Perry D. Slocum.

Nymphaea 'Venus' (Perry D. Slocum 1991)
N. 'Pink Starlet' × *N.* 'Pamela.' 29–32 petals. Good bloomer.
Blooms held 3–6 in. (8–15cm) above water. White petals,
blushed a very pale pink, form stellate flowers that measure 6–7
in. (15–18 cm). Leaves measure 10.5 in. (27cm) and spread 4–5
ft. (1.2–1.5 m).

Nymphaea 'Virginalis'
Photo by H. Nash.

Nymphaea 'Virginalis' (Joseph B.L. Marliac 1910)
21–22 petals. Excellent bloomer. Pristine white, cup-shaped flowers measure 4.5–5.5 in. (11–14cm). Leaves measure 9 in. (23cm) and spread 3–4 ft. (1–1.2 m).

Nymphaea 'Virginia'
Photo by Bob Romar.

Nymphaea 'Virginia' (Charles Thomas 1962)
N. odorata 'Sulphurea Grandiflora' × *N.* 'Gladstoniana'. 23–27 petals. Inner petals are a soft yellow with white outer petals. Flowers measure 7–8 in. (18–20 cm); leaves measure 10 × 8.5 in. (25 × 22 cm) and spread 5–6 ft. (1.5–2 m).

YELLOW

Nymphaea 'Colonel A.J. Welch' (Joseph B.L. Marliac)
Viviparous from the blossom. 22–23 petals. Sparse bloomer. Closely resembles N. 'Sunrise'; 'Col. A.J. Welch' is a coarser lily with fewer blooms and considerably more foliage. Usually recommended for deeper earth ponds, planting it at 2–3 ft. (0.6–1 m) deep and allowing it to spread into deeper waters. Petals are lemon-yellow with an inner row of a slightly deeper hue. Stellate flowers measure 5.5–6 in. (14–15cm). New leaves are often flecked with purple, but then turn to olive-green. Round, 9 in. (23cm) leaves spread to 6 ft. (2 m).

Nymphaea 'Colonel A.J. Welch'
Photo by H. Nash.

Nymphaea 'Gold Medal'
Photo by Perry D. Slocum.

Nymphaea 'Gold Medal' (Perry D. Slocum 1991)
Seedling of *N*. 'Texas Dawn.' Fragrant. 27–31 petals. Good bloomer. Inner petals of rich yellow are framed by petals of a lighter hue. Flowers measure 6–8 in. (15–20 cm). Olive-green leaves, mottled purple, measure 10 in. (25cm) with a spread to 4–5 ft. (1.2–1.5 m).

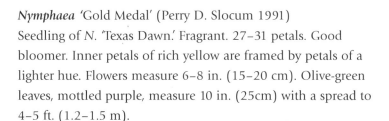

Nymphaea 'Helvola'
Photo by Perry D. Slocum.

Nymphaea 'Helvola' (syn. 'Yellow Pygmy') (Joseph B. L. Marliac 1879)
Probably *N. tetragona* × *N. mexicana*. 16–17 petals. Excellent bloomer. Does well in colder climates. Opens and closes later in day than most others. ST. Cup-shaped, medium yellow flowers evolve into stellate form and measure only 2–3 in. (5–8 cm). Green leaves, heavily mottled and blotched deep purple, measure 5 × 3.5 in. (13 × 9 cm) with a spread of 2–3 ft. (0.6–1 m).

Nymphaea xmarliacea 'Chromatella'
Photo by Perry D. Slocum.

Nymphaea x*marliacea* 'Chromatella' (syn. 'Golden Cup,' 'Marliac Yellow';) (Joseph B.L. Marliac 1887)
22–25 petals. Excellent bloomer. Blooms in part shade. Light yellow cup-shaped flowers measure 4–5.5 in. (10–14cm). Green leaves, blotched and mottled purple, measure 8–9 in. (20–23cm) with a spread to 3 ft. (1 m).

***Nymphaea odorata* 'Sulphurea Grandiflora'**
Photo by Perry D. Slocum.

***Nymphaea* 'Sunrise'**
Photo by Bob Romar.

***Nymphaea* 'Texas Dawn'**
Photo by Perry D. Slocum.

Nymphaea odorata 'Sulphurea Grandiflora' (Joseph B. L. Marliac 1888)

Parentage probably *N. odorata* var. *gigantea* × *N. mexicana*. 23–28 petals. Good bloomer in Zone 6 and above. Requires extra winter protection in zones colder than 5. Easily confused with *N.* 'Sunrise.' Walter Pagel notes 'Sunrise' has hairy stems while *N. odorata* 'Sulphurea Grandiflora' has smooth stems. LN. Outer petals of the stellate-shaped blooms are a lighter yellow than the inner ones. The 7–9.5 in. (18–24 cm) flowers seem to glow on the water. Tiny purple mottles mark the 11 × 10 in. (28 x25 cm) leaves that spread 4–5 ft. (1.2–1.5 m).

Nymphaea 'Sunrise'

At this writing, confusion exists as to the existence of *N.* 'Sunrise.' As noted above, Walter Pagel believes there are two, albeit nearly identical, varieties. The story is that around 1930, Johnson Water Gardens in Hynes, California, renamed *N. odorata* 'Sulphurea Grandiflora' as 'Sunrise.' Walter believes that Kirk Strawn has the true *N.* 'Sunrise.' Having secured our 'Sunrises' from Kirk, we can corroborate that the stems do have a slight hairiness.

Nymphaea 'Texas Dawn' (Kenneth Landon 1985)

N. 'Pink Starlet' × *N. mexicana* No. 1. Fragrant. 26–28 petals. Excellent bloomer. Flowers may be held 10 in. (25 cm) above water. One of the very best of yellow hardies. Give extra winter protection in Zone 5 and colder. Inner petals are a rich yellow with outer petals blushed pink on the long, narrow petals that form a 6–8 in. (15–20 cm) stellate bloom. Leaves measure 8 in. (20 cm) and spread 3–5 ft. (1–1.5 m).

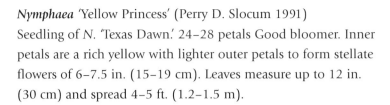

Nymphaea 'Yellow Princess' (Perry D. Slocum 1991)
Seedling of *N.* 'Texas Dawn.' 24–28 petals Good bloomer. Inner petals are a rich yellow with lighter outer petals to form stellate flowers of 6–7.5 in. (15–19 cm). Leaves measure up to 12 in. (30 cm) and spread 4–5 ft. (1.2–1.5 m).

Nymphaea **'Yellow Princess'**
Photo by Perry D. Slocum.

Nymphaea 'Yellow Queen' (Perry D. Slocum 1991)
Seedling of *N.* 'Texas Dawn.' Fragrant. 30–32 petals. Good bloomer. Rich yellow inner petals and lighter outer petals curl upward to form unique star-shaped flower of 7–10 in. (18–25cm). Leaves are heavily mottled with purple and measure up to 12 in. (30 cm) and spread 4–5 ft. (1.2–1.5 m).

Nymphaea **'Yellow Queen'**
Photo by Perry D. Slocum.

Nymphaea 'Yellow Sensation' (Perry D. Slocum 1991)
N. alba from New Zealand × *N. mexicana* No. 2. 33–36 petals. Good bloomer. Blooms held up to 6 in. (15cm) above water. Needs room to prevent leaves piling. Rich yellow, cup-shaped flowers measure 5–8 inches (13–20 m). Leaves measure up to 10 in. (25 cm) and spread 3–5 ft. (1–1.5 m).

Nymphaea **'Yellow Sensation'**
Photo by Perry D. Slocum.

Other Water Lilies Available to the Trade.

Nymphaea 'Castaliflora'— a tropical day bloomer. Photo by H. Nash.

Nymphaea 'Aquarius'—a Patrick Nutt day-blooming cultivar. Photo by H. Nash.

Nymphaea 'Marmorata'—a tropical day bloomer. Photo by H. Nash.

Nymphaea 'Angela'— a Don Bryne day-blooming tropical cultivar.
Photo by H. Nash.

Nymphaea 'Ruby'—a day-blooming tropical
Photo by H. Nash.

Nymphaea 'Crystal'—
Don Bryne's white tropi-
cal day bloomer, the
first viviparous intro-
duction since N.
'Isabella Pring' in 1922.
Photo by H. Nash.

Nymphaea 'Floyd
Wolfort'—a William
Frase cultivar.
Photo by H. Nash.

Nymphaea 'Shirley Bryne'—a Don Bryne day-blooming
tropical. Photo by H. Nash.

Nymphaea 'June Allison' Photo by H. Nash.

Nymphaea
'Sturtevanti'
Photo by Bob
Romar.

Nymphaea 'Afterglow' (Martin E. Randig 1946)
Unknown parentage. Tropical day bloomer. Fragrant. 21 petals. Good bloomer. Yellow petals have orange tips. Sepals are a deep pinkish orange. Flowers are shaped like a sunflower after the first day and measure 6–10 inches (15–25 cm). Nearly round, green leaves are smooth with wavy edges, measure 11.5 × 11 in. (29 × 28 cm), and spread 6–8 ft. (2–2.5 m). Red undersides bear prominent green veins.

Nymphaea 'Alice Tricker' (Charles Tricker 1937)
May be seedling, hybrid, or mutation of *N.* 'Mrs. George H. Pring.' Tropical day bloomer. Fragrant. Good bloomer with long bloom season. 21 petals. White broad petals form 7–9 in. (18–23cm) stellate flowers graced with golden yellow stamens. New leaves are mottled with purple and then age to green. Egg-shaped, they measure 15 × 12 in. (38 × 30 cm) and spread 6–8 ft. (2–2.5 m).

Nymphaea 'Amabilis' (syn. 'Pink Marvel') (Latour-Marliac Nursery 1921)
Hardy water lily. 20–23 petals. Good bloomer. Medium pink shade with lighter pink tips on petals in a stellate-shaped flower measuring 6–7.5 in. (15–19 cm).

Nearly round, leaves of 9.5 in. (24 cm) spread 5–7.5 ft. (1.5–2.3 m).

Nymphaea 'Aurora' (Joseph B.L. Marliac 1895)
Hardy water lily. 24–25 petals. Excellent bloomer. Flowers stay open late in day. ST. A sunset or changeable, first day color: yellow-apricot with darker center; second day: orange-red with a slight flecking; third day: deep burgundy-red slightly flecked. Stamens are a glowing, golden orange. Flower is cup-shaped and evolves into flatter form, 4–4.5 in. (10–11 cm). Leaves, 6–6.5 in. (15–16 cm), are green with new leaves blotched with purple. Spreads 3 ft. (1 m).

Nymphaea 'Aviator Pring' (George H. Pring 1956)
N. 'Sulfurea' × *N.* 'St. Louis.' Tropical day bloomer. Fragrant. Excellent bloomer. 25–26 petals. Yellow flowers are star-shaped and measure 8–10 in. (20–25 cm). Slightly ovate leaves measure 12 × 10.5 in. (20 × 25 cm) and spread 6–8 ft. (2 × 2.5 m).

Nymphaea 'Cherokee' (syn. 'Orange Hybrid') (Perry's Water Gardens 1989)
N. 'Colonel A.J. Welch' × *N.* 'Aurora.' Hardy water lily. Occasionally viviparous from

flower. 21 petals. Good bloomer. Subject to crown rot. ST. Petals open a rich red with outer petals cream-flushed-pink, becoming a deep red by third day. Cup-shaped flower measures 3–4 in. (8–10 cm). 4–6 in. (10–15 cm) green leaves are mottled maroon when new. Spreads 3–4 ft. (1–1.2 m).

Nymphaea 'Formosa' (Joseph B.L. Marliac 1909)
Hardy water lily. 26 petals. Excellent bloomer. Cup-shaped flowers of highly flecked, vivid, medium pink with deeper hues in center measure 5–6 in. (13–15 cm). Olive-green leaves measure 8 in. (20 cm) and spread 4–5 ft. (1.2–1.5 m).

Nymphaea 'Golden Fascinator' (Martin E. Randig 1946)
Unknown parentage. Tropical day bloomer. Fragrant. 18–22 petals. Excellent bloomer. Yellow cup-shaped and then stellate blossoms of 6.5–9 in. (16–23cm) feature orange-pink outer petals and tips. With overlapping lobes, the 11–12 in. (28–30 cm) green leaves bear some jagged points and wavy edges. Spreads to 6–7 ft. (2–2.2 m).

Nymphaea 'Golden West' (Martin E. Randig 1936)
Seedling of *N.* 'St. Louis.' Tropical day bloomer. 21 petals. Fragrant.

Excellent bloomer. Peach-colored petals and peach sepals marked with greenish gray lengthwise veins form 8–10 in. (20–25 cm) flat blossoms. New leaves are heavily mottled purple, then turn green and measure 10–11 in. (25–28 cm) with a spread of 5–6 ft. (1.5–2 m).

🌿 🌿 🌿 🌿 🌿 🌿 🌿 🌿 🌿 🌿

Nymphaea 'Green Smoke' (Martin E. Randig 1965)
Unknown parentage. Tropical day bloomer. Fragrant. 21–22 petals. Excellent bloomer. Uniquely colored, the inner petals are a greenish yellow, tipped blue, with the outer petals blue. Sepals are a light blue with a greenish yellow base. Cup-shaped blossoms measure 5–6 in. (13–15 cm). Greenish leaves bear some faint purple blotches. New leaves are pinkish to bronze with faint purple blotches. Ovate leaves with rounded and wavy edges measure up to 12 × 10.5 (30 × 27cm) and spread 5–6 ft. (1.5–2 m).

🌿 🌿 🌿 🌿 🌿 🌿 🌿 🌿 🌿 🌿

Nymphaea 'Red Beauty' (Perry D. Slocum 1966)
Seedling of *N. capensis* var. *zanzibariensis*. Tropical day bloomer. Fragrant. 34 petals. Good bloomer. Leaves are longer than they are wide, 12.5 × 14 in. (32 × 35 cm) with jagged and wavy edges. New leaves are bronze with purple mottling. They later turn green and retain some faint purple blotches. Spreads 5–6 ft. (1.5–2 m).

🌿 🌿 🌿 🌿 🌿 🌿 🌿 🌿 🌿 🌿

Nymphaea 'Henry Shaw' (George H. Pring 1917)
Seedling of *N.* 'Castaliflora.' Day-blooming tropical. Fragrant. 28–30 petals. Good bloomer. Campanula blue petals with lighter sepals form cup-shaped blossoms that evolve into flat, open blooms measuring 8–10 in. (20–25 cm). Indented and wavy-margined leaves are green with sparse light brown spots and measure up to 15 × 13.5 in. (38 × 34 cm) with a spread of 6–8 ft. (2–2.5 m).

🌿 🌿 🌿 🌿 🌿 🌿 🌿 🌿 🌿 🌿

Nymphaea 'Jack Wood' (John Wood 1972)
Unknown parentage. Tropical day bloomer. Fragrant. 25–26 petals. Excellent bloomer. Raspberry-red petals and deep red sepals form 8–10 in. (20–25cm) stellate blossoms. Nearly round, dentate-edged green leaves show some purple blotching on new leaves. Measuring 10–12 in. (25–30 cm), they spread 6–7 ft. (2–2.2 m).

🌿 🌿 🌿 🌿 🌿 🌿 🌿 🌿 🌿 🌿

Nymphaea 'Joanne Pring' (George H. Pring 1942)
A mutation of *N. tetragona*. Hardy water lily, but must be propagated by seed. 15–16 petals. Good bloomer. May be subject to crown rot. ST. Inner petals are light to medium pink with outer petals a pale pink. The cuplike, 3–4 in. (8–10 cm) flowers deepen in color with age. Purple blotched leaves

measure 5.5 in. (14 cm) and spread to 3 ft. (1 m).

🌿 🌿 🌿 🌿 🌿 🌿 🌿 🌿 🌿 🌿

Nymphaea 'Judge Hitchcock' (George H. Pring 1941)
One parent is probably *N. stuhlmannii*. Day-blooming tropical. Fragrant. 24 petals, 4 sepals. Excellent bloomer. Nearly purple blue petals and veined sepals form cup-shaped blossoms 6–8 in. (15–20 cm) across. Many purple blotches radiate from the center of the nearly round green leaves that measure 10 in. (25 cm) and spread to 5 ft. (1.5 m).

🌿 🌿 🌿 🌿 🌿 🌿 🌿 🌿 🌿 🌿

Nymphaea 'Juno' (1906)
N. lotus is one parent. Tropical night bloomer. 19–20 petals. Good bloomer. 6–10 in. (15–25 cm) white, cup-shaped flowers evolve into flat platelike form. Nearly round, jagged, green leaves measure 13 × 12 (33 × 30 cm) and spread 5–6 ft. (1.5–2 m).

🌿 🌿 🌿 🌿 🌿 🌿 🌿 🌿 🌿 🌿

Nymphaea 'Louise' (Charles Thomas 1962)
N. 'Escarboucle' × *N.* 'Mrs. C.W. Thomas.' Hardy water lily. Fragrant. 20 petals. Good bloomer. Red, cup-shaped flowers measure 6 in. (15 cm). Leaves are 9–10 in. (23–25 cm) and spread 4–5 ft. (1.2–1.5 m).

🌿 🌿 🌿 🌿 🌿 🌿 🌿 🌿 🌿 🌿

Nymphaea 'Margaret Randig' (Martin E. Randig 1939) Unknown parentage. Day-blooming tropical. Fragrant. 22 petals. Excellent bloomer. 8–11 in. (20–28 cm) blue blossoms are flat and round. Nearly round, deep green, mature leaves show large, round serrations around the edges. Leaves grow to 13 × 12 in. (33 × 30 cm) and spread 8–9 ft. (2.5–2.7 m).

Nymphaea 'Marian Strawn' (Kirk Strawn 1969) *N.* 'Mrs. George H. Pring' × unknown. Tropical day bloomer. Fragrant. 22 petals. Excellent bloomer. Full, stellate, flowers of pristine white measure 8–9 in. (2.5–2.7cm). Irregular purple blotches radiate from the center of the green leaves that measure up to 13 × 11 (33 × 28 cm). Margins are wavy, serrated, and spread 7–8 ft. (2.2–2.5 m).

Nymphaea 'Mark Pullen' (Charles Winch 1987) Unknown parents. Day-blooming tropical. Lightly fragrant. 37–44 petals. Good bloomer. Rich violet-blue petals and pale bluish green sepals form cup-shaped blossoms that evolve stellate, measuring 7–8 in. (18–20 cm). Nearly round and wavy-edged green leaves measure up to 12 × 11.5 in. (30 × 29 cm) with one

lobe usually slightly raised. Spreads 5–6 ft. (1.5–2 m).

Nymphaea 'Mrs. George C. Hitchcock' (George H. Pring 1926) Seedling of *N.* 'Omarana.' Tropical night bloomer. 20 petals. Excellent bloomer. Prolific seed producer. Light to medium pink petals with darker-hued sepals form large, flat 10–11 in. (25–28 cm) flowers. Bronze-tinted leaves bear some purple blotching in newer pads and are longer than they are wide. Jagged and wavy edges on leaves up to 15 × 13.5 in. (38 × 34 cm). Spreads 7–8 ft. (2.2–2.5 m).

Nymphaea 'Moorei' (Adelaide Botanic Gardens 1900) 25–26 petals. Good bloomer. May be subject to crown rot. Medium yellow cup-shaped flowers evolve into stellate form and measure 4–5 in. (10–13 m). Green leaves, mottled purple, measure 9 in. (23 cm) and spread 3–4 ft. (1–1.2 m).

Nymphaea 'Paestlingberg' (Wendelin Buggele) Hardy water lily. 19–20 petals. Good bloomer. LN. White stellate petals form a cup-shaped flower 6–7 in. (15–18 cm). Leaves are 13 × 12 in. (33 × 30 cm) and spread 6 ft. (2 m).

Nymphaea 'Peach Blow' (George H. Pring 1941) Unknown parentage. Viviparous. Tropical day bloomer. Fragrant. 34–36 petals. Excellent bloomer. Greenish yellow sepals beautifully contrast with the light pink inner petals and medium pink outer petals. A full, peony-style flower form measures 8–10 in. (20–25 cm). Nearly round, up to 12 in. (30 cm), somewhat jagged-edged leaves are a light green with some purple flecking. They spread 7–8 ft. (2.2–2.5 m).

Nymphaea 'Perry's Pink Beauty' (Perry D. Slocum 1989) Probably *N. alba* plant from New Zealand and *N.* 'Vesuve.' Hardy water lily. 23 petals. Fragrant. Good bloomer. Flowers small in relation to leaves. Medium to light pink cup-shaped flowers, 4–5 in. (10–13 cm). Leaves 8.5 in. (22 cm) spread 4–5 ft. (1.2–1.5 m).

Nymphaea 'Perry's Pink Bicolor' (Perry D. Slocum 1989) *N. alba* from New Zealand and *N.* 'Fabiola'. Hardy water lily. 20–21 petals. Slightly fragrant. Good bloomer. Center petals of the stellate-shaped, 5.5–6 in. (14–15 cm) blossoms are a deep pink with outer petals a whitish pink marked with pink veins. Leaves measure up to 11 × 10 in.

(28 × 25 cm) and spread 5–6 ft. (1.5–2 m).

🌿 🌿 🌿 🌿 🌿 🌿 🌿 🌿 🌿 🌿

N. *'Perry's Red Glow'* (Perry D. Slocum 1989)
Probably *N.* Alba Plenissima × *N.* 'Atropurpurea.' Hardy water lily. 23–30 petals. Good bloomer. Very deep red petals and deep green sepals form a stellate bloom 3.5–4 in. (9–10 cm). Leaves measure 6–7 in. (15–18 cm) and spread 3 ft. (1 m).

🌿 🌿 🌿 🌿 🌿 🌿 🌿 🌿 🌿 🌿

Nymphaea 'Perry's Red Star' (Perry D. Slocum 1989)
N. 'Vesuve' × *N.* 'Colonel A.J. Welch.' Hardy water lily. 23 petals. Good bloomer. Sometimes viviparous from flower early in season. Bright red petals with pale pink sepals form a stellate bloom 5–6 in. (13–15 cm) across. Flowers display a unique chartreuse stigmal area. Leaves measure 7 in. (18 cm) and spread 30–36 in. (75–90 cm).

🌿 🌿 🌿 🌿 🌿 🌿 🌿 🌿 🌿 🌿

Nymphaea 'Perry's Stellar Red' (Perry D. Slocum 1989)
Probably *N. tuberosa* 'Richardsonii' No. 2 × *N.* 'Charles de Meurville.' Hardy water lily. 24 petals. Good bloomer. Inner petals are a deep red and the outer petals a lighter hue with pink tips to form stellate-shaped flower of 6–8 in.

(15–20 cm). Leaves are 9 in. (23 cm) across and spread to 4 ft. (1.2 m).

🌿 🌿 🌿 🌿 🌿 🌿 🌿 🌿 🌿 🌿

Nymphaea 'Pink Pearl' (August Koch)
N. 'Mrs. George H. Pring' is one parent. Tropical day-bloomer. Fragrant. 40–42 petals. Excellent bloomer with blooms held up to 12 in. (30 cm) above water. Pinkish lavender cup-shaped flowers measure 7–8 in. (18–20 cm). Nearly round, deep green leaves measure up to 10 in. (25 cm) and spread 4–5 ft. (1.2–1.5 m).

🌿 🌿 🌿 🌿 🌿 🌿 🌿 🌿 🌿 🌿

Nymphaea 'Pink Perfection' (Joseph Lingg 1951)
Unknown parentage. Tropical day-bloomer. Very fragrant. 24–26 petals. Excellent bloomer. Lavender pink, stellate flowers with long, pointed sepals measure 8–10 in. (20–25 cm). Nearly round leaves are lusciously patterned with reddish purple and green. Measuring 10–12 in. (25–30 cm), they spread 5–7 ft. (1.5–2.2 m).

🌿 🌿 🌿 🌿 🌿 🌿 🌿 🌿 🌿 🌿

Nymphaea 'Pink Platter' (George H. Pring 1941)
Unknown parentage. Viviparous. Tropical day-bloomer. Slightly fragrant. 26–30 petals. Excellent bloomer. Medium pink petals are framed by sepals of a deeper hue. Large, round, flat flowers measure 7–10 in. (18–25 cm). Nearly round, wavy olive-green leaves are lightly mottled with purple, more prominently so on new leaves. Measuring 9–10 in. (23–25 cm), they spread 5–6 ft. (1.5–2 m).

🌿 🌿 🌿 🌿 🌿 🌿 🌿 🌿 🌿 🌿

Nymphaea 'Pink Star' (syn. 'Stella Gurney') (James Gurney 1900-1905?)
Chance seedling of *N.* 'Mrs. C.W. Ward.' Tropical day-bloomer. Fragrant. 17–18 petals. Excellent bloomer. Withstands more cold than most other tropicals. Produces many leaves. LN. Pink petals and slightly deeper hued sepals form a stellate bloom of 7–8 in. (18–20 m). Leaves, longer than they are wide, measure 17 × 15.5 in. (43 × 39 cm) and spread up to 10–12 ft. (3–3.5 m) .

🌿 🌿 🌿 🌿 🌿 🌿 🌿 🌿 🌿 🌿

Nymphaea 'Red Cup' (Kirk Strawn 1986)
N. 'Red Flare' × unknown. Tropical night-bloomer. 18–20 petals. Good bloomer. Flowers borne early in the season are a dark red; in late summer and fall, they are a deep pink. Vase-shaped

blossoms measure 5–8 in. (13–20 cm). Bronze-brown leaves are jagged with wavy edges and measure up to 13 × 18 in. (33 × 45 cm). Spreads 5–12 ft. (1.5–3.5 m).

🌿 🌿 🌿 🌿 🌿 🌿 🌿 🌿 🌿 🌿

Nymphaea 'Red Star' (syn. 'Mrs. C.W.Ward') (William Tricker 1899?) *N. flavovirens* is one parent. Tropical day-bloomer. Fragrant. 15–16 petals. Excellent bloomer. Blooms held 12 in. (30 cm) above water. Reddish pink, narrow petals and slightly deeper-hued sepals form stellate, 6–8 in. (15–20 cm) blooms. Ovate, somewhat wavy, green leaves measure 12–15 in. (30–38 cm) and spread 8 ft. (2.5 m).

🌿 🌿 🌿 🌿 🌿 🌿 🌿 🌿 🌿 🌿

Nymphaea 'Robinsoniana' (syn. 'Robinsoni, ' 'Robinsonii') (Joseph B.L. Marliac 1895) Hardy water lily. 24–27 petals. Good bloomer. May be subject to crown rot. Orange-red petals with lighter tips form an inner cup-shaped form and outer stellate form that measures 4.5–5 in. (11–13 cm). Light purple with deeper purple blotches on new leaves turn green with mature leaves measuring 8 in. (20 cm) and spreading 4–5 ft. (1.2–1.5 m).

🌿 🌿 🌿 🌿 🌿 🌿 🌿 🌿 🌿 🌿

Nymphaea ×*marliacea* 'Rosea' (syn. 'Marliac Rose') (Joseph B.L. Marliac 1879) Hardy water lily. 22 petals Excellent bloomer. Light pink, cup-shaped flowers measure 4–5 in. (10–13cm). Deep olive-green leaves measure 8–9 in. (20–23 cm) and spread 4–5 ft. (1.2–1.5 m).

🌿 🌿 🌿 🌿 🌿 🌿 🌿 🌿 🌿 🌿

Nymphaea 'Rosennymphe' (Junge) Hardy water lily. 32 petals. Good bloomer. Medium pink with one or two darker pink lengthwise stripes on the petals of star-shaped blossoms that measure 5.5–6.5 in. (14–16 cm). Leaves measure up to 10 × 9.5 in. (25 × 24 cm) and spread 3.5–5 ft. (1.1–1.5 m).

🌿 🌿 🌿 🌿 🌿 🌿 🌿 🌿 🌿 🌿

Nymphaea ×*marliacea* 'Rubra Punctata' (Joseph B.L. Marliac 1889) Hardy water lily. Fragrant. 20–22 petals. Good bloomer. ST. Deep purple-red, cup-shaped flowers measure 4 in. (10 cm). Round green leaves measure 9 in. (23 m) and spread to 3 ft. (1 m).

🌿 🌿 🌿 🌿 🌿 🌿 🌿 🌿 🌿 🌿

Nymphaea 'Somptuosa' (Joseph B.L. Marliac 1909) Hardy water lily. 35 petals. Good bloomer. Inner petals of the 5–6 in. (13–15 cm) peony-shaped flower are a deep pink that turn a glowing red with age as the outer

petals turn from white to blush pink. Considered a pink-and-white bicolor. Leaves bear faint purple mottling and measure 8 in. (20 cm) and spread 4–5 ft. (1.2–1.5 m).

🌿 🌿 🌿 🌿 🌿 🌿 🌿 🌿 🌿 🌿

Nymphaea 'Tammie Sue Uber' (Van Ness Water Gardens 1970) Unknown parentage. Tropical day-bloomer. Highly fragrant. 18 petals. Excellent bloomer. Fuchsia pink petals and lighter-hued sepals form a cup-shaped flower, 7–8 in. (18–20 cm). Nearly round, smooth-edged green leaves are heavily mottled with purple when new. Leaves measure 10 in. (25 cm) and spread 5–6 ft. (1.5–2 m).

🌿 🌿 🌿 🌿 🌿 🌿 🌿 🌿 🌿 🌿

Nymphaea 'William Falconer' (syn. 'Chateau le Rouge') (Henry A. Dreer 1899) Hardy water lily. 25 petals. Excellent bloomer in cool-summer areas. Inner flowers burn and plant stops blooming in hot periods. Very deep red petals form a cup-shaped flower 4.5–5 in. (11–13 cm) across. Leaves measure 8 × 7.5 in. (20 × 19 cm) and spread to 3 ft. (1 m).

Cultivars from Dr. Kirk Strawn

Dr. Kirk Strawn, owner of Strawn Water Gardens in College Station, Texas, has hybridized and introduced many beautiful hardy water lily cultivars. Those pictured here are available to the trade.

Nymphaea 'Berit Strawn' was produced by crossing *N.* 'Rembrandt' with *N. mexicana*. It is especially good for small garden and tub culture.

Nymphaea 'Colorado' Kirk crossed *N.* 'Louise Villemarette' and *N. mexicana* to come up with this beauty. It may need extra protection in the winters of Zone 5 and colder.

Nymphaea 'Georgia Peach' (Kirk Strawn 1998) A real showstopper, this hardy water lily is an exclusive Lilypons introduction.

Nymphaea 'Peachglow' (Kirk Strawn 1997) Really peach overall, this is another Lilypons exclusive introduction.

Nymphaea 'Berit Strawn'
Photo by Perry D. Slocum.

Nymphaea 'Colorado'
Photo by H. Nash.

Nymphaea 'Georgia Peach'
Photo by H. Nash.

Nymphaea 'Peachglow'
Photo by H. Nash.

Nymphaea 'Mayla' (Kirk Strawn 1993)
Incredibly rich fuchsia color creates a sensation in the water garden. Best in the larger pond.

🌱 🌱 🌱 🌱 🌱 🌱 🌱 🌱

Nymphaea 'Pink Grapefruit' (Kirk Strawn 1997)
A natural cross of *N.* 'Texas Dawn' and *N.* 'Fabiola'. 5–7 inch electric, yellowish pink petals are held 6 in. above water. Excellent bloomer

🌱 🌱 🌱 🌱 🌱 🌱 🌱 🌱

Nymphaea 'Pink Sparkle' (Kirk Strawn 1997)
Reddish apricot-pink, 4–inch blooms darken in color toward center. Orange-yellow stamens. Heart-shaped leaves measure 3.5 in. across and are dark green with purple splotches. Suited to small ponds and tub culture.

🌱 🌱 🌱 🌱 🌱 🌱 🌱 🌱

Nymphaea 'Gypsy' (Kirk Strawn 1997)
With red petals that darken to cherry-red with age, this hardy water lily offers a long bloom season.

🌱 🌱 🌱 🌱 🌱 🌱 🌱 🌱

Nymphaea 'Mayla'
Photo by Bob Romar.

Nymphaea 'Pink Grapefruit'
Photo by H. Nash.

Nymphaea 'Gypsy'
Photo by Bob Strawn.

Nymphaea 'Pink Sparkle'
Photo by H. Nash.

Nymphaea 'Red Spider' (Kirk Strawn)
Uniquely crinkled stellate petals!

🌿 🌿 🌿 🌿 🌿 🌿 🌿 🌿 🌿 🌿

Nymphaea 'Laura Strawn' (Kirk Strawn 1997)
A pure white lily good for the medium to large pool.

🌿 🌿 🌿 🌿 🌿 🌿 🌿 🌿 🌿 🌿

Nymphaea 'Starbright' (Kirk Strawn 1997)
An exclusive LilyPons introduction with 30 slender petals of sparkling white to create a star-shaped blossom. Sepals have pink tint on edges. Medium-size leaves are a very dark green with a black inky mottling.

🌿 🌿 🌿 🌿 🌿 🌿 🌿 🌿 🌿 🌿

Nymphaea 'Charlene Strawn' (Kirk Strawn 1969)
27–29 petals. Fragrant. Excellent bloomer. May need to prune leaves for maximum flower enjoyment. Inner petals are a rich yellow with outer petals a lighter hue. Stellate-shaped flowers measure 6–8 in. (15–20 cm). Nearly round leaves measure 8–9 in. (20–23 cm) and spread 3–5 ft. (1–1.5 m).

🌿 🌿 🌿 🌿 🌿 🌿 🌿 🌿 🌿 🌿

***Nymphaea* 'Red Spider'** Photo by H. Nash.

***Nymphaea* 'Laura Strawn'**
Photo by Bob Strawn.

***Nymphaea* 'Starbright'** Photo by Bob Strawn.

***Nymphaea* 'Charlene Strawn'**
Photo by Perry D. Slocum.

Nymphaea 'Innerlight' (Kirk Strawn 1997)
An exclusive LilyPons introduction, full, bold blossoms of yellow petals with cream-colored centers are perfect for the medium-size pool. An excellent bloomer.

Nymphaea 'Joey Tomocik' (Kirk Strawn)
Holding its bright yellow blossoms above the water, this lily is a hobbyist favorite. Good for the medium-to-large pool.

Nymphaea 'Barbara Dobbins' (Kirk Strawn 1995)
N. mexicana × *N.* 'Rembrandt.' 25 petals. Creamy pink flowers are held out of the water on vigorous plants. Leaves bear light flecks of maroon.

Nymphaea 'Walter Pagel'
A charming white lily suited to the small pool or tub culture.

Nymphaea 'Betsy Sakata' (Kirk Strawn 1997)
A delightful yellow hardy that grows well in the small pond or tub garden. 'Betsy' has a long bloom season, too.

Nymphaea 'Innerlight'
Photo by H. Nash.

Nymphaea 'Barbara Dobbins'
Photo by Kirk Strawn.

Nymphaea 'Betsy Sakata'
Photo by Bob Strawn.

Nymphaea 'Charlie's Choice'
Photo by Kirk Strawn.

Nymphaea 'Joey Tomocik' Photo by Bob Romar.

Nymphaea 'Walter Pagel'
Photo by Bob Romar.

Nymphaea 'Clyde Ikins.' Photo by Bob Strawn.

chapter seven

LOTUS

Although lushly tropical in appearance, lotuses are perennials. There are only two recognized species of the genus *Nelumbo*: *N. lutea*, the native American species, and *N. nucifera*, native to the Orient, the Philippines, north Australia, Egypt, and the Volga River delta at the Caspian Sea. Only one variant of *Nelumbo lutea*, a natural hybrid, *N. lutea* 'Yellow Bird,' discovered in 1975 at Lilypons Water Gardens in Buckeystown, Maryland, is recognized. Several variants exist of the *N. nucifera*. While the first hybrid cultivar was produced by Joseph Bory Latour-Marliac (*Nelumbo* 'Flavescens'), the cultivars available today are modern cultivars, produced primarily through the efforts of Perry D. Slocum.

In North America, lotuses do well over most of the U. S. and southern Canada as long as there is enough summer heat to bring the plants into flower. Likewise,

lotuses do not fare well in the extreme south and southwest, where the temperatures range *beyond* their ideal two to three

Lotuses are among the most beautiful flowering aquatic plants.
Photo by Marilyn Cook.

months in the 75–85°F (24–29° C) range. Excessive humidity may also be a problem. Summer weather in the British Isles and northern Europe is too cold for lotuses to bloom except in a greenhouse or conservatory.

Although lotuses are a sun-loving species, they will still bloom in partially shaded conditions so long as the water temperature is in the appropriate range.

All lotuses are day-bloomers that open early in the morning and close by midafternoon for three successive days. First-day flowers close earlier. *Nelumbo nucifera* produces variants in white, pink, red, and bicolor types and in both single and double blooms. To call a lotus "changeable" means that its flower color gradually changes over a three-day period. Lotuses do not bloom as early in the season as water lilies. Even their leafy growth is later showing in the spring. Typically, lotus tubers (technically rhizomes)

The above photo of *Nelumbo nucifera* 'Rosea Plenum' was featured on the cover of *Landscape and Nursery Digest*.
Photo by Bob Romar.

Nelumbo speciosum (aka *N. nucifera*) is commonly called the Hindu lotus.
Photo by Bob Romar.

are available by mail order during March, April, and, in some areas, into May. Potted lotuses may be purchased from nurseries during the growing season.

Lotus tubers are notoriously fragile; break the growing tip, and the plant may die. For that reason, lotuses are best planted in large, roomy, round containers. This prevents the growing tips from jamming and breaking in corners. For standard-size lotuses, a container approximately 3 to 4 feet (1 to 1.2 m) in diameter provides enough space for ample growth and satisfactory blooming. Smaller or dwarf-type lotuses can be planted in bushel basket–size containers or in half barrels. Since even the half-barrel container is difficult to manage, many people opt to plant lotuses in their own container gardens. Lined, sealed, or otherwise watertight containers allow for increasing water depth over the soil's surface as the plant grows in the spring. If the container is too small to allow keeping fish for mosquito control, use *Bacillus*

thuringiensis bacteria, conveniently sold in a floating form known as "dunks" or "doughnuts."

Teacup or Bowl Lotuses

Very recently, importers have brought in a variation on the standard and dwarf form of lotuses— the "bowl" lotus, miniature plants that grow to only 10–12 in. (25–30 cm). Seed capsules are very tiny to nonexistent. Many of the 2–4 in. (5–10 cm) flowers are incredibly double with ruffled

Note the difference in size between leaves of the dwarf lotus 'Momo Botan' and those of the teacup or bowl lotus. Photo by H. Nash.

Teacup or bowl lotuses are imported from China. Typically, they have very small or nonvisible seed heads. They must be grown in very shallow water and are treated as tropical plants. Bowl lotus 'Pink Radiance' is shown above.
Photo courtesy of Scherer Water Gardens.

petaloids in the center. Thought to originate in China, information is still very sparse on how to grow these relatively tiny plants. Growers' experiences in the past two years indicate that if the plants are kept in water deeper than 2 in. (5 cm), they may not survive. They apparently should not be wintered in the outdoor pond, unless you live in a Zone 9 or 10. They are being successfully wintered in moist soil with up to 2 inches (5 cm) of water over the plant's crown in heated greenhouses.

Nelumbo lutea. American yellow lotus Photo by Perry D. Slocum.

Lotus Species, Variants, and Cultivars

Each plant is listed with its botanical name and any synonyms, hybridizer or introducer, and description of flower, leaf, and height.

Nelumbo lutea. American yellow lotus
Native to eastern and central United States. 22–25 rich yellow petals with slightly lighter tips form flowers measuring 7–11 in. (18–28 cm) and bearing a slight fragrance. Round leaves measure 13–17 in. (22–42 cm), but they may grow twice that size if the growing medium is enriched with composted cow manure or compost. With flowers held above the leaves, the plant grows to 2.5–5 ft. (0.8–1.5 m).

Nelumbo lutea 'Yellow Bird'
Photo by Perry D. Slocum.

Nelumbo lutea 'Yellow Bird'
Considered a seedling or mutation of the American yellow lotus, the species presents much broader petals with more rounded tips than the species.

Nelumbo nucifera. Hindu lotus
Photo by Bob Romar.

Nelumbo nucifera. Hindu lotus, Egyptian lotus, sacred lotus, and speciosa
24 deep pink petals with creamy yellow bases delicately pale over the life of the 9–12 in. (23–30 cm) fragrant flower. Leaves measure 20–36 in. (50–90 cm) with the plant growing to 3–5 ft. (1–1.5 m).

Nelumbo 'Alba Striata'
Photo by Bob Romar.

Nelumbo nucifera var. ***caspicum.*** Russian lotus or red Russian lotus
Pinkish red flowers average 22 petals and measure 8.5–12.5 in. (21–31.5 cm). Leaves average 20–24 in. (50–60 cm) in diameter and grow to 3–5 ft. (1–1.5 m) above the water.

N. nucifera var. 'Rosea.' The rose lotus
This native of China and Japan bears 8–10 in. (20–25 cm) flowers rose-pink with yellow centers and exudes a rich anise fragrance. Leaves are 18–20 in. (45–50 cm) and held 4–5 ft. (1.2–1.5 m) above the water.

Nelumbo 'Alba Striata.' Syn. *N.* 'Empress'
White petals bear prominent uneven red margins in flowers measuring 10–12 in. (25–30 cm) with 18–19 petals per flower. Leaves measure 19–20 in. (48–50 cm), but can grow to 28 in. (70 cm) across when grown in rich soil. The plant grows to 4–5 ft. (1.2–1.5 m).

Nelumbo 'Angel Wings'
Photo by Perry D. Slocum.

Nelumbo 'Angel Wings' (Perry D. Slocum 1984)
N. nucifera 'Shirokunshi' × *N.* 'Pekinensis Rubra.' U.S. plant patent No. 5799 issued in 1986. 20–24 white petals form flowers of 8–10 in. (20–25 cm). Petals roll inward at the edges. Highly convoluted leaves, with a deep cup in the center of each, measure 18–23 in. (45–48 cm) and grow to 2–4 ft. (0.6–1.2 m).

N. 'Baby Doll'
Photo by Perry D. Slocum.

N. 'Baby Doll' (Perry D. Slocum 1985)
A seedling of *N.* 'Angel Wings.' With 21 petals, slightly fragrant blooms measure only 4–6 in. (10–15 cm). 9–11 in. (23–28 cm) leaves grow to 24–30 in. (60–75 cm). Tiny seed capsules measure only 0.75 in. (2 cm) across.

N. 'Ben Gibson'
Photo by Perry D. Slocum.

N. 'Ben Gibson' (Perry D. Slocum 1988)
N. nucifera 'Alba Plena' × *N.* 'Momo Botan.' Petal bases are a pale yellow with red veins that move into the pink tips to form flowers 5.5–6 in. (14–15 cm). 96–115 petals make for a delightful double form. Leaves measure 10–13 in. (25–33 cm) and grow to 3–4 ft. (1–1.2 m). Inherited from parent 'Momo Botan,' this cultivar's flowers last up to a week and older flowers may stay open all night. Blooms are held above the leaves.

N. 'Carolina Queen'
Photo by Perry D. Slocum.

N. 'Carolina Queen' (Perry D. Slocum 1984)
N. lutea × *N.* 'Pekinensis Rubra.' Pink petals with creamy bases number 21 to form 9–11 in. (23–28 cm) flowers. Flowers are held well above foliage. Leaves measure up to 25 in. (63 cm) and grow to 3–6 ft. (1–2 m).

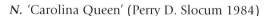

N. 'Charles Thomas'
Photo by Perry D. Slocum.

N. 'Charles Thomas' (Perry D. Slocum 1984)
N. nucifera 'Shirokunshi' × *N.* 'Pekinensis Rubra' U.S. Plant Patent No. 5794 in 1986. Lavender-pink petals pale with age and number 21 per flower that measures 6–8 in. (15–20 cm). Leaves measure 14–22 in. (35–56 cm) and grow 2–3 ft. (0.6–1 m) tall.

N. 'Chawan Basu'
Photo by Bob Romar.

N. 'Chawan Basu'
Unknown parents. Deep pink margins and veins mark the ivory petals that number 21–22 and form a flower of 5–9 in. (13–23 cm). Flowers wilt in hot summer climates, while in cool climates they may not bloom at all. Leaves measure 14–17 in. (35–43 cm) with the plant growing to 2–3 ft. (0.6–1 m).

N. 'Debbie Gibson'
Photo by Perry D. Slocum.

N. 'Gregg Gibson'
Photo by Perry D. Slocum.

N. 'Debbie Gibson' (Perry D. Slocum 1988)
N. nucifera 'Alba Plena' × *N. lutea.* Cream-colored petals lighten in hue toward the flower's center. With 23 petals, the flowers measure 10 in. (25 cm). Blossoms held high above foliage. Leaves measure 18 in. (45 cm), and the plant grows to 5–6 ft. (1.5–2 m).

N. 'Glen Gibson' (Perry D. Slocum 1986)
N. nucifera var. *caspicum* × *N. lutea.* 19–20 pink petals with yellowish orange bases form flowers that measure 8–9 in. (20–23 cm) across. Blooms are held high above leaves. Leaves measure 15–18 in. (38–45 cm) and grow to 3 ft. (1 m) tall.

N. 'Gregg Gibson' (Perry D. Slocum 1985)
Seedling of *N.* 'Charles Thomas.' Lavender-pink petals pale with age in these flowers measuring 6.5–7 in. (16–18 cm) with 22 petals each. Inner petals offer curving edges. Leaves measure 13 in. (33 cm) with the plant growing to 24 in. (60 cm).

N. 'Maggie Belle Slocum'
Photo by Perry D. Slocum.

N. 'Maggie Belle Slocum' (Perry D. Slocum 1984)
N. nucifera 'Shirokunshi × *N.* 'Pekinensis Rubra' U.S. Patent No. 5798 in 1986.

A very rich, deep lavender-pink color in the petals merges with pale yellow bases. Flowers measure 10–12 in. (25–30 cm) with 22 petals. Leaves measure 20–25 in. (50–63 cm) and grow to a height of 4–5 ft. (1.2–1.5 m).

N. 'Momo Botan'
Photo by Perry D. Slocum.

N. 'Momo Botan'
Unknown parents. Very deep rosy-pink petals yellow toward their bases. Flowers measure 5–6 in. (13–15 cm) with 106–118 petals for a pronounced double effect. Flowers stay open for several days longer than those of most lotuses, as well as later in the day. An extra-long bloom season is a plus, too. Leaves measure 12–15 in. (30–38 cm) and grow to a height of 2–4 ft. (0.6–1.2 m).

N. 'Mrs. Perry D. Slocum'
Photo by Bob Romar.

N. 'Mrs. Perry D. Slocum' (Perry D. Slocum 1964)
N. lutea × *N.* 'Rosea Plena.' Considered a changeable lotus, first-day blossoms are pink flushed with yellow; the second day they are a distinct pink and yellow; and the third day they open a cream flushed with pink. Flowers of 86 petals measure 9–12 in. (23–30 cm). Leaves measure 18–23 in. (45–58 cm) with the plant growing 4–5 ft. (1.2–1.5 m).

N. 'Nikki Gibson'
Photo by Perry D. Slocum.

N. 'Pekinensis Rubra'
Photo by Perry D. Slocum.

N. 'Perry's Giant Sunburst'
Photo by Bob Romar.

N. 'Nikki Gibson' (Perry D. Slocum 1988)
Seedling of *N.* 'Mrs. Perry D. Slocum.' Pink tips top whitish yellow petals with yellow bases in flowers of 20 petals that measure 10–12 in. (25–30 cm). Blooms open cup-shaped and then flatten out on the second day. Leaves measure 18–20 in. (45–50 cm) and grow to 5 ft. (1.5 m).

N. 'Patricia Garrett' (Perry D. Slocum 1988)
N. 'Maggie Belle Slocum' × *N. lutea.*' Pink petals have slightly darker tips and apricot-yellow centers. With 22 petals, the flowers measure 7–10 in. (18–25 cm). Flowers are held up to 30 in. (75 cm) above the leaves.

N. 'Pekinensis Rubra.' Red lotus
Unknown parents. Rosy red petals fade to a deep pink after the first-day bloom. With 16–17 petals, the flowers measure 8–12 in. (20–30 cm). Leaves measure 20–24 in. (50–60 cm), and the plants grow to 4–6 ft. (1.2–2 m). Similar to *N. nucifera* var. *caspicum*, 'Pekinensis' flowers are deeper in color and smaller, although the seed capsule of 'Pekinensis' is larger.

N. 'Perry's Giant Sunburst' (Perry D. Slocum 1987)
N. nucifera 'Alba Plena' × *N. lutea.* Creamy petals with outer petals of pale green grace these 10–13.5 in. (25–34 cm) blooms of 24–25 petals. Blooms held high above foliage. Leaves measure 16–18 in. (40–45 cm), and the plant grows to 4.5–5.5 ft. (1.4–1.7 m).

N. 'Perry's Super Star'
Day One.

N. 'Perry's Super Star'
Day Two.

N. 'Perry's Super Star' (Perry D. Slocum 1988)
Seedling of *N.* 'Mrs. Perry D. Slocum.' A changeable; first-day petals are a rich pink, but by day two they are mostly yellow. On the third day they are mostly cream with some pink tips. 75 such petals and petaloids combine in a flower 7–8 in. (18–20 cm) across. (Six to eight green-tipped petals at the flower's center are known as petaloids.) Leaves measure 17–21 in. (43–53 cm) with a plant height of 3–4 ft. (1–1.2 m).

N. 'Perry's Super Star'
Day Three.
Photos by Perry D. Slocum.

N. 'Rosea Plena.'
Photo by Bob Romar.

N. 'Rosea Plena.' Double rose lotus.
Unknown parents. Very deep rose-pink petals yellow toward their base. With 89–102 petals, including petaloids, per flower, the flowers measure 10–13 in. (25–33 cm). Seed capsules are very small. Leaves measure 18–20 in. (45–50 cm), with the plant growing to 4–5 ft. (1.2–1.5 m) or more in rich soil.

N. 'Sharon' (Perry D. Slocum 1987)
N. nucifera 'Alba Plena' × *N.* 'Momo Botan.' Pink petals deepen in color with pink veins. 80 petals, including petaloids, form a flower 8 in. (20 cm) across. Leaves measure 12–14 in. (30–35 cm) with the plant growing to 4 ft. (1.2 m).

N. 'Sharon'
Photo by Perry D. Slocum.

N. 'Suzanne' (Perry D. Slocum 1988)
Seedling of *N.* 'Alba Striata.' 22 medium pink petals are marked with darker pink stripes to form a flower 6–8 in. (15–20 cm) across. Leaves are 15–20 in. (38–50 cm) with the plant growing to 4–5 ft. (1.2–1.5 m).

N. 'The Queen.' (Perry D. Slocum 1984)
N. 'Alba Striata' × *N. lutea.* Outer petals are green with cream-colored petals inside. 21 petals make for a 10 in. (25 cm) flower held high above leaves up to 14–23 in. (35–58 cm) in diameter. The plant grows to 4–5 ft. (1.2–1.5 m).

N. 'The Queen'.
Photo by Bob Romar © Maryland Aquatic Nurseries, Inc.

Other Lotuses Available to the Trade

N. 'Momo Botan Minima'
Photo by Perry D. Slocum.

N. 'Paleface'
Photo by Perry D. Slocum.

Shiroman lotus, *N.* 'Alba Plena'
Photo by Perry D. Slocum.

Asiatic lotus, *N.* 'Alba Grandiflora'
Photo by Perry D. Slocum.

N. nucifera **'Japanese double white lotus'**
Photo by Perry D. Slocum.

Shirokunshi, the tulip lotus
Photo by Perry D. Slocum.

chapter eight

MARGINAL AQUATICS

Marginal aquatics are also known as emergent plants, their roots growing under water and their foliage emerging above. While often referred to as "bog plants," most of these plants are not true bog plants at all. True bog plants grow in saturated, acidic and peaty soils, while marginal or emergent aquatics grow in the rich topsoil and clay-based soils found in freshwater marshes, in swamps, and around ponds, lakes, and streams. See the end of this

Marginal aquatics add interest, texture, and beauty to the shallow waters around the edge of the pond. Photo by H. Nash.

chapter for a section on true bog plants, the carnivorous plants. Additional information on potting, maintenance, and propagation of the plants in this chapter can be found in Chapters 2 and 3. Unless otherwise noted, the plants listed should be fertilized monthly as described in Chapter Two.

The edge-softening effects of marginal aquatics blend even an otherwise plantless koi pond into its surroundings.
Photo by H. Nash.

Marginal aquatics soften the pond edges and blend the water garden into the surrounding landscape.
Photo by John Nagle.

Acorus calamus **'Variegatus'**
Photo by Bob Romar Maryland
Aquatic Nurseries.

Acorus calamus
Photo by Ron Everhart.

Acorus gramineus **'Ogon'**
Photo by Bob Romar.

Acorus calamus. Sweet flag.

Hardiness Zones: 4–11.

Description & habit: Grows 2–3 ft. (0.6–1m) high with long, glossy swordlike leaves that have distinct midribs and crinklings along part of one edge. An unusual flower is the conical spadix resembling a small horn that emerges laterally just below the tip of a leaf. The rhizomatous root grows shallowly across the soil and produces twin offshoots from each side along the length of the rhizome. These offshoots can extend in growth to develop their own twin offshoots as well.

Potting & growing: Plant in a wide-mouthed, 5-gallon (20 l), shallow pot with the cut end of the rhizome against the side of the pot for maximum growing space across the pot and to prevent "jumping out." Grow in sun to part shade.

Propagation: Rooted plantlets can be cut from the main rhizome in spring or summer. If plantlets have not developed enough roots, expose them to water and repot when roots are sufficient to anchor the plant.

Comments: The plant goes fully dormant in winter. It is likely to require annual repotting.

Varieties to look for:

Acorus calamus 'Variegatus.' Variegated sweet flag.

Hardiness Zones: 4–11.

Cream-striped, swordlike foliage grows to 2–3 ft. (0.6–1 m). Not as rapid-growing as its green counterpart, it still requires a wide-mouthed pot and is likely to require annual repotting.

Acorus gramineus. Japanese rush or dwarf sweet flag.

Hardiness Zones: 6–11.

Grassy-leaved species grows in fans from the growing tips of the creeping rhizome. Some fans grow along the rhizome, too, with lateral branching occurring, but primary growth is at the tip. Grows 8–12 in. (20–30 cm) tall. Not reliably hardy in Zone 5 and colder. Winter over indoors in a saucer of water as a houseplant, if in doubt. Also available in variegated and yellow forms. Plant in one-gallon containers and grow with 0–3 in. (0–7.5 cm) of water over crown, in sun to part shade. Propagate by division.

Alisma plantago-aquatica
Photo by Bob Romar.

Alisma plantago-aquatica. (*A. subcordatum*) Water plantain.

Hardiness Zones: 3–7.

Description & habit: Bold, long-stalked leaves grow up to 2 ft. (0.6 m) tall from a basal rosette. Rounded to cordate leaf blades have prominent ribbed, longitudinal veins. Pinkish-white flowers grow in pyramidal panicles and yield masses of seeds that sprout readily in any pot in the pond. While preferring very shallow water, it will grow in as much as 18 in. (45 cm). When grown in deeper waters, submerged leaves grow in ribbonlike form.

Potting & growing: Grow in 1–2-gallon (4–8 l)container in sun to part shade.

Propagation: Occurs naturally by seeds; sow fresh seed in pots or in mud flats.

Comments: The plant can become highly invasive, especially in the natural earth pond where it often appears voluntarily. Flowers can be dried upside down in a cool, dark place and used in floral arrangements. The plant is highly attractive to aphids.

** ** ** ** ** ** ** ** ** **

Arundo donax 'Variegata'
Photo by Bob Romar.

Alternanthera ficoidea. Parrot leaf. Alligator weed.

Hardiness Zone: 10.

Description & habit: Mat-forming perennial that grows only 2 in. (5 cm) high bears narrowly oval, green leaves that are marked with red, yellow, and orange, with wavy margins. 'Versicolor' is an erect form with height and spread to 1 ft. (30 cm). Leaves are rounded to spoon-shaped and shaded brown, red, and yellow.

Potting & growing: Pot in 1-gallon (4 l) container and grow in wet soil in very shallow water. Winter indoors in a greenhouse or under strong light.

Propagation: By tip cuttings or division in spring.

Varieties to look for: *A.* 'Rosefolia' with predominantly red leaves, *A.* 'Bettzickiana' with green leaves, *A. sessilis* with bronze leaves, and ' Variegata' with varigated leaves.

** ** ** ** ** ** ** ** ** **

Arundo donax 'Variegata.' Giant variegated Mediterranean rush.

Hardiness Zones: 7–11.

Description & habit: This Middle Eastern native bears white and green leaves of a bamboo effect to a height of 3–8 ft. (1–2.4 m). It will sometimes flower.

Potting & growing: Grow in 5–20 gallon (20–80 l) containers in 1–6 in. (2.5–15 cm) of water in sun to part shade.

Propagation: Divide rhizomes in spring through summer.

Comments: Best suited to the larger pond.

** ** ** ** ** ** ** ** ** **

Bacopa lenagera is treated as a tropical plant and wintered indoors, perhaps in a hanging basket.
Photo by Bob Romar.

Baumea rubiginosa 'Variegata'
Photo by Bob Romar.

Baumea rubiginosa **'Variegata.'** Variegated rush.

Hardiness Zones: 6(?)-11

Description & habit: An Australian native, this rush produces cylindrical, flat, green leaves with a yellow and dark green variegation. It grows 1–2 ft. (30–60 cm) tall. In Zone 8 and warmer, it is usually evergreen.

Potting: Grow in 2-gallon (8 l) containers at a depth of 1–6 in. (2.5–15 cm) in sun to part shade.

Propagation: Divide clumps in spring.

ᙡ ᙡ ᙡ ᙡ ᙡ ᙡ ᙡ ᙡ ᙡ ᙡ

Butomus umbellatus. Flowering rush.

Hardiness Zones: 3–11.

Description & habit: Very long, dark green, pointed, narrow leaves grow up to 3 ft. (1 m) or more long and 0.5 in. (1.3 cm) wide with sheathed triangular bases. Round flower stalks are borne in leaf axils up to 5 ft. (1.5 m) high with large individual umbels of conspicuous reddish white flowers. Does best in shallow water no deeper than 3–5 in. (8–13 cm).

Potting & growing: Plant in 2-gallon (8 l) containers in sun to part shade.

Propagation: Plant bulbils or divide clumps in spring.

Comments: Generally slow-growing and requires rich soil. While it will grow in zones 8–11, it is happier in cooler climates.

ᙡ ᙡ ᙡ ᙡ ᙡ ᙡ ᙡ ᙡ ᙡ ᙡ

Calla palustris. Bog arum.

Hardiness Zones: 3–6

Description & habit: A creeping plant suited to the water's edge, where it will grow in no deeper than 2 in. (5 cm) of water over the plant's crown, this plant grows from a scrambling rhizome that is conspicuous along the soil's surface. The plant above water is 6–12 in. (15–30 cm) tall. The rhizome will grow from 6–20 in. (15–50 cm) long with oblong heart-shaped, shiny leaves that are leathery and firm. Flowers of a broad white spathe around a spadix covered with tiny yellow flowers are only 2 in. (5 cm) long and bloom from late May into August. They are followed by red berries in late summer and autumn.

Potting & growing: Pot in one-gallon (4 l) containers and grow in sun to part shade. At home in boggy areas, it appreciates some acid in its soil.

Propagation: By rooted cuttings or by stratified seed.

ᙡ ᙡ ᙡ ᙡ ᙡ ᙡ ᙡ ᙡ ᙡ ᙡ

Butomus umbellatus
Photo by H. Nash.

Caltha palustris
Photo by Bob Romar.

Caltha palustris. Marsh marigold.

Hardiness Zones: 2–6.

Description & habit: Nearly round leaves are heart-shaped and have dentate margins. Waxy yellow buttercuplike flowers are produced in early spring. Usually growing 1–1.5 ft. (30–45 cm), the plants can grow in shallow water up to 4–5 in. (10–13 cm) deep or in soggy soil around the natural pond or stream. The plant is notorious for going dormant during the summer, although this happens when the plant is sited in full sun in hot summer temperatures. In its native habitat, the plant flourishes and blooms in the full sunlight of early spring. Such habitats usually become shaded as surrounding vegetation fills in.

Potting & growing: Grow in 2-gallon (8 l) nursery or mum pots in rich topsoil.

Propagation: Sow fresh seeds or divide clumps in late summer.

Comments: An 'Alba' variety produces white flowers, while 'Flore Plena' produces double yellow flowers. Moving the plant to a shadier location where it is sheltered from summer sunlight by taller marginal plantings gives it a better chance of continued foliage display. Should the plant go dormant, set the bare pots in an inconspicuous area of the pond until the following spring or bury the pots to their rims in a semi-shady area of the garden and keep well watered.

🌿 🌿 🌿 🌿 🌿 🌿 🌿 🌿 🌿

Canna yellow hybrid
Photo by H. Nash.

Canna americanallis **var. 'Variegata'** (syn. 'Bengal Tiger')

Hardiness Zones: 9–11.

Description & habit: Usually grows 4–5 ft. (1.2–1.5 m) tall, but may reach 6 ft. (2 m). Yellow-striped leaves are accented by glowing orange flowers in summer.

Potting & growing: Cannas are best grown in full sun and in rich soil. Pot them in 5-gallon (20 l) containers and set in water 1–10 in. (2.5–25 cm) over crowns in sun to part shade. If they have not been adapted to growing in water, gradually introduce them to aquatic life by first keeping them moist and gradually increasing water to an inch (2.5 cm) or so over the plant's crown. Remove from the pond in the autumn and winter and maintain as tropical houseplants. Rhizomes can also be hosed free of soil, dried, and stored in a cool, non-freezing, dark area as is done with terrestrial canna.

Propagation: Rhizomes may be divided in fall if storing them without soil, or in the early spring in conjunction with repotting. To grow from seed, nick the seed coat to enhance germination.

Canna 'Bengal Tiger'
Photo by H. Nash.

Comments: Although primarily a terrestrial plant, canna can be adapted to growing in up to 6 in. (15 cm) of water during the summer season.

Varieties to look for: C. glauca, a Brazilian native, offers many cultivars, most notably the Longwood hybrids. Cultivars include 'Endeavor,' a bright red, 'Erebus,' a salmon-pink, 'Ra,' a yellow, and ' Taney,' a burnt orange. These hybrids are known for their long bloom season and superior performance in the water garden.

Leaf of *Canna* 'Pink Sunburst'
Photo by H. Nash.

***Canna.* Red hybrid** Photo by Bob Romar.

***Canna.* Salmon hybrid**
Photo by Bob Romar.

Colocasia esculenta
Photo by Bob Romar.

**Colocasia esculenta
'Fontanesia,' violet-
stemmed taro**
Photo by Bob Romar.

**Colocasia esculenta
'Black Magic'**
Photo by Bob Romar.

Carex pseudocyperus. Gray sedge

Hardiness Zones: 3–7.

Description & habit: A hardy species with bright green grassy leaves 2–3 ft. (0.6–1 m) long and interesting dark green spikelets in June. The plant resembles umbrella palm and offers hardiness of tropical appearance for northern gardens.

Potting & growing: While preferring slightly acidic soil, the plant does well in rich topsoil. Plant in one to two-gallon (4–8 l) containers in up to 3 in. (7.5 cm) of water in sun to part shade.

Propagation: By division of the clumps in spring.

Comments: Although not commonly considered aquatic plants for water gardens, the *Carex* family offers interesting species that flourish in the pond.

Varieties to look for: C. elata (C. stricta) 'Aurea ' or 'Bowles Golden' offers graceful yellow foliage and grows to a height of 15 in. (38 cm).

'Variegata' is another variety that grows 1–2.5 ft. (0.3–0.8 m) tall with green and white striped foliage.

Colocasia esculenta. Green taro or elephant ears.

Hardiness Zones: 9–11.

Description & habit: From a genus of seven tropical plants, *C. esculenta* is the species most often available to the trade. An erect tuberous rootstock is marked with ringlike scars where former leaves have dropped off. Heart-shaped to arrow-shaped leaves resemble elephant ears, hence its common name. Leaves grow to 3 ft. (1 m) in length, with the plant growing 2–6 ft. (0.6–1.8 m).

Potting & growing: Pot in 5-gallon (20 l) pots or larger in rich topsoil. Grow in full sun to part shade. The plant may be hardy outdoors to Zone 8, but is easily wintered indoors as a houseplant in a saucer of water in a sunny window.

Propagation: Cut off and pot up "pups" produced on terminal ends of stolons.

Varieties to look for: Colocasia antiquorum Imperial Taro. Dark green foliage is overlaid with velvety black between the veins. Grow in sun to part shade in 1–6 in. (2.5–15 cm) of 70° F (21° C) or higher water. *Colocasia esculenta* 'Black Magic.' Black Taro. Growing to 4 ft. (1.2 m), masses of dusty charcoal-black leaves on dark burgundy/black stems are spectacular. *Colocasia esculenta* 'Fontanesia.' Violet-Stemmed Taro. Very dark purple stems contrast with large, green leaves on a plant that grows 2–4 ft. (0.6–1.2 m). *Colocasia esculenta* 'Rubra.' Cranberry or Red-Stemmed Taro. Dusty green leaves top brilliant red stems. Grows to 4 ft. (1.2 m).

Comments: If allowed to grow year-round, either outside in tropical zones or wintered indoors, plants will attain maximum height. Otherwise, a single season's growth is usually around 2 ft. (0.6 m). Some nurseries sell "Taro" that is of the *Alocasia* family. *Alocasia amazonica* 'Hilo Beauty' is a variegated form that is not suited to aquatic cultivation. Hardiness and cultivation are the same for *Alocasia* plants.

Crinum americanum
Photo by Bob Romar.

Crinum americanum. Southern swamp lily.

Hardiness Zones: 8–11.

Description & habit: A tropical native with narrow, evergreen, straplike leaves up to 2 in. (5 cm) wide and 18–24 in. (45–60 cm) long, bears long-petaled, white, and very fragrant flowers. Although preferring water depths of 1–6 in. (2.5–15 cm), it will grow in up to 12 in. (30 cm) of water.

Potting & growing: Pot in 5-gallon (20 l) containers and grow in sun to part shade. In colder zones, move to a greenhouse or indoors with adequate light and water before the first frost. Return to the garden when temperatures have stabilized to 70° F (21° C) or higher in late spring or early summer.

Propagation: Plant bulb offsets or start from seed.

🌿 🌿 🌿 🌿 🌿 🌿 🌿 🌿 🌿

Cyperus alternifolius
Photo by H. Nash.

Cyperus alternifolius. Umbrella palm

Hardiness Zones: 7–11.

Description & habit: Usually growing 1–3 ft. (0.3–1 m), the plant may reach 5 ft. (1.5 m) in optimal conditions. A lovely accent plant crowned with many dark green radiating leaves like a parasol, it can be grown as a houseplant.

Potting & growing: Plant in rich soil in 2–5 gallon (8–20 l) containers or larger and grow with 1–6 in. (2.5–15 cm) of water over the plant's crown in sun to part shade.

Varieties to look for: 'Nana' and 'Gracilis' are dwarf cultivars hardy in zones 9–11. Cultivation is the same as for larger species with wintering indoors as a houseplant recommended in non-hardy zones. 'Variegatus' is another dwarf form with creamy white lengthwise strips along stems and leaves. Prune out any fully green stems to prevent the plant's reverting to nonvariegated form.

Propagation: Division and head cuttings.

🌿 🌿 🌿 🌿 🌿 🌿 🌿 🌿 🌿

Cyperus giganteous
Photo by H. Nash.

Cyperus giganteous. Mexican papyrus.

Hardiness Zones: 8–11.

Description & habit: Very erect stems grow 12–15 ft and are topped by 10 in. (25 cm) spheres of fluffy, starlike foliage.

Potting & growing: Plant in 5–20 gallon (20–80 l) containers at 1–12 in. (2.5–30 cm) water depth in sun to part shade. Winter indoors as a houseplant out of hardiness zones.

Propagation: Divide clumps; this may require two people! Also, by seed. Rolf Nelson reports hybridization of this plant and the Egyptian form.

🌿 🌿 🌿 🌿 🌿 🌿 🌿 🌿 🌿

Cyperus haspan
Photo by Bob Romar.

Cyperus haspan. Dwarf papyrus.

Hardiness Zones: 9–11.

Description & habit: Grows 12–18 in. (30–45 cm) tall, topped with round spiked flower heads of yellow-green florets that turn bronze in late summer. Stems that bend over and touch the water create new plantlets.

Potting & growing: Considered an invasive weed in the Philippines, it is controllable when potted in a 2-gallon (8 l) container and given 1–4 in. (2.5–10 cm) of water over the crown in sun to part shade.

Propagation: Division or by rooted plantets that form when flower heads touch water or by cutting off the flower heads and floating them upside down in water.

Cyperus longus. Sweet galingale or umbrella sedge.

Hardiness Zones: 6–10.

Description & habit: Triangular stems grow 2–4 ft. (0.6–1.2 m) tall and bear bright green, stiffly ribbed leaves radiating from the top with brown spikelets.

Potting & growing: Grow this species in 5-gallon (20 l) or larger pots with 2–4 in. (5–10 cm) of water over its crown.

Propagation: By division; by stratified seed; or by rooting flower heads upside down in water.

Comments: *C. eragrostis* and *C. vegetus* are essentially the same plant available to the trade. This is the one hardy version in this plant family. Give it protection outdoors in Zone 5. If wintering it indoors as a houseplant, do not feed and allow it to rest. Growth resumes in the spring.

Cyperus papyrus. Egyptian paper reed. Giant papyrus.

Hardiness Zone: 10

Description & habit: Pithy stems grow 12–15 ft. (3.5–4.5 m) tall with large mop heads of pendulous leaves and greenish brown flower spikelets that measure nearly a foot across.

Potting & growing: Pot in rich soil in a 20-gallon or larger container. This plant needs strong lighting to maintain its full and lush appearance. Protect from wind. A tropical plant, winter indoors in zones colder than Zone 10.

Propagation: By division of clump, or by seed.

Comments: Because of the size of this specimen, it may be best grown in its own watertight container with water kept over the soil. Set the container on wheels to allow mobility of the plant, especially in zones colder than Zone 10.

Dulichium arundinaceum
Photo by Bob Romar.

Dichromena colorata
Photo by Bob Romar.

Echinodorus radican
Photo by H. Nash.

Dulichium arundinaceum. Water bamboo.

Hardiness Zones: 6–11

Description & habit: Not really a member of the bamboo family, this plant only looks like bamboo. Usually growing up to 18 in. (45 cm) tall, it can grow to 2 ft. (60 cm) or more. Tiny and insignificant flowers appear in summer from among the slender leaves.

Potting & growing: Grow in a one-gallon (4 l) container or larger in up to 4 in. (10 cm) of water in sun to part shade. Winter indoors as a houseplant or in a greenhouse in colder zones.

Propagation: Divide clumps in spring or summer.

🌿 🌿 🌿 🌿 🌿 🌿 🌿 🌿 🌿 🌿

Dichromena colorata. Star grass.

Hardiness Zones: 9–10

Description & habit: An evergreen sedge, star grass grows 12–18 in. (30–45 cm) tall and produces star-shaped flower bracts at its stem tips.

Potting & growing: Plant in 2–5 gallon (8–20 l) containers with slightly acid soil in sun to part shade. Cut back when foliage turns rangy for renewed growth. Winter in heated greenhouses or indoors under adequate growlights in zones colder than 9–10.

Propagation: By division.

🌿 🌿 🌿 🌿 🌿 🌿 🌿 🌿 🌿 🌿

Echinodorus radican '**Marble Queen.**' Melon sword.

Hardiness Zones: 6–11.

Description & habit: Large, melon-shaped foliage displays creamy white to creamy yellow patches. Summer *Sagittaria*-like flowers, produced on arching stems in July through September, are small and pale purple that fade to pink. Plant grows to 3 ft. (1m).

Potting & growing: Grow in 2-gallon (8 l) or larger containers in rich soil with up to 2 in. (5 cm) of water over the crown in sun to part shade. Provide winter protection outside in Zone 6 to ensure survival, or winter indoors as a houseplant.

Propagation: By viviparous plantlets, by root division, or by stratified seed.

Comments: The green form is identical but for the variations.

🌿 🌿 🌿 🌿 🌿 🌿 🌿 🌿 🌿 🌿

Eleocharis montevidensis
Photo by Bob Romar.

Equisetum hyemale
Photo by Carol Chrustensen.

Equisetum scorpoides
Photo by Bob Romar.
© Maryland Aquatic Nurseries.

Eleocharis montevidensis. Spike rush.

Hardiness Zones: 3–11.

Description & habit: Growing 6–12 in. (15–30 cm) tall, this fine grasslike plant is tipped with tiny, round pokers. Spreading by stolons and by seed, it can crop up in every pot in the water garden and become a virtual weed.

Potting & growing: Pot in 1–2 gallon (4–8 l) containers and provide 0–2 in. (0–5 cm) of water over the plant crown in sun to part shade. It does not like to be transplanted and will sulk for several days before deciding to resume growth.

Propagation: By root division, preferably in spring.

Comments: A charming plant for the tub or container garden, it works well as a base camouflage or filler plant in the pots of taller vertical plants.

Varieties to look for: Eleocharis tuberosa, Chinese water chestnut. Hardy to Zone 7. Bright green hollow stems grow to 2 ft. (0.6 m). Edible tubers produced. "Spike rush" also sold under names of *Eleocharis interestincta* and *Eleocharis flavescens.*

🌿 🌿 🌿 🌿 🌿 🌿 🌿 🌿 🌿

Equisetum hyemale. Horsetail or scouring rush.

Hardiness Zones: 4–11

Description & habit: The common form of *E. hyemale* grows to 4 ft. (1.2 m) tall. Hollow stems are furrowed and green with black bands that give it a bamboolike appearance. Male plants bear a brownish pollen cone at the tip, while female plants bear spikelet-like growths on their tips.

Potting & growing: Plant in 2–gallon (8 l) containers in sun to part shade. This plant takes some time to become established, as well as time to adjust to planting in water, if it is not already adapted to aquatic culture. Start it out with moist soil to adapt it if it has not been growing with water over the plant's crown. In a year or two, growth becomes established and the plant assumes vigorous growth. While the plant remains green year-round, old stems that have died are dried and brown. Prune them out for best plant appearance. This plant can become invasive when planted in soil near a pond or stream.

Propagation: By division, making sure that offshoots are well rooted.

Varieties to look for: E. scorpoides. Dwarf horsetail. Hardiness zones: 1–8. An evergreen miniature version of *E. hyemale,* bears evergreen, twisted stems. Grow it in wet soil with a minimum of water over the plant crown to avoid swamping the plant; pot in small containers, and set in sun to part shade. Propagate by root division in spring.

🌿 🌿 🌿 🌿 🌿 🌿 🌿 🌿 🌿

Eriophorum angustifolium Photo by Bob Romar.

Eriophorum angustifolium. Cotton grass.

Hardiness Zones: 6–11.

Description & habit: Flat grasslike leaves and a creeping rootstock characterize this temperate-zoned plant that bears tassels of white cottonlike flowers. The plant grows to 12 in. (30 cm) high.

Potting & growing: Plant in one-gallon (4 l) containers in acidic soil with up to 3 in. (12.5 cm) of water over the crown in sun to part shade.

Propagation: By stolons or division in spring through summer.

Comments: This plant is native to peat bog regions. Planted in the usual clay-based aquatic soil mixture, the plant may only malinger. Feeding with an acid-based fertilizer or enriching the soil mix with peat makes the plant happy.

Glyceria maxima var. 'Variegata.' (G. spectabilis 'Variegata') Variegated manna grass.

Hardiness Zones: 5–8

Description & habit: A rapidly spreading aquatic grass that grows to 2 ft. (0.6 m). Foliage is striped green, white, and cream with pink flushes in spring.

Potting & growing: Grow in one-gallon (4 l) or larger pots in up to 5 in. (13 cm) of water.

Propagation: By separating rooted plantlets from runners; by division.

Comments: Particularly good for binding banks along streams and lakes, it can become invasive in the water garden. Prune out fully green blades to avoid its reverting to green form. Grows well in shade.

Hibiscus moschuetos Photo by Ron Everhart.

Hibiscus moschuetos. Rose mallow or swamp hibiscus.

Hardiness Zones: 5–11.

Description & habit: The common rose mallow found in marshes in temperate zones, this woody shrub grows 4–8 ft. (1.2–2.5 m) high with 6–10 in. (15–25 cm) flowers that bloom in red, pink, or white, usually with contrasting "eye" in center of the bloom. Consider this large shrub for the more naturalized water garden.

Potting & growing: Plant in 5–20 gallon (20–80 l) containers and keep soil wet or provide up to 6 in. (15 cm) of water over crown in sun to part shade.

Propagation: Seed may be sown in heated beds in March or green stem cuttings may be taken in June. Also, crown division when repotting.

Varieties to look for: H. militaris, the soldier rose mallow or halberd-leaved hibiscus, grows 6–9 ft. (1.8–2.7 m) high with 4–6 in. (10–15 cm) pink flowers with red centers.

Houttuynia cordata
Photo by H. Nash.

**Houttuynia cordata
'Variegata'**
Photo by Bob Romar;
© Maryland Aquatic Nurseries.

Hydrocotyle verticilata
Photo by Bob Romar.

Houttuynia cordata.

Hardiness Zones: 6–10.

Description & habit: A hardy, rhizomatous marginal plant that grows 6–12 in. (15–30 cm) or more. Broadly ovate, bluish green, heart-shaped leaves with red edges on red stems gain sparkle from small white flowers at stem tips in early summer.

Potting & growing: Pot in one-gallon (4 l) containers and set in water no deeper than 1–2 in. (2.5–5 cm) over the plant's crown; also good for use as ground cover around the pond edges. Notoriously vigorous in growth, it can be invasive when planted next to a natural pond or stream.

Propagation: Divide clumps in spring or plant rooted cuttings of stem pieces that root at leaf nodes.

Comments: Is grown successfully in Zone 5.

Varieties to look for: The double flowered cultivar 'Plena' is reputedly not as invasive. Plant in 1–2-gallon (4–8 l) containers in sun to shade. *Houttuynia cordata* 'Variegata' is reported hardy to a Zone 4. Red stems bear bluish green, heart-shaped leaves that sparkle with red and cream in sunny exposures. Cone-shaped white flowers appear in early summer. Of creeping habit, it makes an excellent transition plant from pond edge to 1–2 in. (2.5–5 cm) of water. Growing only to 6 in. (15 cm) tall, it will grow in moist soil to shallow water.

🌿 🌿 🌿 🌿 🌿 🌿 🌿 🌿 🌿 🌿

Hydrocotyle. Water pennywort.

Hardiness Zones: 5–11.

Description & habit: Three species of this charming plant may be found available to the trade: *H. americana,* a semihardy species found growing naturally in the southern U.S.; *H. vulgaris,* a hardy species from Europe and North Africa; and the most commonly sold *H. verticilata* . The plants are rapid growers with round penny-shaped leaves that attach to their stems from the center of the leaves. The stems grow from 4–12 in. (10–30 cm) tall, depending upon individual species. Inconspicuous white or pink umbel flowers are held on shorter stalks below the leaves from June through September.

Potting & growing: Grow in one-gallon (4 l) containers with up to 2 in. (5 cm) of water over crowns in sun to part shade. A vigorous grower, it quickly camouflages the pond edge, but may require control.

Propagation: By cuttings of rooted stolons.

🌿 🌿 🌿 🌿 🌿 🌿 🌿 🌿 🌿 🌿

Hymenocallis liriosme. Water spider lily.

Hardiness Zones: 7–11.

Description & habit : A native plant of the southern U.S. from Louisiana west to Texas, straplike and deeply grooved leaves grow to 18 in. (45 cm). Spidery white flowers are produced March-May.

Potting & growing: Plant in rich soil in 2-gallon (8 l) containers with up to 6 in. (15 cm) of water over the plant's crown in sun to shade. In temperate zones, winter as houseplant indoors.

Propagation: Divide clumps after flowering or start from seed.

Varieties to look for: *H. caribaea* 'Variegata ' offers impressive green and white striped foliage that may grow to 2 ft. (0.6 m) tall. White flowers with six narrow, radiating lobes of three petals and three sepals bloom in spring and may repeat in fall.

Ipomea batatas
Photo by H. Nash.

Ipomea batatas. Water spinach.

Hardiness Zones: 10

Description & habit: Growing vinelike and spreading by runners, *Ipomea* forms attractive clumps in the hot summer pond. Attractive pinkish morning glory—like flowers bloom sparingly even in full sun.

Potting & growing: To grow in the pond, pot in a 5-gallon (20 l) container and submerge with up to 3 in. (7.5 cm) of water to cover the plant's crown. Winter indoors or in a heated greenhouse in all zones below 10.

Propagation: By division, cuttings, or runners.

Comments: Cultivated in the Far East for edible shoots, young leaves, and stems, *Ipomea* can be wintered in a heated greenhouse or under strong grow lights. If grown in a tub garden, it will need a garden trellis fitted to the container to provide support for the vining plant. With wheels affixed below the tub, it can be easily moved indoors for wintering.

***Juncus effusus* 'Spiralis'**
Photo by H. Nash.

Juncus effusus. Soft rush.

Hardiness Zones: 3–8.

Description & habit: Soft, grasslike stems grow in clumps that rarely intrude upon other plants in water up to 6 in. (15 cm) deep. Each stem bears a cluster of very small, greenish brown, scaly flowers that bloom in July through September from a point on the stalk near the top. Grows to a height up to 1 ft. (30 cm) tall.

Potting & growing: Grow in rich soil in one-to-two-gallon (4–8 l) pots or larger and repot every 1–2 years. Set out in sun to part shade.

Propagation: By root division, spring through summer, or by seed.

Varieties to look for: Juncus effusus 'Spiralis'. Corkscrew rush. Hardiness zones: 4–9.

A hardy cultivar that grows to 18 in. (45 cm) with contorted-to-corkscrew, dark green needlelike leaves, it is generally prostrate in growth. Plant with 1–6 in. (2.5–15 cm) of water over the crown in 2-gallon pots in sun to part shade. Propagate by division or collect seed and follow the stratification procedure. *Juncus glauca*, Blue rush, grows to 2 ft. (0.6 m), semi-evergreen, hardy to zone 5. *Juncus macrophyllus*, Flat-bladed rush, grows to 1 ft. (30 cm) with dark green stems and small clusters of pink and white flowers. One of the earlier plants to break dormancy in the spring, a heavy feeder. *Juncus* 'Carmen's Japanese, ' a green rush growing to 3 ft. (1 m) with narrow bright green foliage and delicate ivory-yellow flowers. Hardy to a Zone 8.

Lobelia cardinalis
Photo by Bob Romar.

Lobelia cardinalis. Cardinal flower.

Hardiness Zones: 5–11.

Description & habit: Growing to a height of 2–4 ft. (60–122 cm), long, alternate, lanceolate and toothed leaves are produced up the stems. Tubular flowers in elongated clusters are produced at the ends of erect stalks. Flowers are 1–2 in. (3.5 cm) long, 5-petaled with two lips and narrow leaflike bracts beneath them. Blooming season is July–September.

Potting & growing: Requires winter protection in Zones 5–6 to ensure survival. (Move the pot to the garden, dig in, and mulch heavily.) Plant in one-gallon (4 l) or larger containers in rich soil with 1–3 in. (2.5–7.5 cm) of water over plant crown in sun to part shade.

Propagation: Clumps may be divided in early spring or following flowering in warmer zones. Seeds may be started in early spring and may require stratification.

Comments: Native to damp sites, especially along streams, in North America, *Lobelia cardinalis* is particularly attractive to hummingbirds. It may be subject to slug damage in moist soil plantings.

Ludwigia peploides
Photo by Bob Romar.

Lysimachia nummularia
Photo by H. Nash.

Lysimachia nummularia
'Aurea' Photo by H.Nash.

Ludwigia longifolia. Primrose willow.

Hardiness Zones: 9–10.

Description & habit: A tropical species bearing yellow flowers with glaucous, green laceolate leaves on erect red stems that reach 4–6 ft. (1.2–2 m) high.

Potting & growing: Grow in up to 12 in. (30 cm) of water in 5 gallon (20 l) containers containing rich loam or clay-based soil in sun to part shade. Winter indoors as a houseplant or in a greenhouse.

Propagation: Division or rooted stem cuttings.

Ludwigia palustris. Primrose creeper.

Hardiness Zones: 9–10.

Description & habit: Mats of partially submerged vegetation of creeping or floating and branched stems may grow to 12 in. (30 cm) in length with shiny oval short-stalked leaves up to 1 in. (2.5 cm) long and half as wide with pale green upper and whitish green beneath. Leaves above water may be smaller and a deeper green, often with a reddish tint. Cup-shaped, yellow flowers. Considered extremely invasive

Potting & growing: Grow in shallow water in 1–2 gallon (4–8 l) containers of rich loam or clay-based soil in sun to part shade. Winter indoors as houseplant or in heated greenhouse.

Propagation: By division or rooted cuttings.

Lysimachia numularia. Creeping Jenny.

Hardiness Zones: 3–8.

Description & habit: Opposite round leaves are produced along trailing and rooting stems. Yellow flowers are produced at midsummer. Useful as edging plant to the water garden, stems that trail into the water root happily.

Potting & growing: Plant in one gallon (4 l) containers and set in 1–6 in. (2.5–15 cm) water. This variety performs best with dappled sun to shade.

Propagation: By stem cuttings rooted in water, by seed, or by division.

Varieties to look for: L. numularia 'Aurea,' a yellow-leaved form, grows in full sun, the yellow brightening in proportion to sun exposure.

Comments: Green form is often found in wet woods.

Lythrum salicaria
'Robert'
Photo by Bob Romar.
© Maryland Aquatic Nurseries.

Marsilea mutica
'Variegata'
Photo by Bob Romar.

Lythrum salicaria. Loosestrife.

Hardiness Zones: 4–9.

Description & habit: Growing to 3 ft. (1 m), erect-growing perennial clumps of lance-shaped leaves are topped by racemes of 4-petaled flowers in mid to late summer.

Potting & growing: Plant in one-gallon (4 l) or larger container and grow with shallow water over the plant's crown in full sun to part shade.

Propagation: By division in spring. Cultivars are not supposed to bear fertile seeds.

Comments: Banned in many states for its highly invasive nature, loosestrife is a striking plant to grow in the water garden if you can get it.

Varieties to look for: 'Morden's Gleam' bears red-purple flowers. 'Robert' blooms in deep fuchsia pink with a slightly more compact growing habit.

❧ ❧ ❧ ❧ ❧ ❧ ❧ ❧ ❧ ❧

Marsilea mutica 'Variegata.' Variegated water clover.

Hardiness Zones: 6–11.

Description & habit: In very shallow water, greenish yellow-to-brown patterned leaves usually float on the water's surface with a four-leaf clover effect. Planted in several inches of water, the stems may stand 3–4 in. (7.5–10 cm) above the water. A good transition plant, it will grow in moist soil or in shallow water. Highly invasive by vigorous rhizomes.

Potting & growing: Plant in one-gallon (4 l) containers in 1–12 in. (2.5–30 cm) of water in sun to part shade. Winter portion over indoors if necessary.

Propagate : By separating plantlets from rhizome or by cuttings.

Varieties to look for: M. crenata. Dwarf water clover. Zones 6–10. Perfect for small container gardens. *M. drumondii.* Zones 6–10. Cloverlike leaves covered with small white hairs. Sun to part shade. *M. schelpiana.* Cut-leaf water clover. Zones 6–10. Similar to the *quadrifolia* form but with more deeply cut leaves and finer habit. *M. quadrifolia.* Zones 6–10. Smaller European species, less variation in leaves. Sun to part shade.

Comments: Monitor this plant closely in container or tub gardens to prevent it from choking out other plants. Thinning may be required weekly.

❧ ❧ ❧ ❧ ❧ ❧ ❧ ❧ ❧ ❧

Mentha aquatica
Photo by H. Nash.

Mentha aquatica. Water mint.

Hardiness Zones: 5–11.

Description & habit: Rhizomatous roots with long segments grow to a height of 24–36 in. (60–90 cm) with crossed pairs of egg-shaped leaves with serrated margins. Often the leaves are tinged with purple and the undersides of even deeper purplish casts. Reddish stems radiate into the leaf veins. Lilac, globular flowers are produced in terminal whorls in summer. Highly fragrant, the minty aroma suggests anise. The plant scrambles about in the water and along the pond edge to form large (and invasive) colonies.

Potting & growing: Grow in one-to-two-gallon (4–8 l) containers with up to 3 in. (7.5 cm) of water over the crown in sun to part shade.

Propagation: Easily propagated from rooted portions of the stem. (Roots form at nodes where they touch soil or water.)

🌿 🌿 🌿 🌿 🌿 🌿 🌿 🌿 🌿 🌿

Menyanthes trifoliata
Photo by Bob Romar.

Menyanthes trifoliata. Bogbean.

Hardiness Zones: 5–11.

Description & habit: A scrambling plant with a thick, spongy, creeping rootstock, this plant may be slow to establish in the water garden, requiring even 2 to 3 years before lush growth is attained. Olive-green leaves of three leaflets with a long petiole bear flower stalks of 10–16 in. (25–40 cm) topped with short-lived, white, fringed flowers in mid-spring. The plant flowers sparsely, if at all, in Zones 8–11.

Potting & growing: The lush growth of attractive leaves makes this a desirable plant to establish around the pond edge or in very shallow water. When ordered by mail, it frequently arrives as a rooted piece of stem. Bury the roots in rich topsoil and leave the rhizome free across the soil in the pot. Set the pot in very shallow water of 1–3 in. (2.5–7.5 cm) over the rootstock in sun to part shade. Trailing stems may grow some distance from their pot, rooting in other pots or along the pond edge. Provide acidity in the potting mix for quicker establishment of the plant and for more vigorous growth.

Propagation: Cuttings of rooted sections can be taken in spring through summer. Roots may be produced at submerged leaf nodes.

Comments: Native to peat bogs, the addition of acid to the soil, in the form of peat additives, enhances plant performance.

🌿 🌿 🌿 🌿 🌿 🌿 🌿 🌿 🌿 🌿

Mimulus ringens
Photo by H. Nash.

Mimulus ringens. Lavender musk.

Hardiness Zones: 4–10.

Description & habit: Bears many branching, succulent, square stems that grow to 18 in. (45 cm) with narrow dark green oblong leaves. Blue to violet tubular flowers with lobed lips bloom in summer.

Potting & growing: Plant *Mimulus* in 1–2 gallon (4–8 l) containers of rich soil with 0–2 in. (0–5 cm) water over the crown in sun to part shade. The plant may be grown in 3–5 in. (8–13 cm) of water and is not as invasive as other species in the family.

Propagation: By cuttings of rooted nodes and by seed. Reseeds readily.

Comments: The stigma at the end of the pistil of *Mimulus* flowers has two spreading lobes that fold together when touched. If touching the lobes allows pollen from a different plant to be left behind, the lobes remain closed and the pistil sets seed. If there is no pollen, or if the pollen is from the same flower, the lobes soon reopen.

Varieties to look for: M. cardinalis. Scarlet monkey flower. Hardiness zones: 8–10. Vivid scarlet blooms with backswept upper and lower lips. Blooms from April into October. M. cardinalis is more compact than the type, growing only to 3 ft. (1 m). Leaves are paired, oblong, toothed, sticky, and hairy. M. guttatus. Yellow monkey flower. Hardiness zones: 5–10. Yellow native from western North America and Canada, bears reddish brown hairy spots on the flower's throat. Flowers have flat faces and bloom in loose clusters from March into September. Grows to 40 in. (102.5 cm) tall.

🌿 🌿 🌿 🌿 🌿 🌿 🌿 🌿 🌿 🌿

Myosotis scorpioides (M. palustris)
Photo by Ron Everhart.

Myosotis scorpioides (M. palustris). Water forget-me-not.

Hardiness Zones: 3–10.

Description & habit: Creeping underground shoots form dense colonies. M. scorpioides may grow from 4 to 24 in. (10–60 cm) tall, with the tips bearing flat wands of coiled tips of sky-blue, yellow-centered flowers from May through September.

Potting & growing: Plant in one-gallon containers with up to 2 in. (5 cm) of water over the crown in sun to part shade. Pinch plants to develop fuller habit. A hardy species native to Europe and naturalized in North America, this shallow-water plant will grow in slowly moving streams, too, and as a base plant in pots of taller, more vertical plants.

Propagation: Root division in spring to summer or rooted stem cuttings.

Varieties to look for: 'Alba,' a white-flowered form; 'Semperflorens,' a more compact form; and 'Mermaid,' a more free-flowering form.

🌿 🌿 🌿 🌿 🌿 🌿 🌿 🌿 🌿 🌿

Nasturtium officinale
Photo by H. Nash.

Nasturtium officinale. Watercress.

Hardiness Zones: 3–11

Description & habit: Although stems may grow up to 10 ft. (3 m) long, they are usually prostrate and matted in this creeping plant. Shiny leaves are divided into many leaflets, and white flowers bloom in rounded clusters, much like candytuft, in March through November.

Potting & growing: Pot in a one-gallon (4 l) pot or larger in rich garden loam. If the pot is set within the path of moving water, cover the top with a good layer of gravel to prevent the soil from becoming dispersed. Can be grown in a bed of gravel in a stream or waterfall. Dormant in winter, but returns in early spring with a charming carpet of green that quickly grows to fill its space.

Propagation: Rooted stem cuttings and root division.

Comments: A prolific plant for stream planting where it enjoys running water, watercress is also a good vegetative filter plant and can grow at the entry point of the water. Its peppery-tasting leaves are often used in salads and as sandwich garnishings. When collected from running ditches and streams, it may be *Cardamine cordifolia*, heart-leaved bittercress, quite similar in appearance to, but much taller (to 2.5 ft/.8 m) than, the prostrate watercress.

Orontium aquaticum. Golden club.

Hardiness Zones: 5–11.

Description & habit: A lovely, hardy species with bluish green, lance-shaped leaves that grow to 18 in. (45 cm), this species can be grown in water as deep as 12 in. (30 cm), or more (when its leaves float on the surface). Grow it as a marginal to fully appreciate its beauty. Unique pencil-like flowers emerge white-colored from the water and are tipped with a bright yellow. Slow to establish itself, it eventually produces lush growth that fares well in both dense shade and deeper water.

Potting & growing: Plant in rich soil in 2–5 gallon (8–20 l) containers in part sun to shade. In frost and freezing areas, move the plant into deeper part of the pond where it will remain safe from freezing.

Propagate: Divide plants in May-June by carefully pulling apart separate plants and entangled roots. Ripe seed may be sown in June to July.

Orontium aquaticum
Photo by Ron Everhart.

Peltandra virginica
Photo by Bob Romar.

Peltandra virginica. Arrow arum.

Hardiness Zones: 5–9.

Description & habit: Growing 1–2 ft. (30–60 cm) tall, this glossy and arrow-shaped–leaved plant produces an inconspicuous arumlike flower in summer. It does well in dense shade. Slightly green-tinged flowers are followed by green berries. Another native species, *P. sagittifolia* produces red berries. Leathery leaves are very similar in appearance to an arrowhead.

Potting & growing: Slower growing than many other marginal aquatics, it may be left in its 2-gallon (8 l) container for more than one season without requiring repotting. Provide 1–6 in. (2.5–15 cm) of water over the plant's crown and grow in sun to part shade.

Propagation: Divide clumps in spring or start with stratified seed.

Phragmites australis
Photo by H. Nash.

Phragmites australis 'Aurea.' Variegated dwarf common reed.

Hardiness Zones: 6–10.

Description & habit: While *Phragmites* are generally too large and invasive for inclusion in the typical water garden, this variegated species grows less vigorously and to only 3–4 ft. (1–1.2 m) in containers. Plumes produced in late summer can be cut, dried, and used in winter arrangements, and the green/yellow variegation adds delightful life to the waterscape.

Potting & growing: Plant in 5-gallon (20 l) containers and set in water to 4–5 in. (10–12.5 cm) over the plant's crown in sun to part shade. The plant may work in colder gardens if it is moved to the pond bottom for the winter.

Propagation: Root divisions in spring and early summer.

Pontederia cordata
Photo by Bob Romar.

Pontederia cordata 'Alba'
Photo by Bob Romar.

Ranunculus flammula
Photo by H. Nash.

Regnellidum diphyllum
Photo by Bob Romar.

Pontederia cordata. Pickerel weed.

Hardiness Zones: 4–11.

Description & habit: Growing to 18–24 in. (45–60 cm) or slightly more, glossy, erect, deep green leaves are slightly heart-shaped with a distinctive swirling. Soft blue flower spikes grow from leaf bracts at the top of stems. The plant adapts to very shallow water or to depths up to 18 inches (45 cm).

Potting & growing: Plant *Pontederia* in a 5-gallon (20 l) or larger pot to accommodate vigorous and fleshy roots. Grow in sun to part shade.

Propagation: Divide clumps in spring while discarding the rotting portion from the previous year. Stolon cuttings may be taken in summer, or the plant may be started from fresh seed collected in late summer.

Varieties to look for: P. lanceolata, with a more narrow lanceolate leaf form, is native to the southeastern U.S. and grows 4–5 ft. (1.2–1.5 m) high. It is not as hardy. Likewise, the varieties 'Alba' and 'Angustifolia' are not fully hardy in northern regions. These less hardy species, however, can be wintered over in northern ponds by sinking them to the pond bottom with hardy water lilies where the rhizome will escape freezing. Yet another tropical species is *P. rotundifolia,* the tropical pickerel weed, with rounder leaves 2–4 in. (5–10 cm) long and 1.25–4 in. (3–10 cm) wide. Its light blue flower appears more flowerlike than spikelike. A fast-growing species, it can grow immersed, submerged, floating, or creeping. 🌿🌿🌿🌿🌿🌿🌿🌿🌿

Ranunculus flammula. Miniature or lesser spearwort.

Hardiness Zones: 5–10.

Description & habit: Producing semiprostrate reddish stems, dark green oval leaves, and bright yellow flowers, this plant works well in the shallow waters of the informal or wildlife pond. Growing to 12 in. (30 cm), it is better suited for the water garden than *R. lingua,* greater spearwort, which can grow to 5 ft. (1.5 m).

Potting & growing: Plant in 1–2 gallon containers with up to 2 in. (5 cm) water over the crown, in sun to part shade.

Propagation: Divide plants in spring or sow seeds. 🌿🌿🌿🌿🌿🌿🌿🌿🌿

Regnellidum diphyllum. Two leaf clover.

Hardiness Zones: 7–11.

Description and habit: Grows to 6 in. (15 cm) with shiny double leaves. A lighter "heart" is encircled by a reddish-tinged circle that blends into the lighter green of the leaf.

Potting & growing: Pot in a one-gallon (4 l) container and submerge with no more than 2 in. (5 cm) of water over the plant's crown. In colder zones, allow to assume dormancy in a non-freezing location. Do not allow the plant to dry out.

Propagation: By division and stolon cuttings. 🌿🌿🌿🌿🌿🌿🌿🌿🌿

Ruellia squarrosa
Photo by Bob Romar.

Ruellia squarrosa. Bluebell.

Hardiness Zones: 9–11.

Description & habit: Growing only to 10 in. (25 cm), this charming plant spreads to 12 in. (30 cm) with dark purplish green foliage. Petunia-like blue flowers complement the plant in midsummer.

Potting & growing: Plant in 1–2-gallon (4–8 l) containers and cover the crown with 1–3 in. (2.5–7.5 cm) of water in sun to part shade.

Propagation: Seeds can be sown in greenhouses in March for planting in May. Cuttings can be taken in late summer and started in a heated bed and greenhouse. Move into the water garden when water and air stabilize above 70° F (21° C).

Varieties to look for: Ruellia brittoniana is a compact form of the species; Ruellia brittoniana 'Chi Chi' is a named variety.

💮 💮 💮 💮 💮 💮 💮 💮 💮 💮

Sagittaria lancifolia
Photo by H. Nash.

Sagittaria lancifolia. Lance-leaved arrowhead.

Hardiness Zones: 6?–11.

Description & habit: Dark green, spear-shaped foliage is graced by brilliant white flowers with yellow centers. The plant grows 12–20 in. (30–50 cm) tall and is known to tolerate brackish water. Trade indications are a hardiness only to Zone 8, but the plant has proven able to survive in Philadelphia, Zone 6.

Potting & growing: Plant in 2-gallon (8 l) containers in sun to part shade. If unsure of hardiness in your zone, winter over on the pond bottom with the hardy water lilies.

Varieties to look for: S. lancifolia var. rubrum. Red-stemmed Sagittaria. Zones 8–11. Grows 2–3 ft (0.6–1 m) with swordlike leaves growing from burgundy-red stems.

Propagation: By division of stolons or by seed.

💮 💮 💮 💮 💮 💮 💮 💮 💮 💮

Sagittaria latifolia
Photo by H. Nash.

Sagittaria latifolia. Duck potato.

Hardiness Zones: 3–11.

Description & habit: Produces starchy tubers known to attract waterfowl. Distinctive arrow-shaped leaves of this species may reach 32 in. (80 cm) long. Delicate three-petaled white flowers are produced in summer in whorls of three. Can be invasive.

Potting & growing: Plant in 2-gallon (8 l) containers at a depth of 1–6 in. (2.5–15 cm) in sun to part shade.

Propagation: By division of stolons or by seed.

💮 💮 💮 💮 💮 💮 💮 💮 💮 💮

Sagittaria montevidensis
Photo by Bob Romar.

Sagittaria japonica
Photo by H. Nash.

Sagittaria gramina 'Crushed Ice,' variegated arrowhead.
Photo courtesy of Springdale Water Gardens.

Sagittaria montevidensis. Giant arrowhead or Aztec arrowhead.

Hardiness Zones: 8–11.

Description & habit: Multiple blooms are produced all season long with flowers of white petals marked by a red dot at the base of each bloom. The plant grows 2 ft. (60 cm) or more and thrives with 1–5 in. (2.5–12.5 cm) of water over the plant's crown.

Potting & growing: Plant in 2-gallon (8 l) containers or larger in sun to part shade. While classified as an annual or a short-lived perennial in the trade, the plant can be maintained by propagation. Winter in cold zones by moving the plant into a greenhouse; it will experience dormancy.

Propagation: The seed is generally prolific and enables the plant to spread quickly in the wild. Collect seed and start in moist flats. Seedlings should have their crowns kept in water. In early spring, turions produced at the ends of stolons can be dug and planted, too.

🌿 🌿 🌿 🌿 🌿 🌿 🌿 🌿 🌿 🌿

Sagittaria sagittifolia. Common arrowhead.

Hardiness Zones: 3–11.

Description & habit: This European native produces arrow-shaped leaves up to 18 in. (45 cm) long and bears the characteristic white flowers.

Potting & growing: Plant in 2-gallon (8 l) containers at a depth of 1–6 in. (2.5–15 cm) in sun to part shade.

Propagation: Division of stolons or by seed.

Varieties to look for: S. japonica 'Flore Pleno.' Double-flowering arrowhead. Hardiness zones: 3–11. Pompons of round, double-white flowers are held above delicately arrow-shaped leaves. S. graminea. Narrow-leaf arrowhead. Hardiness zones: 4–11. Very narrow arrow-shaped leaves. Flowers typical of species. 'Crushed Ice' variegated form was introduced in 1997 by Springdale Water Gardens in Virginia.

🌿 🌿 🌿 🌿 🌿 🌿 🌿 🌿 🌿 🌿

Saururus cernuus
Photo by Bob Romar.

Saururus cernuus. Lizard's tail.

Hardiness Zones: 4–11.

Description & habit: Heart-shaped, bright green foliage grows 12–24 in. (30–60 cm) high and is graced with gently arched spikes of fragrant white flowers 4–6 in. (10–15 cm) long. Will still flower in dense shade.

Potting & growing: Plant in a 2–5 gallon (8–20 l) pot in 1–6 in. (2.5–15 cm) water in sun to part shade.

Propagation: Divide clumps in spring or take stem cuttings in spring to summer.

Scirpus cyperinus
Photo by H. Nash.

Scirpus cyperinus. Woolgrass bulrush.

Hardiness Zones: 3–11.

Description & habit: Grows 3–5 ft. (1–1.5 m) and bears a compound umbel of many spikelets on branching rays atop a nearly round stem surrounded by leaflike bracks. The spikelets turn woolly when in fruit. A wonderful plant for the wildlife garden!

Potting & growing: Plant in 5-gallon (20 l)containers with rich-to-clay soil in water to 4 in. (10 cm) over the crown in sun to part shade.

Propagation: Divide clumps in spring to summer.

Scirpus 'Zebrinus'
Photo by H. Nash.

Scirpus lacustris **subsp.** *tabernaemontani.* Zebra rush.

Hardiness Zones: 5–11.

Description & habit: This species offers two cultivars of note: 'Zebrinus' bears cream banding horizontally on the stems like porcupine quills and grows 3–6 ft. (1–2 m) tall, and 'Albescens' bears creamy vertical banding in its growth of 3–6 ft. (1–2 m).

Potting & growing: Grow in 2–5 gallon (8–20 l) containers in water up to 6 in. (15 cm) deep in sun to part shade. Divide clumps in the spring every two years.

Propagation: By division or by stratified seed.

Comments: Remove all green stems to prevent reversion to green form.

Scirpus 'Albescens'
Photo by H. Nash.

Thalia dealbata
Photo by Bob Romar.
© Maryland Aquatic Nurseries.

Thalia geniculata form
ruminoides
Photos by H. Nash.

Thalia dealbata. Powdery thalia.

Hardiness Zones: 5–11.

Description & habit: A bold accent plant of tropical appearance, the plant is also known as hardy canna. Growing to 6 ft. (2 m) high with striking ovate to lanceolate, glaucus, blue-green leaves edged in purple, 20 in. (50 cm) long and 10 in. (25 cm) wide, and dusted with white powder, it earns the common name of "powdery thalia." Small violet flowers are carried on 8–in. (20–cm) long, branched panicles.

Potting & growing: Pot in 5–20 gallon (20–80 l) container and grow in up to 12 in. (30 cm) of water over the plant's crown.

Propagation: By division or by cold, moist stratification of seed.

᭬ ᭬ ᭬ ᭬ ᭬ ᭬ ᭬ ᭬ ᭬ ᭬

Thalia geniculata **form** *ruminoides*. Red-stemmed thalia.

Hardiness Zones: 9–10.

Description & habit: Very similar to the *dealbata* plant except for its attractive red stems. In tropical regions, this plant grows 5–6 ft. (1.5–1.8 m), but can reach 8 ft. (2.5 m) in height. Flowers are a soft lavender and stand well above the foliage.

Potting & growing: Grow in 5-gallon (20 l) or larger pots in 1–6 in. (2.5–15 cm) of water in sun to part shade. Plant it in locations protected from strong winds. In temperate zones, winter over indoors as a tropical houseplant.

Propagation: Divide in spring to summer or start from seed. If propagating by seed, 30–40 percent of seedlings will show red-stemmed coloring.

᭬ ᭬ ᭬ ᭬ ᭬ ᭬ ᭬ ᭬ ᭬ ᭬

Collection of various cattails. Photo by H. Nash.

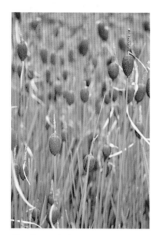

Typha minima
Photo by Bob Romar.

Typha latifolia 'Variegata'
Photo by Ron Everhart.

Typha angustifolia. Narrow-leaf cattail.

Hardiness Zones: 3–11.

Description & habit: Slender leaves grow to 4 ft. (1.2 m) high. Brown flower spikes with male and female flowers separated by a small gap distinguish this plant.

Potting & growing: Plant in 5-gallon (20 l) containers in up to 6–12 in. (15–30 cm) of water in sun to part shade.

Propagation: Divide clumps in spring to early summer or remove portions of rooted rhizomes. Start dry-stratified seed collected the previous year in pots sited in shady beds during April and May.

Typha minima. Dwarf cattail.

Hardiness Zones: 3–11.

Suitable even for small ponds, tub, and container gardens with growth of 12–18 in. (30–45 cm) high. Very narrow grasslike leaves and small, round, dark brown flower spikes make it a charming specimen. The slender rhizomes circle their container in the upper layer of soil and send up vigorous growth. Reports from water gardeners in zones warmer than Zone 5 report sparse production of catkins, indicating the plant requires a period of freezing dormancy to produce blooms. Plant in one-gallon (4 l) containers or larger and set in *shallow* water in sun to part shade.

Typha latifolia 'Variegata.' Variegated cattail.

Hardiness Zones: 4–11. Grows 3–4 ft. (1–1.2 m) tall in containers, but can reach 5–7 ft. (1.5–2.1 m) with rich soil and regular feeding. Tall stalks of white and green-striped broad leaves are topped with 3 in. (7.5 cm) green catkins, which turn brown in summer. Although a *latifolia,* this species is not as vigorous a grower as its green cousin. Plant in 5–10 gallon (4–40 l) pots in 1–12 in. (2.5–30 cm) of water in sun to part shade.

Comments: The common, broad-leaved cattails (*Typha latifolia*) found growing in the wild across North America and Europe are too large for the typical water garden. Their size is overpowering to most garden designs, and large, unwieldy pots are necessary to prevent the plants from blowing over. All *Typha* plant parts are edible, including the pollen, which is used as flour.

Other varieties to look for: T. laxmannii (T. stenophylla). Graceful cattail. Narrow grayish-green, half-round leaves are grooved on one side and rounded on the other and grow to 4 ft. (1.2 m) high. Flower spikes have lighter brown male flowers above with a slight gap from the dark brown female flowers below. Grows in 1–12 in. (2.5–30 cm) of water in sun to part shade.

Zantedeschia aethiopica
Photo by Bob Romar.

Zantedeschia aethiopica. Arum lily or calla lily.

Hardiness Zones: 9–11.

Description & habit: The species grows 2–3 ft. (0.6–1 m) tall with large, fragrant, white aroid flowers 3–10 in. (8–25 cm) long with central yellow spadixes and surrounded by shiny arrow-shaped leaves.

Potting & growing: Plant in 1–2 gallon (4–8 l) or larger containers in rich soil with up to 2 in. (5 cm) of water over the crown. Grow in sun to part shade. Although a frost-tender, tropical, terrestrial plant, *Zantedeschia* is highly adaptable to aquatic culture. In regions where hard freezes are minimal, this plant will survive if the pot is completely submerged below the water's surface. The safest way to ensure its survival is to winter the plant in a heated greenhouse or under grow lights in the house.

Propagation: By offsets in winter.

Varieties to look for: 'Green Goddess' has a yellow spadix and a green and white spathe; 'Crowborough' grows to only 2 ft. (0.6 m); *Z. rehmannii*, pink arum, grows to only 16 in. (40 cm).

❧ ❧ ❧ ❧ ❧ ❧ ❧ ❧ ❧ ❧

Zizania latifolia. Perennial wild rice.

Hardiness Zones: 5–10.

Description & habit: Although growing to 10 ft. (3 m) in the wild, wild rice grows to only 4 ft. (1.2 m) tall as a showy container plant in the water garden. Commonly referred to as "perennial" wild rice, the plant is actually a robust annual and probably returns the following season from seeds. Grow in rich garden loam and fertilize monthly. Turns yellow in autumn.

Potting & growing: Set the 5-gallon (20 l) or larger container so that up to 2 in. (5 cm) of water covers the plant crown. Grow in full sun. Collect seed in fall for next year's plants.

Propagation: By stratified seed.

❧ ❧ ❧ ❧ ❧ ❧ ❧ ❧ ❧ ❧

Zantedeschia rehmannii
Photo by Bob Romar.

BOG PLANTS

Quite often within the trade shallow-water aquatic plants are called "bog plants." Likewise, special shallow-water gardens constructed to grow these plants are called "bog gardens." Bogs, however, are a very distinctive type of wetland. Self-contained and unfreshened by waters other than rainfall, bogs are characterized by a growth of evergreen trees and shrubs with a floor covered by a thick carpet of sphagnum moss. While a bog may have a considerable number of open water spaces, floating vegetation and the sphagnum moss accumulate and decompose to render a highly acidic environment. The depth of peat does not decompose by bacterial action due to severely anaerobic conditions. Hence, peat is deficient in many minerals that are needed for plant growth. Plants which flourish under these conditions are either evergreen or have developed other means of securing the nutrients needed for growth.

Plants Commonly Found in True Bogs

TREES

Black spruce (*Picea mariana*)

Atlantic white cedar (*Chamaecypdris thyoides*)

Northern white cedar (*Thuja occidentalis*)

Tamarack/larch (*Larix laricina*)

Red maple (*Acer rubrum*)

Poison sumac (*Toxicodendron vernix*)

Black ash (*Fraxinus nigra*).

SHRUBS

Leatherleaf (*Chamaedaphne calyculata*)

Sheep laurel (*Kalmia angustifolia*)

Labrador tea (*Ledum groenlandicum*)

Cranberry (*Vaccinium macrocarpon*)

Great laurel (*Rhododendron maximum*)

Highbush blueberry (*Vaccinium corymbosum*)

PLANTS

Pitcher plants (*Sarracenia spp.*)

Sundews (*Drosera spp.*)

Butterworts, (*Pinguicula spp.*)

Grass pink (*Calopogon pulchellus*)

Rose pogonia (*Pogonia ophioglossoides*)

Bladderworts (*Utricularia spp.*)

Water arum (*Calla palustris*)

Cotton grass (*Eriophorum polystachion*)

Goldthread (*Coptis groenlandica*)

Bogbean (*Menyanthes trifoliata*)

Bog rosemary (*Andromeda glaucophylla*)

Orchids (*Habenaria spp.*)

Swamp pink (*Arethusa bulbosa*)

Swamp loosestrife (*Decodon verticillatus*)

Swamp saxifrage (*Saxifraga pensylvanica*)

Yellow-eyed grass (*Xyris iridifolia*).

(*Note that boldface species are commonly adapted to water garden culture; these plants do best when given an acid-enhanced soil medium.*)

While it is conceivable to create a large enough "bog garden" in which to grow true bog trees and shrubs, the home bog garden usually focuses on collections of perennial plants, particularly sundews, Venus flytraps, and pitcher plants, known commonly as *carnivorous plants*. The nutrition of these plants is supplied by insects that are trapped and digested within the plants.

Trapping mechanisms of carnivorous plants vary from passive to active. In the pitcher plant, insects are attracted by nectar that is secreted at the opening of the tall, tubular leaves. The insects slip or crawl down into the hollow leaf, above which is a zone of stiff, downward-pointing hairs or waxy particles that prevent escape. At the bottom of the trap are enzymes that are currently believed to digest the insect for absorption and use by the plant. The Venus flytrap uses an active mechanism that snaps shut when insects touch the trigger hairs on the inside of the leaf. Bladderworts, too, snap shut around their prey as they float in the water.

All carnivorous plants require strong sunlight for six to eight hours a day, a growing medium with a low pH, and an ability to hold moisture, such as commercial-grade whole-fiber sphagnum moss or a mix of equal parts peat moss and coarse vermiculite or sharp sand, and a constant water supply during the growing season.

Exceptions to the above requirements are bladderworts that actually grow in shallow water, and butterworts and the purple pitcher plant (*Sarracenia purpurea*) that both require strong sunlight in the spring but prefer partial shading for the rest of their growing season.

Creating a Bog Garden

Select a very sunny site within your yard. Use containers such as plastic dishpans, old bathtubs, or kiddie wading pools. Make three or four drainage holes halfway up the sides of the container and cover the holes with plastic screening. Bury the container in the ground to within a few inches of its rim. Rob Gardner of the North Carolina Botanical Garden at the University of North Carolina at Chapel Hill also suggests the option of sinking the container only halfway into the ground and mounding excavated dirt around the outside edge.

Fill the container with either whole-fiber sphagnum moss or a peat moss and sand mix. Add water and check that drainage holes are working. This allows the bottom half of the container to be constantly full of water with the planting medium wicking water up to the plants from below.

Allow the planting mix to settle for a few days before planting. Check weekly that water level remains up to the drainage holes. You can construct a bog garden, too, from pond liner membrane; simply follow the same procedure as for preformed units.

Carnivorous plants do require a dormancy period in the winter. Watch that the plants do not remain in soggy conditions over the winter; they should be kept just moist and not allowed to dry out. In cold winter zones, you may wish to provide a thick layer of protective mulch over the bog garden. Forcing the plants into active growth in the spring promotes rotting. Resume normal watering regime once growth has resumed in the spring. Rob recommends as a reference book Donald Schnell's *Carnivorous Plants of the United States and Canada*, as well as the *Carnivorous Plant Newsletter*, the official journal of the International Carnivorous Plant Society.

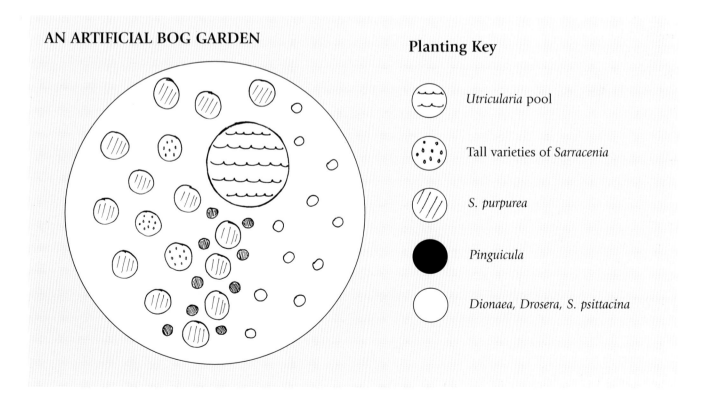

AN ARTIFICIAL BOG GARDEN

Planting Key

Utricularia pool

Tall varieties of *Sarracenia*

S. purpurea

Pinguicula

Dionaea, Drosera, S. psittacina

Carnivorous Plants for a Bog Garden

Dionaea muscipula
Photo by Rob Gardner.

Dionaea muscipula
Photo by Rob Gardner.

Dionaea muscipula
Photo by Rob Gardner.

Dionaea muscipula. Venus flytrap.

Description: A perennial of prostrate growth from a short rhizome to 3 in. (7.5 cm), Venus flytraps bear white flowers in June on 6–12 in. (15–30 cm) stems. Traps form on the end of short expanded petioles. Inner surfaces of traps may be a rich, dark red or green. The amount of sunlight seems to affect how red the leaves become.

Growing: Grow in full sun in a planting mix of whole-fiber sphagnum moss or a mix of equal parts of peat moss and coarse vermiculite or sharp sand.

Fruit and Seed: Flowers must be cross-pollinated to produce seeds; pollen from the same plant will not produce seed. To ensure pollination, use an open pollen-shedding flower from one plant to dust the stigmas of all other flowering plants in the bed. Do this daily for as long as the flowers continue to open. Shiny, jet-black seeds require about a month to develop and mature as rounded seeds that may be clustered together at the end of each flower stalk. If you would collect them, keep a daily watch for the quickly shed seeds.

Collecting Seed: Cut the flower stalk several inches below the cluster of ripe seeds and spread them on newspaper for air drying. Seeds turn black when properly dried. Clean the seeds by putting them through a sieve or metal screen. Place dry, clean seeds in a paper envelope, label, and store in airtight jars in the refrigerator.

Propagation by Seed: Sow seed thinly in a flat or pot containing a mixture of one part peat to one part vermiculite. Do not cover the seeds. Place the container in a shallow tray of water in a warm, protected location with indirect light. Germination normally occurs within 30 days. Following germination, the seedlings can be gradually exposed to full sun. Sown thinly enough, the seedlings can remain undisturbed until large enough to transplant easily.

Rules for successful seed germination of carnivorous plants:
1. Protect from rain or overhead watering. **2.** Supply a constantly damp growing medium. **3.** Supply enough sun or artificial light after germination.

Cultivation: Plant survival depends upon receiving six to eight hours of sunlight per day. A planting medium of equal parts of peat moss and vermiculite or whole-fiber sphagnum moss is recommended. Keep the medium moist constantly during the growing season.

Rob Gardner notes that it takes very little to satisfy the needs of the Venus flytrap. If you must feed it, provide only very small, soft-bodied insects such as spiders or ants. Feeding it a too-large insect can result in the plant's death. "Never feed your plant hamburger, boiled egg, or anything else that comes from the kitchen." Remember that once a leaf trap has closed, it takes several days for it to reopen; "teasing" the plant into shutting can deprive it of normal feeding.

🌿 🌿 🌿 🌿 🌿 🌿 🌿 🌿 🌿 🌿

Drosera Intermedia
Photo by Rob Gardner.

Drosera Capillaris
Photo by Rob Gardner.

Drosera species. Sundews.

Description: Perennial of prostrate growth growing to 8 in. (20 cm). Dozens of slender, crimson, or green-tipped filaments stud each leaf to give the plant a sparkling jewel-like appearance. Each gland secretes a tiny droplet of a clear, mucilaginous substance that entraps tiny insects. Struggling insects stimulate nearby glands to slowly bend toward the prey and secure it even more firmly. Mosquitoes, gnats, damselflies and other small insects are attracted to the plant. Blooming in May through August, slender flower stalks of 6–12 in. (15–30 cm) rise above a rosette of basal leaves. One flower opens each day and can pollinate itself upon closing in the afternoon. The lower flowers are the first to open, with the blooms working their way up the stem. Flowers may be white to pink.

Growing: Grow in full sun in a planting mix of whole-fiber sphagnum moss or a mix of equal parts peat moss and coarse vermiculite or sharp sand.

Fruit and Seed: About five to seven weeks after flowering, small green capsules turn blackish when mature. Minute seeds are black or dark grey. Because the flowers open over such an extended period of time, seeds may be maturing on the lower portion of the stalk as the last flower opens at the tip.

Collecting Seed: Cut the entire flowering stalk just below the lowest seed capsule when the stalk presents the greatest number of mature seed capsules and place it in a paper seed envelope or inside a fold of paper. (The seeds are so fine that too many are lost when being collected into a paper bag.) Lay the stalks on a sheet of white paper to dry. While you may have to break some capsules apart for full seed release, most of them can be shaken out of their capsules when they are completely dry. Place cleaned, dry seeds in a labeled paper envelope and store in the refrigerator in an airtight jar.

Propagation by Seed: In either fall or spring, lightly sow seeds over the surface of your bog. Because the plants reseed so easily, plants maintained in an outside bog garden usually self-sow. However, they can be started in pots. Fill a 3 to 4 in. (7.5–10 cm) plastic pot with slightly moistened peat and vermiculite of equal proportions. Sow the seeds thinly on the surface and place the pot in a tray of shallow water. Always water from the bottom! Germination occurs in 20–30 days, depending upon the

Sundews attract and hold insects to a sticky nectar, known as the fly-paper method.
Photo by Bill Foshee.

time of year. After 2–3 months, seedlings are large enough for transplanting. Because the seedlings produce long hairlike roots that are easily damaged in transplanting, you may wish to carefully plant them in small clumps.

Propagation by Cuttings: Leaf cuttings provide a quicker and easier way of propagating your sundew plants. Cut fresh new leaves from the plant. Avoid selecting leaves that have captured insects, as these cuttings may decay. Place the leaf cuttings "face up" on a medium of either moistened, milled sphagnum moss or peat moss. Pin or weight them down to be sure the entire lower leaf surface touches the medium. If the leaf is not fully touching the soil, its edges curl up and the leaf dies. Water the cutting with water mixed with a fungicide, drain thoroughly, and enclose within a plastic bag to create the necessary humid environment for bud production.

Place the bagged pot under grow lights or in a window with strong but indirect sunlight. Plantlets form in three to five weeks and may be transplanted after they have formed their own roots. Gradually accustom the young plants to shade and then sun outside before moving them into a permanently sunny location.

Alternate Leaf Cutting Method: Thoroughly sterilize baby-food jars and their lids with bleach, rinse, and fill them with sterilized or distilled water at room temperature. Place leaf cuttings in the jar and seal. You can use whole leaves or pieces of leaves. Place the jar under a fluorescent light or where it receives indirect lighting. Plantlets form in 15 to 30 days, depending upon time of year. Well-budded leaves can be transplanted on a premoistened planting medium by gently pressing the plantlets into the medium with your finger. Keep new transplants in the shade for several days and gradually introduce them to stronger light.

Cultivation: Sundews require a constant moisture supply, a low pH growing medium such as peat moss, and at least 6 to 8 hours of sunlight daily. Plant them on low mounds in the bog garden to help prevent overwatering.

**Pinguicula lutea,
yellow butterwort**
Photo by Rob Gardner.

Pinguicula planifolia
Photo by Rob Gardner.

Pinguicula species. **Butterworts.**

Description: Perennial herbaceous plants with glandular, yellow-green or purplish leaves in a basal rosette, these carnivorous plants capture insects such as gnats and mosquitoes. Minute glands completely cover the upper surface of each leaf. Droplets of sticky fluid capture struggling insects, their struggle stimulating even more sticky fluid to be secreted until the insect is hopelessly stuck to the leaf. Digestive enzymes are then secreted that dissolve the soft parts of the insect for absorption by the plant. Solitary flowers of yellow, pink, purple, and white are held 3–10 in. (7.5–25 cm) above the leaves on slender stalks in April and May.

Growing: Grow in full sun to partial shade in a planting mix of whole-fiber sphagnum moss or a mix of equal parts peat moss and coarse vermiculite or sharp sand.

Fruit and Seed: Green capsules about 1/8 in (3 mm) in diameter swell slightly and gradually turn buff or brown with maturity, bearing tiny brown or black seeds.

Collecting Seed: Three to four weeks after flowering in late spring, the capsule turns brown and the seeds are ready for collection. Break ripe capsules open and shake out the seeds. Store them in a paper envelope in an airtight container in the refrigerator.

Propagation by Seed: Fill a pot with moistened peat moss, milled sphagnum moss, or a mix of one part peat moss to one part vermiculite. Water with a mixture of water and fungicide. Sow seeds on the surface of the medium. Do not cover them. Place the pot in a shallow tray of water. Water from below to avoid displacing the seeds. Maintain high humidity and ensure germination by covering the top of the pot with glass or plastic wrap. Watch for fungal infections and keep the pot out of direct sunlight.

Cultivation: Butterworts need a moist area in full sunlight. Plant them on a low mound in the bog garden to help prevent overwatering.

**Sarracenia minor,
hooded pitcher plant**
Photo by Rob Gardner.

Sarracenia species. Pitcher plants.

Description: The pitcher plant bears highly modified tubular leaves 6 in. to 3 ft. (15–91 cm) in length. Yellow or maroon flowers are solitary on long stalks that bloom usually in April or May. After a bloom period of 7–8 days, the petals drop to leave the rest of the flower structure in place as the seeds mature.

Growing: Grow in full sun in a planting mix of whole fiber sphagnum moss or a mix of equal parts peat moss and coarse vermiculite or sharp sand.

Fruit and Seed: A green, five-chambered capsule remains on the tall scape for the entire growing season. In the fall it turns brown when ripe with numerous, small, tear-shaped seeds of tan to brown or purplish brown.

Collecting Seed: Collect in the fall when the capsule sutures begin to crack open when the capsule starts to turn from green to greenish yellow or tan. If you collect before the capsule begins to split, the seeds may not be mature; on the other hand, waiting too long may find the seeds already dispersed. You may wish to contain the capsules in muslin bags towards the end of summer. Cut or break off the ripe capsules and dry them for a few days in a paper bag on a sheet of paper. Once they have dried, break them open, sieve the seeds to clean them, and store in an airtight jar in the refrigerator. If the seeds are collected fresh and stored correctly, a fairly high rate of germination may be expected for up to five years from the time of collection.

Propagation by Seed: Rob recommends equal parts of peat and coarse vermiculte as a germination medium for *Sarracenia* seeds. Sterilize a 4-inch(10-cm) plastic pot with a bleach solution, rinse it well, and fill it to 1/2 in. (1.3 cm) below the rim with

**Flowers of *Sarracenia
flava*** Photo by Rob Gardner.

Right: Habitat of Sarracenia flava
Photo by Rob Gardner

Far right: Sarracenia psittacina
Photo by Rob Gardner.

Sarracenia leucophylla, **white-topped pitcher plant** Photo by Rob Gardner.

moistened planting media. Water in the soil with the label-recommended strength of a fungicide such as Benlate and allow the medium to drain for several hours to avoid excess moisture. Sow the seeds thinly on top of the mixture; do not cover them, but press them lightly into the planting medium. Enclose the pots in a plastic bag and place in the refrigerator for 60 days. Then remove from the refrigerator; take the pots from the plastic bag and place them in a shallow tray of water that reaches one-fourth to one-third up the side of the pot. Use distilled, de-ionized, or rainwater if possible. Do not water from above, even after germination. Germination begins 20 to 40 days after the seeds have been removed from the refrigerator. Bottom heat speeds the rate of germination but is not required. Place seedlings in a greenhouse or other protected place for the first year to give adequate time for establishment. Do not leave them outside where rain can damage them. Transplanting is usually performed in the spring of the second growing season. Good ventilation and monthly applications of a fungicide help prevent soil fungi and damping off.

Propagation by Division: Crown division offers the easiest means of propagation. Mature, healthy plants form many crowns. Carefully break or cut the rhizome to separate the individual crowns, taking special care not to damage the roots. Replant immediately.

Cultivation: Whatever soil mixture you use for *Sarracenia*, it must have a low pH and

Sarracenia leucophylla
Photo by Rob Gardner.

good moisture-retentive quality. Many growers consider whole-fiber sphagnum moss the best medium, but any of the variations discussed for other carnivorous plants are acceptable.

Pitcher plants require at least 6 to 8 hours of direct sunlight each day during the growing season. Without enough sun, they will be weak, display poor color, and eventually die. (The purple pitcher plant, however, benefits from direct morning sunlight, but enjoys shading from intense afternoon sun.) Requiring a constant supply of water, the plants should be planted 5 or 6 inches (12.5–15 cm) *above* the water table of your bog garden. Particularly if you are growing your pitcher plants in pots, you may notice a thin whitish crust accumulating on top of the growing medium— salt. Since pitcher plants are particularly sensitive to salt in the water supply, you should periodically flush out the plants with extra water two or three times a season to wash away these deadly concentrations. Many growers use rain, distilled, or deionized water to avoid this problem. Pitcher plants have such specialized growing requirements in strong light and high humidity that they do not adapt well to indoor cultivation.

Sarracenia flava
Photo by Rob Gardner.

Growing habit of
Utricularia
Photo by Ron Everhart.

Utricularia. Bladderwort. Several species of this unique native, carnivorous, fully aquatic plant may be available to the trade. *U. inflata*, swollen bladderwort, is found throughout the U.S. and Nova Scotia. *U. minor*, lesser bladderwort, is found in the northeastern U.S. and Great Lakes region. *U. purpurea*, purple bladderwort, is found in acid lakes and ponds in the southeastern U.S. to Minnesota and southern Canada. *U. resupinata*, reversed bladderwort, is found in the eastern U.S. *U. vulgaris*, common bladderwort, is found throughout Europe, Asia, and the U.S., except in the extreme south. Small, submerged bladders triggered by touch-sensitive hairs allow insects and small crustaceans and fish to be trapped inside for digestion by the plant. The plants may bear yellow or purple flowers that are usually held above the water, sometimes supported by a whorl of spongy, floating leaves. Temperate species over-winter by winter buds that float to the pond bottom. Still, shallow water is the only real requirement. Slightly acidic water is favored.

ю ю ю ю ю ю ю ю ю ю

Close-up of flower of
Utricularia
Photo by Ron Everhart.

chapter nine

WATER IRISES

Water gardeners are only beginning to discover the realm of possibilities within the world of irises. Several iris species of the 15-member subsection Apogon thrive in damp soil. Two of these species even stand in water contantly: *Iris laevigata* from the Far East and *I. pseudacorus,* the European native yellow flag that is now naturalized across North America. While truly aquatic species carry their own "watermark" as dark blotches in the veins of their leaves, a rainbow of colors and species in this beloved flower family grows in the shallow margins of the water garden throughout the season.

Irises offer a whole world of garden color in the water garden.
Photo by Bob Romar.

I. 'Cowee'
Photo by Perry D. Slocum.

Above, *I.* 'Sauterne'
Photo by Perry D. Slocum.

Iris laevigata
Photo by Bob Romar.

Iris Laevigata

Iris laevigata occurs in many parts of eastern Siberia, China, Japan, and Korea. It is the one iris that grows best in standing water. Bearing rich blue flowers with broad pendant falls and somewhat narrower, upright standards, the falls have a central ridge of light yellow. Smooth, thin, light green leaves droop at their upper ends. Stems are rounded and straight. With two or three flowers at the top, one or two blooming side branches are usually produced, as well. *Iris laevigata* blooms June to July and may repeat-bloom.

Atop stems usually about 30″ (80 cm) high, the flower size depends upon the richness and dampness of soil. Maximum flower production occurs in full sun. When planted with 2–8 in. (5–20 cm) of water over its soil, the plant rewards us with much larger flowers than those produced in ordinary garden conditions.

Plant *laevigata* rhizomes at least 2–3 in. (5–7.5 cm) below the soil surface in an acidic, lime-free medium. The plants slowly spread beneath the fibrous remains of the previous season's growth. Do not plant them too closely to other plants or disturb their soil during the growing season, except for transplanting in spring or early summer following bloom. (If your climate permits enough time for root establishment, they may be transplanted in early fall, too.) When grown in the terrestrial garden, they are topped off with a dressing of well-rotted manure or rich compost for their dormant winter period. In the water garden, this risks polluting the water and endangering your finned pets. Within their hardiness zones, simply trim the tops back when they begin to die down and leave the plants until mid-spring, when they will send out new growth. Outside their hardiness zones, move the pots into a sheltered garden site where they can be buried to their pot rims and mulched with a rich compost.

Propagating easily by seed, seed capsules are brown and bear D-shaped seeds with a thick, glossy seed coat. Forms available to the trade include 'Semperflorens' (blue), 'Regal' (plum-colored), 'Alba' (white), *albopurpurea* (white with blue spots), and *albopurpurea colchesterensis* (blue with a white star). *I. laevigata* 'Variegata' bears boldly striped foliage topped with bluish purple blossoms typical of the species.

Iris laevigata 'Variegata'
Photo by H. Nash.

Iris pseudacorus 'Plena'
Photo by Perry D. Slocum.

Iris pseudacorus
Photo by Bob Romar.

Iris pseudacorus

Commonly known as yellow flag iris, this native plant of England is now naturalized in North America. A true swamp and aquatic plant, it grows in even deeper water than *I. laevigata* and makes good growth in as much as 13–15 in. (35–38 cm) of water.

I. pseudacorus is the only yellow-flowered species in the *Iris* series. Normally growing to a height of 28–38 in. (70–98 cm) in containers, it can grow as tall as 4 ft. (1.2 m) in the wild. It has deep green to gray-green leaves, 4 to 12 flowers (the number depending on the dampness of its site and the crowding of the clump), and usually some brown or purplish veining on the falls with a darker yellow zone. The variety *bastardii* lacks the dark blotch. Standards and crests are narrow, erect, and about equal in size. The falls are much larger and spread out horizontally. *Pseudacorus* blooms in early summer from the end of May and into June. Although clumps grow vigorously and develop into large stands, crowding reduces the number of blooms produced. Seeds germinate freely to produce new stands. In the water garden, clip off the seed heads before they mature to prevent unwanted spreading.

Happiest in water or water-soaked, slightly acidic soils, the species survives well in dry conditions. A very hardy plant, it should be left in place through the winter, the dead foliage trimmed back above the water level in northern-grown plants. Southern-grown plants may remain green year-round. Divide and repot in autumn or following the bloom season. Adding well-rotted cow manure in the fall is beneficial, but not advisable if the nutrients might leach into the pond water.

A variegated form that bears paler flowers is not as robust as the type. Although its pale gold leaves with a light green edging turn green as summer progresses, it provides sparkle to the pond for at least half the season. New tetraploid cultivars offer improvements in the species.

🌿 🌿 🌿 🌿 🌿 🌿 🌿 🌿 🌿 🌿

Iris ensata
Photo by Bob Romar.

Wild *Iris ensata*.

Iris ensata (I. kaempferi)

I. ensata and its hybrid strains have been cultivated in Japan for more than five hundred years. By nature a meadow plant, *I. ensata* is traditionally flooded by Japanese gardeners when it is in bloom. Formerly known as *I. kaempferi*, the name has changed in the trade to *I. ensata* according to the rule of precedence in botanical naming.

Modern hybrids are available in the typical single form with three petals, a double form with six petals, or the "dinner plate" size of the triple, peony forms. Colors range from white to purple, blue, plum and pink, and some varieties offer contrasting bands of color or veins. Standards are considerably smaller than the falls. Blossoms last for several days as the flowering peaks in July. The flower stem may be unbranched or bear one lateral branch with three or four flowers. Wide leaves have a very prominent midrib, which distinguishes the plant from *I. laevigata*, whose leaves are completely smooth.

Ensata must have plenty of moisture during the growing season and into late summer to allow full root development. It must be dry in the winter to avoid root rot. Although the leaves wither in the fall, they should not be cut off until spring. *I. ensata* that is grown in the water garden during the summer should be removed from the pond and buried to the rim of its pot in the terrestrial garden. Supply a protective mulch in zones colder than 5. *Iris ensata* appreciates acidic soil. If yellow leaves (chlorosis) occur, cover the plant with peat and water it with a solution of aluminum sulfate.

Divide the plants immediately after flowering about every three years and plant the rhizomes about 1–2 in. (2.5–5 cm) deep. Like other irises, they also appreciate a dressing of composted cow manure in the autumn or early spring before their return to the pond.

Tetraploid forms of Japanese iris, *Iris ensata*.

Iris versicolor
Photo by Bob Romar.

Iris versicolor. Blue flag iris.

Iris versicolor is native to the northeastern U.S., including Virginia, Ohio, the Great Lakes region, and southeastern Canada. It is suited to shallow waters that are maintained *at a constant level* of 2–4 in. (5–10 cm) over the plant crown. A clump-forming species, it is considered coarse in growth with heavily ribbed foliage that measures about 1 ⅛″ (3 cm) wide. It spreads by tough, creeping, wiry rhizomes. A purplish red base colors the fans where they rise from the rhizome.

Stems grow to approximately 24 in. (60 cm) with 1–2 branches that are slightly shorter than the leaves. Blossoms appear in clusters of 2 to 4 flowers in shades of violet, blue-purple, lavender, or dull purple during the first part of June. The falls are round to oval and often have a greenish yellow blotch or signal covered with a faint down at the center of the ovate blade. A wider area marked with purple veins continues down the fall. The standards are very narrow and slanting. There is a white form, as well as the popular *I. kermesina*, a lovely rose purple that is smaller in growth than the type.

Seed is freely produced with well-tended seedlings flowering in the second year. Seed capsules are 2 in. (5 cm) long, oblong-ovate, with a wartlike surface, and bear dark brown, D-shaped fruit. Fully hardy, the plant survives colder northern winters. An application of well-rotted cow manure in the fall produces luxuriant growth the following year.

Iris versicolor flourishes in moist sites but does not fail in dryer conditions. Lime in the soil causes chlorosis. Aquatically grown specimens are usually propagated by division following bloom. Pink forms and white forms with blue veins are now available to the trade.

🌱 🌱 🌱 🌱 🌱 🌱 🌱 🌱 🌱 🌱

Iris virginica grows lushly in its natural habitat, here shown with cinnamon fern.
Photo by Stuart Schuck.

Iris virginica
Photo by Bob Romar.

Iris virginica

Iris virginica, known as the Southern blue flag iris, is found on the eastern seaboard of the U.S., south from Virginia along the Atlantic coast to include Florida, Georgia, the Carolinas, and southeast Louisiana. However, it is hardy in cooler, more northern climates. *Virginica* commonly grows in the very acid soils of swamps and sandy flood plains with the Louisiana irises. You can tell *Iris virginica* from the Louisianas by the pronounced midrib in the center of its leaves and by the foliage remaining green after the Louisianas have discolored. Water often covers the roots for several months of the year.

I. virginica is very similar to *I. versicolor*, but some growers consider it not as easy to grow. It has a bluer flower than *I. Versicolor*, the two species distinguished chiefly by the size of their standards. While the standards of *virginica* are almost exactly the same size as the falls, *versicolor* standards are considerably smaller and shorter than the falls, clearly veined, and broadened through the blade. Falls of *virginica* are more oblong-ovate, with an indicator mark that fuses with the veining.

I. virginica var. *shrevei*, now usually classified as a separate species, *I. shrevei*, is considered easier to grow in the garden. Its basal foliage varies considerably, from 8–35 in. (20–90 cm) long of rich, dark green with conspicuous ribbing. Scapes vary from 11.5–40 in. (30 cm–1 m). Blossoms are relatively large, lavender or violet-blue, with purple-blue veining. Falls are 1.5–3 in. (4–8 cm) long. On the upper base of the blade, a striking, yellow signal spot is covered with dense, fine hairs. Standards are 1 1/8 to 2 3/4 in. (3–78 cm) long. Fragile seed capsules that are often destroyed before the fruit ripens are almost spherical with a wartlike surface and bear rounded or D-shaped seeds with dull, corklike surfaces. A vigorous plant, it comes freely from seed.

Iris virginica may be left in very shallow water year-round. Aquatically grown plants are divided and repotted after flowering. While it does not require as acid a soil as the type, avoid lime in its potting mix.

Iris siberica

Siberian irises are more easily grown and more lime-tolerant than most other moisture-loving irises. *I. sibirica* grows in normal, well-watered garden soils, but it will grow almost twice as large in the water garden. Its roots may be covered by 2–4 in. (5–10 cm) water during their growing season. Remove its pots from the water garden by fall and bury to the rim in the garden for a well-drained dormancy. The plants are sun lovers, although in climates hotter than their native habitat they still perform well with only half-day sun. Grown in full shade, foliage is produced, but few, if any, flowers.

Flowers of different species vary in form, but all are slender in outline, except for the modern, flat tetraploids. Most of the species have straight and thin hollow stems peculiar to the group. Their bloom period coincides with the end of the tall bearded iris season and continues well into summer. Some varieties rebloom in late summer and early autumn.

I. sibirica attracts butterflies. The species has small light blue or blue-purple flowers that are usually veined on the falls. Standards are rigidly upright and the falls pendant. The uppermost branch produces 3 to 4 flowers while the side branches produce another two.

Foliage of slender, grasslike leaves grows from very close-set, wiry rhizomes that are buried under thick tufts of growth. Most of the Siberians reseed readily. The different species within each group also cross very easily. If you attempt hybridizing, pull off the falls and hand-pollinate.

All Siberians die down in late autumn. If you cut them back in the fall, leave enough foliage to prevent frost damage and waterlogging conditions through the winter.

Plant them in rich, lime-free, somewhat acidic soil. The hardiest species are *I. sibirica* and *I. sanguinea.* Two of the most popular hybrids commonly available to the trade are *I.* 'Caesar' and *I.* 'Caesar's Brother.'

LOUISIANA IRISES

A bed of *Iris* 'Dixie Deb.'
Photo by Perry D. Slocum.

Louisiana irises are naturally distributed in the warm and wet habitats of south and southwest Louisiana and into the marshy areas of the Gulf Coast from Texas to Florida. *I. brevicaulis* and *I. fulva* can be found up the Mississippi Valley, and *I. hexagona* is native to the southeastern Atlantic and Gulf coasts. Early trappers and fishermen called them "les gles de marais," the glads of the marsh, a reference to their broad and vibrant range of color.

The American Iris Society lists five species in the series Hexagonae: *I. hexagona, I. fulva, I. brevicaulis, I. giganticaerulea,* and *I. nelsonii.*

The Louisiana iris grows from a rhizome like other irises. A flower stalk emerges at the growing tip of the rhizome when the plant is mature. Growing to its full height,

TYPES OF STALKS

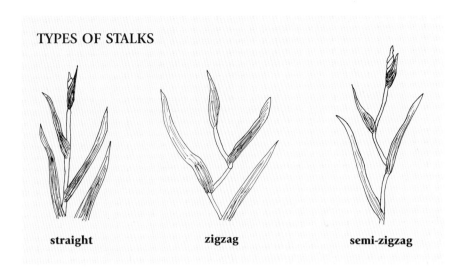

straight   zigzag   semi-zigzag

the stalk grows with three or four sheath leaves. Bloom buds usually emerge at the junctions of the sheath leaves to the stalk. Lower sheath positions may also bear secondary branches that bear blooms at their ends. Typical Louisiana irises produce five to seven blooms and sometimes as many as 10. Each bloom lasts two or three days depending on the weather and opens sequentially. Two or even three blooms may be open at one time. The entire stalk blooms for five to nine days.

The flower's standards tend to stand upright and are more narrow than the falls which droop

RHIZOME AND ROOT STRUCTURE OF LOUISIANA IRIS

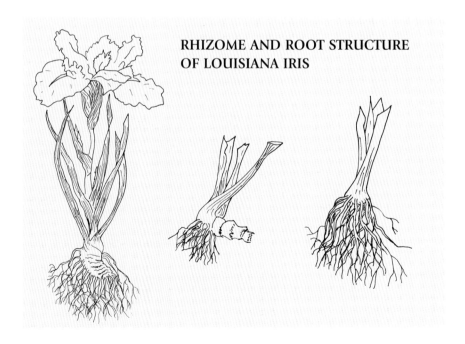

FLOWER PARTS

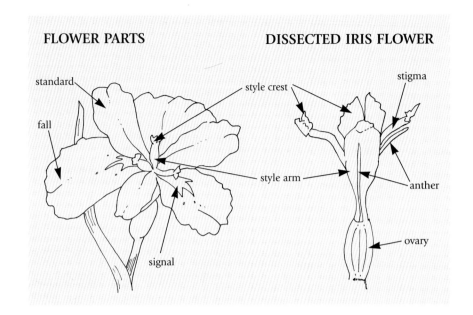

standard

fall

style crest

signal

DISSECTED IRIS FLOWER

stigma

style arm

anther

ovary

September through November. Latitudes of 25–45 degrees allow good adaptive conditions.

Trends in hybridizing are larger flowers up to 6–7 inches (15–18 cm) across, laciness or a ruffling of the falls, and unusual and exotic color combinations. Color breakthroughs include true bicolors, styles of contrasting color, and color variations of white or yellow edging or halos on the segments.

down from the bloom. Three style arms radiate from the center of the flower and extend one-third to one-half the length of the falls. These styles are extensions of the ovaries that later expand to form the seed pod if the flower is pollinated. A pronounced marking in yellow or orange, known as a "signal," is often located on the falls where the beards are located in bearded iris.

In spite of their name, Louisiana irises can be grown successfully in over 80 percent of the United States. The snow cover of the Midwest allows them to survive dormancy well, but the cold weather of the Pacific Northwest often occurs at budding and bloom time. The Louisiana Iris Society recommends *Iris brevicaulis* as a species to try in that difficult region. Internationally, the species do well in Australia and New Zealand, where they bloom in

FLOWER TYPES IN LOUISIANA IRISES

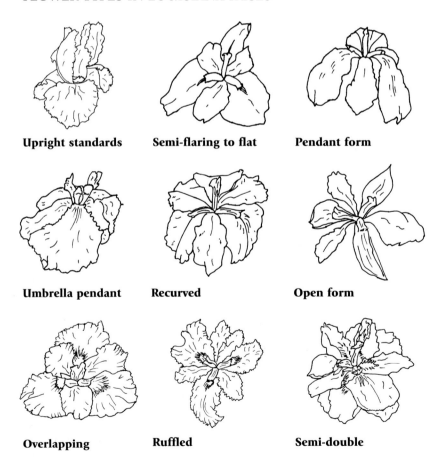

Upright standards   **Semi-flaring to flat**   **Pendant form**

Umbrella pendant   **Recurved**   **Open form**

Overlapping   **Ruffled**   **Semi-double**

The Louisiana Species

Among the five species of Louisiana iris, two are commonly found in the trade: *I. fulva* and *I. brevicaulis.*

I. fulva

A bed of *Iris fulva*   Photo by Perry D. Slocum.

This red iris varies in color from brick or rust-red to cardinal-red. Occasionally, yellow blooms are produced. The flowers droop, sometimes with a slight flare. Falls are 1–1.25 in. (2–3 cm) wide and 2.25–2.5 in. (5–6 cm) long. Leaves measure 18–24 in. (45–60 cm) long and up to an inch wide. Nearly straight flower stalks stand 24–36 in. (60–90 cm) tall. Lower bud positions on the unbranched stalk occur singly, with the tip or terminal position two-flowered. The signal is very small or fully absent. *I. fulva* is often found in water up to 6 inches (15 cm) deep in swampy areas, as well as along streams and in roadside ditches. Intolerant of dense shade or salty water, it is native to acidic, organically fertile soil in south Louisiana, Arkansas, Missouri, and Ohio.

I. brevicaulis

Flaring flowers of 3.5–4.5 in. (9–11 cm) in shades of pale blue, medium blue, and blue-violet bloom among the leaves. The signal is inconspicuous and often on a white background. Thick and short flower stalks, usually 10–14 in. (25–35 cm) are usually zigzagged and sometimes prostrate. All flower positions are two-flowered. The cauline leaves measure 16–19 in. (40–48 cm), are strap-shaped, and grow up to an inch (3 cm) wide. Lateral branches often occur at leaf nodes. The latest-blooming of all the species, it flowers in early to mid-May in Louisiana. Considered quite hardy, it offers the greatest adaptability to low temperatures and so

Iris brevicaulis   Photo by Bob Romar

has been used in breeding hardier varieties.

GROWING LOUISIANA IRISES IN WATER

Even Louisianas grown in large pots usually require annual repotting. Use a soil mix that is lime-free and enriched with well-rotted cow manure or other organic compost. After the iris is planted, cover the soil's surface with coarse gravel or small stones to prevent fish from disturbing the soil and the plant. Place the plant in the pond so that the water level is no more than 3 in. (7.5 cm) above the soil. Feed once monthly with an acid-base fertilizer. While irises that grow directly in water are not as sensitive to moving water as water lilies, they should not be set directly in the flow of the water's current. Growing them in water seems to make the level of acidity less important. After flowering, remove stalks and seed pods unless seeds are to be planted. Plants grown in a bog garden should still be mulched in summer to control dormancy. Since wet mulch deteriorates quickly, apply fresh mulch as necessary.

Louisiana irises are untidy in the heat of summer, as their foliage begins to turn brown. Remove them from the pond, divide if necessary, and leave them in a sheltered spot, buried to the pot's rim and mulched heavily to prevent freezing in colder zones. Louisianas may also be left in place in the non-freezing pond. After the last hard frost in the spring, pull back the mulch and resume regular watering. When the first shoots appear, scrape away the top 1.5–2 in. (4–5 cm) of soil and add fresh compost and rotted manure. Return to the shallow waters of the pond. Plants left in the pond for the winter should be removed and prepared for the growing season in the same way.

HOW TO MAKE A LOUISIANA IRIS BED

To create a bed along the edge of a pond or stream, plan for a width of 2–3 ft. (0.6–1 m). Well composted leaves or peat and well rotted cattle manure provide necessary richness. For sandy soils, add loam; for clay soils, add river sand. Regular applications of acidic mineral fertilizer make these acid-loving plants happy.

After the irises have bloomed,

A bed of 'Glowlight' frames the pond edge. Photo by Sue Bridges.

do not disturb them. Mulch them to protect surface-rooting rhizome from sun-scald and to prevent complete dormancy. In late summer, they may be divided and replanted. Feed heavily after the first warm rains of spring and then feed lightly in the autumn in southern regions when the growing season begins again. In northern regions, cover the plants with a thick layer of mulch.

VEGETATIVE PROPAGATION AND GROWING FROM SEEDS

At least two shoots or offsets form on the main rhizome before the plant blooms. These can be cut off and planted. The rhizome blooms only once and then deteriorates. Vegetative propagation is more productive when the plants are grown in water.

Harvest iris seeds just before the seed capsule reaches complete maturity. If taken too soon, the kernel shrivels and may not germinate at all; if taken too late, the seeds may be lost from the fragile capsules. Stake any pod-bearing stems that are not strong and erect. To ensure harvest, tie a paper or muslin bag around the unripe seed pod.

The pods should be harvested when they are completely ripe. However, if the seed is not fully developed, remove the entire upper part of stalk. Put the stalk

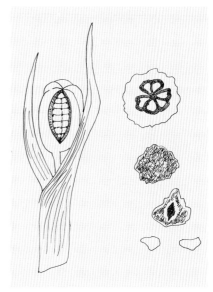

Seed pods and seeds of Louisiana irises

in a container of water if the seeds are still quite green. If they have begun to dry, lay the stalk on a piece of paper in a dry shady place. Tag or label each seed pod while it is still in the garden.

When the seeds mature, remove them from their pods. Place the seeds in a bowl and stir by hand to clean. Store in paper bags; they may mold if they are stored in glasses, jars, or plastic bags, even if the tops are left open. They can be stored in airtight containers only after they have completely dried. Should you see mold developing among the seeds, clean the container and wipe the seeds with a soft cloth that is slightly dampened with a light bleach solution.

While seed may be sown during any season of the year, sowing them as soon as they are mature and dried results in the most successful germination. However, if you sow them immediately upon harvest, they may still retain enough moisture to encourage mold and rotting. Double-check the habit of the specific species and try to duplicate its timing and conditions. Many irises that are not considered fully cold-hardy are native to regions in which the winter temperatures dip below 40° F (5° C). Seeds from such plants require stratification at 40° F for 4–5 weeks. (See Chapter 3.)

If the seeds have been stored, rehydrate them before planting by soaking them in a stoppered bottle of water for two or three days. Chip the seed coat (scarify) at the point where the seed was attached to the seed pod and remove 10 to 15 percent of the seed coating.

Plant seeds according to the standard gardening rule: at a depth of three times the thickness of the seed or approximately 1/2 in. (1.3 cm). Space seeds sown outdoors about 6 inches (15 cm) apart, or leave 1/2 to 1 inch (1.3 to 2.5 cm) between flat-sown seeds. While you may use any weed-free medium comparable to heavy garden soil, preferably amended with sand, many growers recommend a mixture of equal parts of well-composted manure and sand. Press the soil lightly over the seeds and keep them evenly moist in a shaded area, never allowing them to dry out. Too much moisture, on the other hand, combines with high temperatures and sunlight to invite rotting.

Seeds germinate in 3–12 months with a 50 percent germination considered average. Feed small seedlings with soluble fertilizer every two to four weeks. Protect them from prolonged exposure to cold as temperatures below 25° F (-4° C) can kill them. When the young plants are 6–8 inches (15–20 cm) tall, line them out in the ground at two-foot (60 cm) intervals if there is no possibility of severe cold. Plan for three months of active growth to develop roots before moving them into more permanent sites or pots. Keep the seedlings well watered and shaded during the summer. They will bloom in two seasons.

HYBRIDIZING IRISES

1. In the early morning, collect your pollen from your chosen pollen parent by forcing open the flower in the loose bud stage by twisting in the direction opposite the way the bud is furled. Break off the falls. (The falls are the stigma lips that allow bees to pollinate.) It is not necessary to remove the standards. Remove the anthers with tweezers and save the pollen on a piece of paper. Let the pollen dry on the paper for six hours inside at room temperature. At the same time, remove the falls and anthers of the flower selected as your seed parent.

2. Allow the seed-parent bloom with the removed falls and anthers to age during the six hours that the

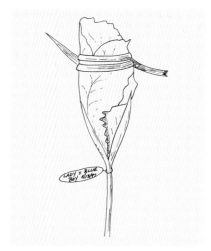

Wrap the fertilized flower within its standards to prevent unwanted insect fertilization.

pollen is drying. This allows the stigmatic lips to loosen and the stigmas to become more receptive.

3. Use a soft brush to place a very small quantity of pollen under the lip (between the lip and the style). Do both lips if possible. Make no more than two pollinations on each scape, usually on the uppermost and the next lower positions. Pollinate only the first bloom and remove the second bloom when it appears. If you wish to protect the integrity of your crossing, fold the standard petals around the fertilized stigma, as shown in the drawing above, and/or tie a labeled muslin bag around the pollinated flower. Do not enclose the flower in a plastic bag as this may "cook" the developing seeds.

4. Three months later, the seed pod will be ready for harvest. The pods may still be green. Mature seeds are tan to brown in color. If the seed pods have begun to turn yellow or brown, you can either plant the seeds immediately or store them in dry conditions until the following spring. However, in mild climates, plant the seeds immediately for best germination.

SAVING POLLEN

Pollen can be saved to hand-cross early- and late-blooming varieties. Remove the anthers from the selected pollen parent with tweezers and place them on sheets of paper for a six-hour drying period. Then remove the pollen from the anthers and funnel it into a small dry jar. (Baby-food jars or plastic 35-mm film containers work well.) Label the bottle with the date and the pollen-parent's name and seal it. Keep as dry as possible. The pollen remains viable for the full season.

A RAINBOW OF IRISES

I. **'Kissie'**
Photo by Bob Romar.

I. **'Roy Davidson'**
Photo by Perry D. Slocum.

I. **'La Peruse'**
Photo by Perry D. Slocum.

I. **'Billy'**   Photo by Perry D. Slocum.

I. **'Sun Fury'**
Photo by Perry D. Slocum.

I. **'Ann Chowning'**
Photo by Perry D. Slocum.

I. **'President Hedley'** Photo by Perry D. Slocum.

I. **'King Kong'**
Photo by Perry D. Slocum.

I. **'Count Pulaski'** Photo by Perry D. Slocum.

I. **'Cajun
Caper'**
Photo by Perry
D. Slocum.

I. **'Bayou Comus'**
Photo by Perry D. Slocum.

I. **'Whooping Charlie'**
Photo by Perry D. Slocum.

I. 'Professor Hedley'
Photo by Perry D. Slocum.

I. 'Snowdrift' Photo by Bob Romar.

I. 'Tokyo Rose' Photo by Perry D. Slocum.

I. 'Uralba Gold'
Photo by Perry D. Slocum.

I. 'Joy Roberts'
Photo by Perry D. Slocum.

I. 'Bellevue's Mike'
Photo by Perry D. Slocum.

I. 'Handmaiden'
Photo by Perry D. Slocum.

I. 'Godzilla'
Photo by Perry D. Slocum.

I. 'Wine Cooler' Photo by Perry D. Slocum.

I. 'Charlie'
Photo by Perry D. Slocum.

I. 'Decoy'
Photo by Perry D. Slocum.

I. 'Margaret Hunter'
Photo by Perry D. Slocum.

chapter ten

PESTS & DISEASES

A water garden is an interactive microcosm of the larger world around it—plants, insects, and microbes all interrelating. While we seek to ensure the best health of our plants, we try to do this in the most natural ways possible to avoid impacting both the water garden and the greater world beyond. Should the problems you encounter merit chemical intervention, we encourage restraint and safe applications. Remember that if you have fish in your water garden, any treatments you apply should be performed in separate

The familiar whirligig beetles are scavengers and predators that do not harm the plants in your pond. Photo by Ron Everhart.

treatment tanks. Ultimately, preventive maintenance in the water garden can keep most problems under control.

INSECT PESTS

Insects impact the water garden in three ways: as predators, as detritivores, and as herbivores. Predators prey upon tiny fish and each other, while detritivores gather to feast upon decomposing vegeta-

tion. The herbivores that eat the healthy, living plants are our prime concern. Certain herbivores are commonly noted in available literature:

Aphids (Family *Aphididae*)

This large group of plant-feeding insects may be terrestrial, but they will still venture into the water garden. Emergent vegetation and floating leaves present a banquet table. Aphids especially like water lilies (*Nymphaea*), Spatterdock (*Nuphar*), Arrowheads (*Sagittaria*), Bog Bean (*Menyanthes*), Pickerel (*Pontederia*), and Water Plantain (*Alisma*). Some hobbyists speculate that aphids are attracted to the waning leaves of water lilies as

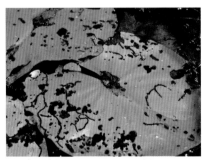

Prevention and early intervention can prevent problems from getting out of control.   Photo by H. Nash.

Above: Healthy plants reward you with your own private haven. Photo by H. Nash.

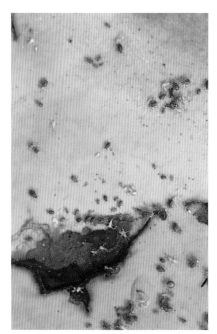

Aphids seem more attracted to dying and injured water lily leaves, but they will feast upon fresh, green growth. Photo by Ron Everhart.

Aphids disfigure and kill leaves on emergent vegetation such as water plantain. Photo by Ron Everhart.

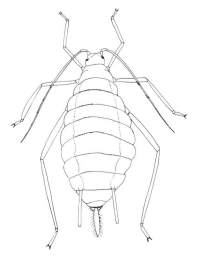

During the spring, wingless females are produced every few days by the winged female aphids that overwintered in plum and cherry trees near the pond.

they begin to yellow or that aphids target injured plant sites. Certainly, keeping damaged and/or older leaves pruned from the garden makes the garden look better. If this practice happens to keep aphids away, so much the better. Understanding insects' life cycle further aids our preventive and control efforts.

THE APHID LIFE CYCLE

The late summer brood of adults lays eggs on the boughs of plum and cherry trees in the late autumn. These overwinter and hatch into winged females during the following spring. Every few days as the winged females feed upon plants, asexual reproduction produces live, wingless females. During the summer, both winged

males and females are produced. Uniting sexually, the females then deposit their eggs in the plum and cherry trees to begin the process again.

THE DAMAGE

Damage can begin in spring and continue throughout the summer. Foliage is skeletonized, turning yellow and brown as it dies. Severe infestation can kill a plant.

PREVENTION AND CONTROL

1. Spray nearby plum and cherry trees with horticultural oil spray in the winter to destroy the overwintering eggs. (Horticultural oil spray is also known as "dormant oil." It is a petroleum-based spray that is sprayed in solution on trees and shrubs during their dormant period for the control of overwintering pests such as aphids, scales, and mites. The temperature must be above 40° F [4° C] for the spray to be effective. It is not safe for use with many plants. A lighter-weight "summer spray" is also available.)

2. During the growing season, keep aging, yellowing, and injured foliage pruned from plants.

3. Supply your garden with beneficial insects such as ladybugs.

4. Light infestations may be controlled by hosing the aphids into the pond water where fish will eat them. Often, however, the aphids scramble back onto plants before the fish notice them.

5. An oil spray of two parts vegetable oil to eight parts water with a dash of dishwashing detergent to enable mixing can be sprayed onto the insects and the surface of the water. This effectively suffocates the insects. Remember to remove the oil film from the water as it also prevents gas exchange and may jeopardize the fish below. (Remove oil film by flooding the pond or by soaking it up with paper or special oil-collection rags.)

6. Sprinkling diatomaceous earth on the infested water lily leaves may kill the invaders. (Diatomaceous earth is a powder made from the ground-up shells of fossilized diatoms, one-celled sea-dwelling organisms. The abrasive particles damage the tissue of soft-bodied insects and kill them in the process.)

7. Worst-case infestation: remove affected plants from the pond and place them in separate treatment tanks for applications of insecticides. Rinse plants well before returning them to the pond.

Beetles (Genus *Donacia*, Family *Chrysomelidae*; *Galerucella nymphacae*)

Other than the familiar whirligig beetle, many beetles that plague our ponds are not aquatic insects at all; their aquatic larvae create the problems. With over 40 either

aquatic or semi-aquatic species, most of these species are of the widespread genus *Donacia*. These aquatic larvae feed on underwater parts of floating or emergent vegetation. Some inhabit the substrate of the water garden, where they feed upon roots. Air is obtained from the host plant by insertion by the larvae of sharp terminal spurs into the plant tissue. Infestations of these pests are highly disfiguring to plants and may weaken or eventually kill some plants.

Donacia

The *Donacia* Life Cycle: Adults of metallic purple, green, or brown may occasionally be found on emergent parts of a host plant. Females bite holes in vegetation to lay their eggs on the underside in a semicircular cluster. Eggs may also be deposited in aquatic plant tissue, on algae or floating vegetation, on aquatic substrates, or even in adjacent moist soil. Within a few weeks the eggs hatch. Usually only one generation is produced each year.

Beetles often lay their eggs on the undersides of water lily leaves.
Photo by Ron Everhart.

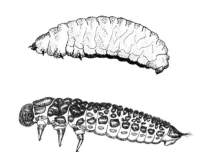
Donacia **larva.**

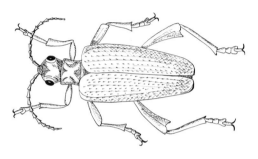
Donacia **palmata.**

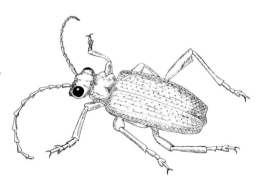
Aquatic leaf beetle, *Donacia* adult

Larvae are robust and grublike with the abdomen segmented into eight or nine sections. Heads and legs are quite small. Most species undergo three changes before they pupate. Pupation (encasing themselves in hard shells for a dormant

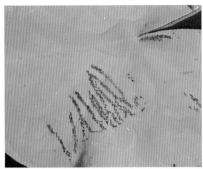

Beetle larvae pierce plant material to obtain oxygen. These piercings leave behind a stippling effect that mars the leaf's appearance.
Photo by Ron Everhart.

period during which they make the final change into adult forms) occurs in the bottom material of the pond, often around plant rhizomes and roots. Adults overwinter in dead foliage near the water's edge.

THE DAMAGE

Larvae chew holes around the edges of floating vegetation as well as throughout it. The injured plant tissue then begins decomposing and dies. Hatching larvae pierce the host plant to acquire air and leave behind a brown stippling. These plant wounds are usually small enough to "heal" with only a series of brown dots marring the plant's appearance.

PREVENTION AND CONTROL

1. Prune and clear away dead vegetation around the pond in the fall.

2. Wipe away eggs from the underside of water lily leaves with your thumb or a soft cloth. Reportedly, free-floating eggs will not hatch, but to make sure, you can "collect" them and dispose of them outside the pond.

3. Remove affected leaves and dispose of them elsewhere.

4. The use of diatomaceous earth and Bt is not usually effective, as both remedies must touch the larvae that are usually submerged and inaccessible. (Bt is the abbreviated name for *Bacillus thuringiensis*, bacteria that feed upon an insect's intestines, parasitizing and killing the caterpillars.)

5. Handpick those larvae you encounter.

6. In severe infestations, remove affected plants to a separate treatment tub for insecticidal remedies.

Water Lily Beetle, *Galerucella*

THE *GALERUCELLA* LIFE CYCLE

Commonly called the water lily beetle, *Galerucella nymphacae* are small dark brown beetles 0.25 in. (0.6cm) long that lay clusters of eggs in June on the surface of water lily leaves. In seven days they hatch into shiny black larvae with yellow bellies. These beetles pupate on emergent foliage and overwinter in brown, dormant foliage around the pond's edge.

THE DAMAGE

As the larvae feed on the lily leaves, surface tissue is skeletonized and rots away.

PREVENTION AND CONTROL

1. Remove dead foliage of dormant plants around the pond.

2. Hose eggs/larvae into the water for consumption by fish.

3. Sprinkle diatomaceous earth on infested water lily leaves.

4. Spray affected leaves and larvae with Bt solution.

5. Handpick.

Larvae of the *Galerucella nymphacae* hatch and feed upon the surface of water lily leaves.
Photo by Harry Hooper.

Noctuid (diver moth) larva

Noctuid (diver moth) adult

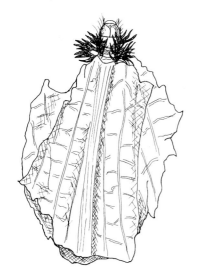

Parapoynx larva

Parapoynx adult

Moths (*Lepidoptera, Families Pyralidae* and *Noctuidae*)

About 50 species of the over 10,000 species of *Lepidoptera* in North America are known to be aquatic. As many as 100 other species are considered to be semi-aquatic as miners and borers in emergent plants. Only the sub-family *Nymphulinae* of the family *Pyralidae* is primarily aquatic. Their larvae are known as caterpillars and have distinctive heads, simple eye spots and mouth parts adapted for chewing.

LIFE CYCLE AND HABITS OF AQUATIC/SEMI-AQUATIC MOTHS

Larvae undergo between five to seven instars or molts. In most cases, the larvae is the overwintering stage. Some semi-aquatic species overwinter by hibernating out of water around the pond edge.

Silk is spun from the lower lip of the caterpillars to build their pupation homes. Pupation may occur submerged, on exposed emergent plant parts, or within burrows in plant stems. The pupal stage usually lasts only a month. Adults make their way to the water's surface upon emergence, often aided by swimming hairs on their middle and hind legs. This may happen in the spring, summer, or early fall, usually at night. A half hour or longer may be nec-

Ostrinia larva and pupa

Parargyractis adult

essary for the wings to dry and spread. The new adult lives from 24 hours to two months, depending upon species and sex. Females often live longer than the males. Generally nocturnal in activity, moths tend to remain in the area of their emergence. They feed on plant liquids.

Females lay rows or rings of eggs on the underside of floating leaves by bending their abdomen over the edge of the leaf or by inserting it through holes cut by aquatic leaf beetles. It is not uncommon to turn over a water lily leaf that bears a hole and discover both rows of eggs lined up away from the hole, along with a

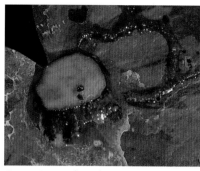

Sometimes the China Mark Moth larva, "the sandwich man," uses a piece of leaf as the upper covering of his "home" and feeds directly upon a leaf's surface.
Photo by H. Nash.

neat concentric circle of eggs around the hole's perimeter—the beetle making the hole and laying the rows of eggs, followed by a moth who uses the same door to deposit eggs around it. The eggs hatch in one to two weeks.

Larvae of the China mark moth, *Nymphula stagnata* and *N. nympheata*, capture pieces of floating debris or chew off pieces of water lily leaves to form a protective shelter from which they feed. They may enclose themselves

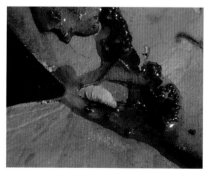

The moth larva works its way into the leaf stem where it will pupate.
Photo by H. Nash.

between two such pieces or they may use one piece overhead as they work their way across a water lily leaf to the petiole that they burrow into, feeding as they go. It is easy to see why they are nicknamed "the sandwich man."

A few species of the *Noctuidae* family are known as "diver moths" for their habit of mining vegetation and burrowing into stems of water lilies. The yellow water lily borer, *Bellura gortynoides*, mines in leaves as a young caterpillar and then becomes a stem borer. This caterpillar must periodically back out of his burrow to breathe. Larvae swim to shore for overwintering in dry areas. Other plants favored by these caterpillars are lotuses, water hyacinths, arrowheads, pickerel weeds, burr-reeds, bulrushes, rushes, and cattails. *Cosmopterygid* moths are miners and stem borers in some sedges and cattails, and serpentine moths of the family *Nepticulidae* are miners and stem borers in spike rush and bulrush. *Crambinae* larvae are semi-aquatic miners and borers of rice, rush, bulrush, and water hyacinth. *Pyraustinae* caterpillars are leaf-surface feeders and borers of water lilies.

Ostrinia (Pyraustinae) is commonly known as the lotus borer. However, it also feeds upon water lilies, submerged grasses, duckweed, and sedges and rushes. It is usually noticed when it first rolls itself up within an edge of a leaf. It can be handpicked at this time. Later, once it has burrowed into

the plant's stems, it is nearly impossible to eradicate without resorting to separate treatment tanks with insecticides.

THE DAMAGE

Disfiguration and destruction of affected vegetation.

PREVENTION AND CONTROL

1. Remove dry, dead vegetation from around the pond in autumn.

2. Wipe eggs from underside of water lily leaves.

3. Remove any floating debris and bits of leaves from the water.

4. Handpick larvae.

5. Remove affected foliage. With severe infestations, you can remove all water lily leaves, if necessary. New leaves are soon produced.

6. Spraying Bt and insecticides is not as effective as the caterpillars are usually protected. However, use of the floating rings of Bt may provide some assistance in control of caterpillars encased within floating debris and exposed to the water.

Flies (Order *Diptera*)

Caddis flies are perhaps the most well known of aquatic plant flies. While the adults are very much mothlike, their wings usually have hairs rather than scales as found in moths. Of the over 1200 species in North America, these insects can be grouped by their methods of feeding: net spinning or fixed retreat forms, free-living forms as in the saddle case makers and the purse case makers, and the tube case makers. Whichever habit they follow, they feed primarily on algae and vegetable detritus. They are not usually a serious pest of healthy, growing plant material. Control them by keeping the pond clear of aged and dying vegetation.

Other flies are more likely to be true pests to your aquatic plants. Gall gnats of the family *Cedidomyiidae* produce small, maggotlike larve, often in brightly colored forms. Larvae of several species develop within galls formed on the leaves or stems of aquatic plants such as sedges and reeds. These galls look like warts or globular masses of plant tissue. Their damage is confined to the unsightly swellings of plant tissue. Remove affected vegetation.

Some species of dung fly (family *Scatophagidae*) produce white maggotlike forms that mine in the leaves, petioles, and culms of aquatic plants. Remove affected vegetation.

Midge

Midges (Family *Chironomidae*)

Midge Life Cycle and Habit

In the early evening, you might notice what look to be swarms of gnats or mosquitoes near the water surface of your pond. Chances are the insects in this swarm are midges that are laying eggs in the water. Larvae of the false leaf-mining midge (*Cricotopus ornatus*) are quite tiny and slender-bodied, but they can devastate a water lily leaf in short order. The tiny larva is protected at the head of its trail by its shallow "burrowing" into the leaf's tissue. Pupae of most species live within cylindrical or conical cocoons. The

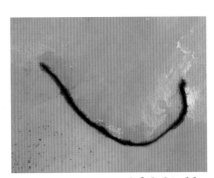

The narrow traceries left behind by the leaf-mining midge larvae dry and rot through the leaf.
Photo by Ron Everhart.

"bloodworm" larvae, reddish-colored from hemoglobin that stores oxygen within their bodies to enable them to feed on detritus in the low-oxygen levels of the pond bottom, do not damage healthy aquatic plants.

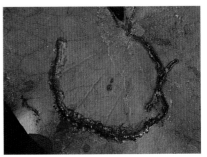

The larva of the midge is known as the "false leaf miner" since it only burrows into the surface layers of the plant's leaf. A flick of a fingernail reveals the tiny larva.
Photo by H. Nash.

THE DAMAGE

Following a meandering path over the surface of a water lily leaf, *Chironomid* midge larvae feed upon the surface layers of the leaf. Injured tissue left behind quickly turns brown and begins to rot all the way through to leave the leaf in tatters.

PREVENTION AND CONTROL

1. While a hose spray may knock the shallow burrowing larvae from the leaf and into the water for fish consumption, be careful not to use so strong a jet as to injure the plant foliage.

2. Larvae may be handpicked.

3. Remove affected leaves and dispose of them elsewhere.

4. Floating doughnuts of Bt in the pond may parasitize the larvae before they can make their way to the top of water lily leaves. Spraying Bt or insecticides is not effective as the larvae are protected within their surface mining.

5. Systemic insecticides can be used in a separate treatment tank, if desired.

Other Insect Pests:

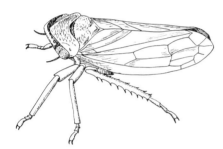

Leafhopper

Leafhoppers (family *Cicadellidae*) venture into the well-planted water garden to feed. They are especially attracted to piling water lily leaves. If your water lilies are climbing over each other, prune out some of the excess leaves or move the plant into deeper water where it has room to spread.

Water weevils live within plant stems, often below the waterline. Pupation and egg-laying takes

Grasshoppers can be especially destructive to emergent plants such as water irises.

place within the host plant. The rice water weevil (genus *Lissorhoptrus*) is an important pest of rice and has been introduced to help control aquatic weeds. Remove affected vegetation in the pond.

Red spider mites (*Tetranychus*) may appear on the undersides of raised water lily leaves and other emergent vegetation, particularly during hot, dry summers. Foliage yellows and dies as they spin silky threads to protect themselves while they feed. Remove affected leaves. Spray your plants with the garden hose to discourage and remove them. Insecticidal soaps or insecticides can be applied in separate treatment tanks, if necessary.

Japanese beetles (*Popillia japonica*) are voracious feeders more commonly encountered in the terrestrial garden. However, they will dessicate marginal aquatics! Bug traps may work for light infestations. Heavy infestations, however, may be the one case that sends you to a treatment tank with insecticides in hand.

A severe infestation of Japanese beetles in a stand of pickerel weed, *Pontederia*. Photo by H. Nash.

Japanese beetles are voracious feeders upon emergent aquatic foliage. Photo by H. Nash.

LEAF ROLLERS AND DAMAGE

Leaf roller damage begins inconspicuously with the larva cutting the edge of a leaf and hiding inside its rolled edge.
Photo by H. Nash.

Allowed to feed upon the plant leaf, the leafroller creates serious destruction.
Photo by H. Nash.

Handpicking the larva is the best way to handle the pest in light infestations.
Photo by H. Nash.

Beneficial Insects to Include in Your Water Garden Yardscape

Dragonflies: Eat mosquitoes and flies.

Lacewings and their larvae: Eat many kinds of soft-bodied insects, especially aphids.

Ladybugs: Consume soft-bodied insects.

Parasitic wasps, such as *braconids, ichneumons,* and *trichogrammas:* Very tiny, they suck the fluids from caterpillars.

***Syrphid* flies:** Resembling small bees or wasps, their larvae attack aphids.

This *Thalia dealbata* plant displays how badly deformed the leafroller can make its host plant.
Photo by H. Nash.

Other Pests: Snails

The three most commonly encountered snails in the water garden: the great pond snail, left (most destructive and totally undesirable), the ramshorn snail, above (commonly acceptable scavenger), and the trapdoor snail, lower (a live-bearing, acceptable scavenger).
Photo by Ron Everhart.

How well I remember discovering what I thought was a mutated water lily plant, each leaf all but symmetrically scalloped. Then I spotted the creators of my new plant: great pond snails! *Limnaea stagnalis* are the snails with tall, narrow shells that often hitchhike into your pond with a new plant. They multiply quickly by laying gelatinous strands of eggs on the undersides of lily pads and on submerged vegetation. (Besides eating your plants, they also serve as the intermediary host to anchor worms that attack your pond fish.) Carefully inspecting and cleaning all new plant introductions helps prevent their taking up residence in your garden. If they're already present, float Styrofoam, cabbage, or lettuce heads, and collect the snails as they gather. Wipe away egg patches with a soft cloth or remove the plants for cleaning outside the pond. A severe infestation may warrant a total cleaning of the pond.

Other snails commonly suggested as scavengers for your pond may also nibble on your plants. Both ramshorn and apple snails are known nibblers. Keep an eye on the "good guy" snails to be sure they are not making mischief.

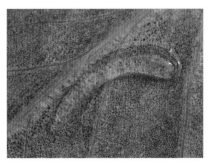

The eggs of the great pond snail are laid on the undersides of water lily leaves and on submersed vegetation. While the ramshorn snail lays its eggs in round patches, the great pond snail lays its eggs in an elongated shape.
Photo by Ron Everhart.

Water gardeners report that koi in the water garden can be troublesome, with the grazing fish nibbling away at aquatic plants, particularly submerged grasses.
Photo by H. Nash.

Whether invited or not, young turtles are vegetarians that will eat aquatic plants in the water garden. As adults, they often add "meat" to their diet—your small fish!
Photo by Ron Everhart.

PLANT DISEASE IN THE WATER GARDEN

Rust attacks on emergent plants, such as this _Glyceria_, are controlled by removing the affected leaves or by treating the plant in a separate treatment tub.
Photo by H. Nash.

***Cerospora* fungus makes the edges of water lily leaves curl up like brown paper. Remove affected leaves.**   Photo by H. Nash.

Fungal Attacks

Plant disease attacks in the pond are rare and usually of fungal nature. Leaf spot diseases, known as "black spot" or "brown spot" are caused by the fungi _Ovularia_ and _Ramularia nymphaearum_ that occur during wet seasons of persistent rains. It seems ironic that a water lily leaf resting upon the water should be subject to such a plight. Remove affected leaves. In severe cases, move the plants into separate treatment tubs for applications of fungicides. Dry brown spot, _Cercospora_, is essentially the same fungus, but it attacks sepals of water lilies or the edges of leaves, causing them to crispen and curl. Rarely does an attack of _Cercospora_ merit treatment other than removing affected vegetation.

A form of bacterial wilt or fungal disease occasionally attacks lotuses and causes them to turn a light green before dying. Perry D. Slocum recommends an application of Manzate for this.

Another, much more serious fungal attack that proves deadly to

Early indications of crown rot in water lilies are the leaves turning yellow prematurely and flower buds rotting away before hitting the surface of the water.
Photo by Perry D. Slocum.

water lilies grown in climates cooler than Zones 9 and 10, as well as contagious to other lilies within the same water, is crown rot, _Phytophthora_ spp. Symptoms are premature yellowing of leaves, rotting of flower buds before reaching the surface, and, ultimately, decomposition of the rhizome. A quick feeling of the submersed rhizome of plants displaying surface symptoms indicates if the rhizome is turning soft. Pulling the plant from the pond

A rhizome infected with crown rot smells rank and is soft and rotting.   Photo by Harry Hooper.

and feeling further around the rhizome confirms your suspicions, as does hosing the soil from the rhizome and noting the putrifying odor and rot. Unless it is a very special cultivar, discard it. It is possible that growing eyes along the rhizome may be unaffected. They can be removed and potted in small containers and grown in a separate tank for a full year until you are sure they are unaffected. Treat them with a systemic fungicide, too. (Truban or Subdue, for example: immersion in the solution for an hour or two for bare rhizomes or for two days with potted plants is usually advised. An alternate preventive treatment is to apply Manzate during the growing season, always in a separate tub.) Any other water lilies in the pond should be removed to a treatment tub for the fungicidal treatment as a preventive measure. Water lilies considered more prone to the disease are generally the yellow and changeable varieties. Specific cultivars known to be susceptible to crown rot are:

'Attraction,'

'Gloriosa,'

'Chromatella,'

'Comanche,'

'Chrysantha,'

'Paul Hariot' and *laydekeri* 'Alba.'

Abnormal growth in a plant may result in deformed flowers.
Photo by Harry Hooper.

Abnormal cell growth results in deformed leaves.
Photo by Harry Hooper.

Deformed Plants

A rare occurrence among water lilies is known as "fasciation," an abnormal cellular acceleration of only portions of the plant. This can result in deformed leaves and flowers. Pull the plant from its pot and check for any growing eyes along the rhizome. Chances are that repotting it will produce a perfectly normal plant. Discard the main rhizome affected with the disease. Cultivars that have shown a propensity to fasciation are 'Ellisiana,' 'Gloriosa,' and 'Chromatella.'

Appendix

Plants for Streamside Planting

The plants included in this list may be planted along the edge of a gently flowing stream. If the flow is gentle enough, you may find them venturing out into the flow of your stream. Whether they stay confined along the edge or move out into the flow, monitor their growth to be sure they do not cause the water level to rise from their massing roots and emergent growth or from sediment collection. Be prepared to prune them as necessary to prevent water loss from the stream bed.

Parrot feather—*Myriophyllum aquaticum*

Alligator weed—*Alternanthera ficoidea*

Arrow arum—*Peltandra virginica*

Arrowhead—*Sagittaria*

Bulrush—*Scirpus*

Cattail—*Typha*

Creeping Jenny—*Lysimachia nummularia*

Lizard tail—*Saururus cenuus*

Loosestrife—*Lythrum salicaria*

Lotus—*Nelumbo*

Manna grass—*Glyceria*

Pickerel weed—*Pontederia*

Powdery thalia—*Thalia dealbata*

Soft rush—*Juncus*

Spatterdock—*Nuphar advena (N. lutea)*

Spike rush, water chestnut—*Eleocharis*

Sweet flag—*Acorus calamus*

Tape grass—*Vallisneria*

Two-leaf clover—*Regnellidum diphyllum*

Umbrella palm—*Cyperus alternifolius*

Variegated rush—*Baumea rubiginosa*

Water bamboo—*Dulichium arundinaceum*

Water celery—*Oenanthe javonica*

Water clover—*Marsilea*

Watercress—*Nasturtium officinale*

Water forget-me-not—*Myosotis*

Water irises—*Iris pseudacorus, Iris laevigata, Iris versicolor, Iris virginica*

Water pennywort—*Hydrocotyle*

Water plantain—*Alisma plantago-aquatica*

Water primrose—*Ludwigia*

Water spinach—*Ipomea batatas*

Plants Suited to Vegetative (Phyto-) Filters

(Especially effective at nutrient removal.)

Watercress—*Nasturtium officinale*

Water celery—*Oenanthe javonica*

Water hyacinth—*Eichhornia crassipes*

Water lettuce—*Pistia*

Cattails—*Typha*

Submerged grasses

Water irises

Rushes and reeds

Shade-Tolerant Water Plants

Water lilies:

Most blue topicals, especially 'Director George T. Moore' and 'Isabella Pring', a white.

Hardies:

'James Brydon', 'Masaniello', 'Lucida, Hal Miller', 'Chromatella', 'Attraction', 'Escarboucle', 'Froebeli', 'Comanche', 'Paul Hariot', 'Chrysantha', Parrot's feather, Cabomba, non-flowering marginals.

Common Plant Names and Corresponding Botanical Names

Alligator weed	*Alternanthera ficoidea*
Amazon water lily	*Victoria amazonica*
Anacharis	*Egeria densa*
Arrow arum	*Peltandra virginica*
Arrowhead	*Sagittaria*
Arum lily	*Zantedeschia*
Banana lily	*Nymphoides aquatica*
Bladderwort	*Utricularia*
Blue bells	*Ruellia squarrosa*
Blue flag iris	*Iris versicolor*
Blue water hyacinth (rooting, nonbulbous)	*Eichhornia azurea*
Bog Arum	*Calla palustris*
Bogbean	*Menyanthes trifoliata*
Bulrush	*Scirpus*
Butterwort	*Pinguicula*
Button bush	*Cephalanthus occidentalis*
Calla lily	*Zantedeschia*
Canadian pondweed	*Elodea canadensis*
Cardinal flower	*Lobelia cardinalis*
Cattail	*Typha*

Common reed	*Phragmites*
Coontail	*Ceratophyllum demersum*
Cotton grass	*Eriophorum angustifolium*
Creeping Jenny	*Lysimachia nummularia*
Curled pondweed	*Potamogeton crispus*
Duck potato	*Sagittaria latifolia*
Duckweed	*Lemna minor*
Dwarf *Sagittaria*	*Sagittaria natans*
Fairy moss	*Azolla*
Flat-bladed rush	*Juncus macrophyullus*
Floating fern	*Ceratopteris pteridoides or C. thalictroides*
Floating heart	*Nymphoides peltata*
Flowering rush	*Butomus umbellatus*
Frogbit	*Hydrocharis morsus-ranae*

Giant water snowflake	*Nymphoides indica 'Gigantea'*
Golden club	*Orontium aquaticum*
Gorgon plant	*Euryale ferox*
Gray sedge	*Carex pseudocyperus*
Hair grass	*Eleocharis acicularis*
Horsetail rush	*Equisetum*
Ivy-leaf duckweed	*Lemna trisulca*
Japanese iris	*Iris ensata*
Lavender musk	*Mimulus ringens*
Lizard tail	*Saururus cernuus*
Loosestrife	*Lythrum salicaria*
Lotus	*Nelumbo*
Manna grass	*Glyceria*
Marsh marigold	*Caltha palustris*
Mediterranean rush	*Arundo donax*
Melon sword	*Echinodorus radican*
Monkey flower	*Mimulus*
Mosaic plant	*Ludwigia sedioides*
Orange snowflake	*Nymphoides hydrocharioides*
Papyrus	*Cyperus*
Parrot feather	*Myriophyllum aquaticum*
Parrot leaf	*Alternanthera ficoidea*

Sweet flag	*Acorus calamus*
Tape grass	*Vallisneria*
Taro	*Colocasia*
Two-leaf clover	*Regnellidum diphyullum*
Umbrella palm	*Cyperus alternifolius*
Variegated rush	*Baumea rubiginosa*
Variegated Water snowflake	*Nymphoides cristatum*
Venus flytrap	*Dionaea*
Watercress	*Nasturtium officinale*
Water bamboo	*Dulichium arundinaceum*
Water chestnut	*Eleocharis tuberosa*
Water cClover	*Marsilea*
Water fern	*Salvinia* or *Ceratopteris pteridoides,* or *C. thalictroides*
Water forget-me-not	*Myosotis palustris* and *M. scorpioides*
Water hawthorne	*Aponogeton distachyus*
Water hyacinth	*Eichhornia crassipes*
Water lettuce	*Pistia stratiotes*
Water meal	*Wolffia*
Water mint	*Mentha aquatica*
Water plantain	*Alisma plantago-aquatica*
Water poppy	*Hydrocleys nymphoides*
Water primrose	*Ludwigia peploides*
Water soldier	*Stratiotes aloides*
Water spider lily	*Hymenocallis liriosme*
Water spinach	*Ipomea batatas*
White rush	*Scirpus lacustris* 'Albescens'
Wild rice	*Zizania latifolia*
Woolgrass	*Scirpus cyperinus*
Yellow flag iris	*Iris pseudacorus*
Yellow fringe	*Nymphoides geminata*
Yellow pond lily	*Nuphar sp.*
Zebra rush	*Scirpus lacustris* subsp. *tabernaemontani*

Pennywort	*Hydrocotyle*
Pickerel weed	*Pontederia*
Pitcher plant	*Sarracenia*
Powdery *Thalia*	*Thalia dealbata*
Prickly water lily	*Euryale ferox*
Red-stemmed *Thalia*	*Thalia geniculata* form *ruminoides*
Rose mallow	*Hibiscus moschuetos*
Santa Cruz water lily	*Victoria cruziana*
Sensitive plant	*Neptunia aquatica,* *Aeschynomene fluitans*
Soft rush	*Juncus*
Southern blue flag iris	*Iris virginica*
Southern swamp lily	*Crinum americanum*
Spatterdock	*Nuphar advena, N. lutea*
Spearwort	*Ranunculus*
Spike rush	*Eleocharis*
Star grass	*Dichromena colorata*
Sundew	*Drosera*
Swamp hibiscus	*Hibiscus moschuetos*

Glossary

Acid soil—Soil having a pH below 7.0 and containing no limestone.

Aerenchyma—Spongy tissue full of air pockets, typical leaf and stem adaptation of plants to allow leaves and stems to float on the water's surface.

Alkaline soil—Soil having a pH above 7.0, usually found where limestone is present and/or rainfall is sparse.

Alluvial—Of sediment deposited by flowing water.

Alternate—Term used to describe leaves or buds produced at intervals on either side of a stem, with no two leaves being directly across from one another.

Anaerobic—With very low or nonexistent levels of oxygen. Some aquatic species can grow anaerobically while initiating new growth in water. Ex: *Typha* and *Peltandra*.

Anatomy—The structure of a plant or an animal.

Annual—A plant that completes its entire life cycle—germination, growth to maturity, and seed production—in one growing season.

Anther—The part of a flower stamen that produces pollen.

Apex—The growing tip of a shoot, or end of a leaf.

Aphid—Common small insect that sucks plant juices and damages plants. Often found clustered on young shoots and in leaf axils.

Aroid—Any of various plants of the *Aracea* family, which includes the arums (plants with arrow-shaped leaves and small flowers on a spadix surrounded by or enclosed within a spathe, such as calla lilies).

Awn—A stiff, hairlike extension on a seed, fruit, flower petal, or leaf, most often found on the ends of grass seeds, a feature of many ornamental grasses.

Axil—The point where a leaf or petiole joins a stem. Many plants form growth buds in leaf axils that grow into new shoots when the stem above that point is pinched back.

Bare-root—Describing a plant with no soil or planting provision around its roots.

Bio-load—Referring to ponds and water gardens, the amount of living animals such as fish and frogs which produce wastes, and the amount of plants both in and around the water that produce dying and decomposing plant matter within the water, both of which combine to create a level of oxygen required by the nitrogen cycle.

Blade—The flat part of a leaf, often used in reference to the leaves of grasses.

Bordeaux mixture—A fungicide containing hydrated lime and copper sulfate. Always apply to aquatic plants in a separate treatment tank if fish are present in the water!

Bract—A modified leaf, usually found at the base of a flower, flower stem, or cluster of flowers. Some plants with insignificant flowers are noted for their colorful bracts—arrow arum (*Peltandra)*, for example.

Bulb—A storage organ, usually underground, consisting of a modified short stem, often enclosed in protective swollen leaf bases. A bulb contains enough nutrients to support the plant through a season of growth.

Bulbil—A small bulblike structure, produced above ground, that can be used to propagate a new plant. Often produced in leaf axils. Ex: *Butomus*, Flowering Rush.

Calcaceous—Referring to soil, containing calcium or calcium carbonate (lime).

Callus—Tissue formed by a plant to seal an injury to a stem or root. Cuttings form callus where they are severed from the plant and then are able to produce roots instead of rotting.

Calyx—Protective outer layer of a flower, usually made of modified leaves, that encloses the flower bud as it develops; the collective name for sepals. In an open water lily, the calyx often looks like the petals or lends a bicolor effect to the bloom.

Carbohydrates—Any of a group of chemical compounds, including sugars, starches, and cellulose, containing carbon, hydrogen, and oxygen only, with the ratio of hydrogen to oxygen atoms usually 2:1.

Catkin—A compact and often drooping cluster of reduced, stalkless, and usually unisexual flowers. Catkins produced by *Typha* (cattail) species are singularly male and female with the female catkin growing slightly below the male catkin.

Cauline—Of, having, or growing on a stem.

Changeable water lily—One with flowers opening up lighter-colored, deepening on second and third days.

Chlorosis—Yellowing or lightening of plant tissues caused by nutrient deficiency, especially iron or potassium, or disease.

Clone—A plant that is genetically identical to its parent, produced by vegetative (asexual) methods of propagation. Most water lilies available in the trade are produced in this way.

Complete flower—A flower that contains petals and sepals, and both male (stamen) and female (pistil) reproductive organs.

Compost—Decomposed remains of plants and other organic materials used to supply organic matter and nutrients to garden soil. Used in conjunction with "cow manure," the term indicates the natural decomposition and rotting of the organic matter.

Compound—Made up of more than one part, used to describe leaves composed of two or more leaflets, or flowers consisting of more than one floret.

Container-grown—Referring to plants propagated and maintained within a container such as a nursery pot.

Cordate—Heart-shaped, term used to describe leaves.

Corolla—Collective term for a flower's petals.

Crenate—Having a notched or scalloped edge, describing leaf edges.

Crisped—Finely waved edge of a leaf or a flower.

Cross-pollination—The transfer of pollen from one plant to another.

Crown—The point of a plant where the roots meet the stem, at or immediately below the surface of the soil.

Culm—The hollow-jointed stem of a bamboo or grass.

Cultivar—A plant variety developed in cultivation, short for cultivated variety.

Cuticle—Waxy coating on leaves that sheds water and helps prevent

immersion, as on the upper surface or epidermis of water lily leaves.

Cutting—A part of a plant removed and induced to form roots and shoots, eventually growing into a new plant genetically identical to the parent.

Damping off—The general name for a group of fungal diseases that afflict germinating seeds. The most common symptom is the girdling and withering of young seedlings at the soil, resulting in the death of the seedling.

Deadhead—To remove faded, spent flowers to keep them from forming seeds.

Dentate—Term describing a leaf with evenly toothed edges, the teeth facing outward.

Division—Method of vegetative propagation in which a plant clump is cut apart into several sections, which are replanted to produce new plants. Most aquatic plants can be propagated in this way.

Double—A flower that has more than the usual number of petals.

Emergent—Describing plants that grow from a submersed soil to present growth above the water surface.

Emersed—Having emerged above the surface; standing above the surface of the water.

Entire—Leaves having smooth edges without teeth or indentations.

Evergreen—Plant that keeps its foliage longer than one growing season, remaining green year round. Semi-evergreen plants lose some of their leaves each growing season while retaining others. Most tropical aquatics qualify as evergreens.

Evolved—Referring to plants, the development of a plant's form and habit over a period of time.

Eye—Dormant bud from which new growth can develop under the right conditions. Water lilies are typically propagated from growing eyes found along the rhizome.

Fall—Lower petal, especially of an iris, that droops downward.

Family—Group of related plant genera that share certain characteristics and differ in others.

Fertile—Having the capacity to produce viable seed.

Filament—Slender stalk which supports the anthers of a flower. Anther and filament collectively are called the stamen.

Finger rhizome—Refers to size of the rhizome; small finger or thumb-sized rhizome; grows erectly.

Floret—One of the small individual flowers that make up a composite flower or flower cluster.

Force—Induce a plant to grow, bloom, or set fruit out of its natural season.

Gall—Abnormal growth on a plant caused by insects or disease.

Genus—Group of related plant species that share many common characteristics and are believed to have evolved from the same ancestor.

Germinate—To develop a young plant from seed.

Glaucous—Blue-green or gray-green leaf. Also refers to covering of whitish powder as in *Thalia dealbata,* commonly called powdery thalia.

Habit—A plant's characteristic form of growth.

Hardening off—A process of adapting plants started indoors to outdoor garden conditions by placing them outdoors in protected conditions for gradually increasing lengths of time over a period of days.

Hardy—Able to withstand the coldest winter temperatures normal in a given location without protection. When a range is given, hardiness also describes a plant's ability to tolerate the hottest summer temperatures normally experienced.

Hardy water lily—A perennial aquatic herb.

Hastate—Having a triangular shape like a spearhead, describing leaf shape.

Herbaceous—Non-woody perennial plants whose top growth dies back to the ground each winter while the roots live on underground.

Heterophylly—Presence of more than one kind of leaf on the same plant, as floating or aerial leaves and submersed leaves on the same plant.

Humus—Fully decomposed organic matter, produced naturally or as a result of composting.

Hydrophily-Flowers are borne beneath the water's surface and the transfer of pollen takes place under water. Relatively rare, *Vallisneria* is one example.

Hydrophyte—A plant that grows in and is adapted to an aquatic or a very wet environment.

Inflorescence—Group of flowers arranged on a stem, such as a corymb, cyme, panicle, raceme, or umbel.

Insecticidal soap—A soap formulated to kill, repel or inhibit the growth of insect pests. Usually used in separate treatment tubs or tanks.

Internode—The plant section found between two successive nodes or joints.

Invasive—Tending to spread very freely and vigorously, often outcompeting other plants in the area.

Lacunae—System of interconnecting gas-filled canals and spaces that permeate submersed stems, petioles, and leaf blades of aquatic plants and serve as both storage and transportation system of gases.

Lacustrine—Of or having to do with lakes.

Lanceolate—Lance-shaped.

Lateral—Shoot or stem growing from a bud on the side of a stem or root.

Larva—A post-hatching immature stage that differs in appearance from the adult and must metamorphose before assuming adult characters. Refers to insects and tadpoles.

Leaflet—One section of a compound leaf.

Loam—Soil containing a mixture of sand, silt, and clay. Loam is generally fertile and well drained. Most water garden experts recommend a good garden loam for the planting of aquatics; the key inference in such recommendations is the presence of clay in the soil mixture.

Lobe—Portion of a leaf or flower petal separated from the rest of the structure by an indentation. Most water lily leaves are lobed.

Mainstem—The vertical center of a flower.

Marliac rhizome—A thick type of hardy water lily rhizome developed by Joseph B.L. Marliac; plants with this type of rhizome are notable for freedom of bloom.

Metamorphosis—Change in the structure and habits of an animal during normal growth, as in a caterpillar emerging a butterfly or a tadpole changing into a frog or toad.

Monoecious—Plants that produce both male and female flowers on the same plant, such as *Typha* (cattails).

Morphology—The biological study of the form and structure of living organisms.

Mulm—Residue of organic decomposition that collects on pond bottoms.

Mutant—A plant with inheritable characteristics that differ from those of the parents.

Naturalized—A plant established in a garden in congenial conditions and allowed to grow and reproduce as it would in the wild. *Iris pseudacorus,* the yellow flag iris European native, has naturalized in North America.

Neutral—Soil or water with a pH of 7.0, that is neither acid nor alkaline.

Nitrogen—A nonmetallic element essential to plant growth, most commonly absorbed by plants in the form of the compound nitrate.

Nodes—Points on a stem from which leaves, shoots, or flowers grow.

Obovate—Egg-shaped, the broad end located at the top, frequently used to describe leaf shape.

Odorata rhizome—A slender type of rhizome common to hardy water lily species, particularly in eastern North America.

Offset—Young plant that grows from the base of the parent plant and may be separated and transplanted. Or a young bulb that forms at the base of the parent bulb, and may be separated and

planted to eventually grow to blooming size. Tropical water lilies may be propagated in this manner.

Opposite—Leaves produced directly across from each other on two sides of a stem. Ex: *Lysimachia nummularia,* Creeping Jenny.

Ovary—A female flower organ located at the base of the pistil, that holds ovules and will eventually grow into a fruit if fertilized.

Ovate—Egg-shaped, the broad end located at the top, describing leaf shape.

Palmate—A leaf that has lobes resembling fingers on a hand.

Palustrine—Of or having to do with a marsh, bog, or swamp.

Panicle—Branched inflorescence, with the branches carried along an axis; a branched raceme.

Peat, peat moss—Partially decayed plant remains that collect in bogs. Sphagnum peat comes from sphagnum moss, sedge peat from decayed sedges and other plants. Peat moss adds organic matter but no nutrients to garden soil. It is acidic by nature.

Peduncle—The stalk of a single flower or the stalk of a cluster flower.

Peltate—Shaped like a shield, describing leaf shape.

Perfoliate—Having a base surrounding the leaf stem; base appears perforated by the stem.

Perianth—The outer part of the flower, including the calyx and corolla.

Perennial—A plant that lives three growing seasons or more and uses the same roots system to produce new plants.

Perigynous—Refers to flower structure: having sepals, petals, and stamens attached to the rim surrounding the ovary but unattached to the ovary itself.

Perianth—Collective name for the corolla and calyx of a flower.

Petal—A part of a flower's colorful corolla. Petals are actually modified leaves.

Petiole—The stem on which a leaf is carried; a leaf stalk.

pH—A measurement of soil's or water's acidity or alkalinity; the measurement of hydrogen ion content. Measured on a 14-point scale; 7.0 is neutral, readings above 7.0 indicate alkalinity and readings below 7.0 indicate acidity. Each number on the pH scale indicates a degree of acidity or alkalinity 10 times the value of the number preceding it.

Phosphate—As a major plant nutrient, the form of phosphorus most readily accessed by plants.

Photosynthesis—Chemical process by which plants use energy from sunlight and chlorophyll to convert carbon dioxide and water into sugars that fuel plant growth.

Phytofiltration—Process of removing nitrates and nutrients from water by plants.

Pineapple rhizome—A thick, upright-growing rhizome typical of certain hardy water lilies.

Pinnate—Compound leaf made up of individual leaflets arranged in pairs on opposite sides of a stem.

Pistil—Female organs of a flower, composed of the stigma, style, and ovary.

Pollen—Spores formed in the anthers that produce male cells in flowers.

Pollination—Fertilization of a flower by the transfer of ripe pollen from anthers to a receptive stigma.

Potash—Any of several compounds containing potassium, especially soluble compounds used chiefly in fertilizers.

Procumbent—A term describing a low-growing plant that creeps along the ground or water's surface; prostrate.

Propagation—Growing new plants from old under controlled circumstances.

Pruning—Removing branches, stems, or roots, or parts thereof, to removed damaged or diseased tissue or to rejuvenate or reshape the plant.

Pubescence—Surface fuzz, hairs, or down; sometimes present on peduncle or petiole of water lilies.

Pump—In aquatic plants, refers to action of plant roots to absorb nutrients from soil.

Pupa—The inactive stage of insects during which the larva transforms into the adult, completing its metamorphosis.

Raceme—An unbranched elongated cluster of flowers with the flowers carried along a central stalk; the youngest flowers are at the tip of the raceme.

Radical—Of, pertaining to, or growing from a root.

Radicle—The part of the plant embryo that develops into the primary root.

Recurved—Curved backwards, describing flower petals.

Reflexed—Bent sharply backward, describing flower petals.

Reniform—Kidney-shaped, describing leaf shape.

Respiration—The metabolic process by which an organism assimilates oxygen and releases carbon dioxide and other products of oxidation.

Rhizome—Swollen, creeping underground stem that stores nutrients like a bulb. Roots and shoots grow from the rhizome. Distinguished from roots by the presence of nodes that are often enlarged by food storage. Hardy water lilies grow from rhizomes.

Rockwool—A porous composition of friable rock used in the hydroponic growing of plants.

Rosette—Cluster of leaves that fan out from a point. *Ludwigia sedoides,* the mosaic plant, grows in rosettes.

Rosulate—Forming a rosette, describing leaf arrangement.

Runner—Slender horizontal stem that trails across the soil or water surface and may form roots at the nodes. Ex: *Menyanthes trifoliata*, bogbean.

Scarify—Nick or abrade a hard seed coat to make it easier for the seed to absorb the moisture it needs to germinate. Lotus seeds are usually scarified.

Self-pollination—Ability of a plant to fertilize its pistils with its own pollen.

Self-seed—A plant expels mature seeds that germinate and grow into new plants on their own, with no help from the gardener. Ex: Water plantain, *Alisma plantago-aquatica*.

Sepal—Outer part of a flower's calyx. Sepals may be green or as showy as the petals.

Sessile—Describes leaves or flowers that have no stalk and grow directly from the stem.

Simple—Describes a leaf that is one piece and not divided into leaflets.

Sink—In aquatic plants, refers to absorption by stems and leaves of nutrients from the water.

Sinus—Area between the lobes of the water lily leaf.

Sodi soil—Highly alkaline soil with a pH above 8.5, found in some desert areas. Also called alkali soil.

Spadix—Fleshy spike found in tiny flowers, usually enclosed in a spathe. Ex: *Peltandra*.

Spathe—A leaflike organ that encloses or spreads from the base of the spadix of certain plants, such as the calla lily.

Species—Group of closely related plants that differ only in small ways. The basic unit of plant classification; species are in turn gathered into genera. Some genera contain only one species.

Sphagnum—Type of very porous moss found in bogs. Used in the true bog garden, it supplies the acidic conditions required of typical carnivorous plants.

Spike—Narrow, elongated, unbranched cluster of sessile flowers produced along a central axis.

Spore—Reproductive structure of a plant that has no flowers and therefore no seeds. Ferns, mosses, and fungi are examples.

Sport—Plant mutation that results in a shoot or new plant different from the rest of the plant or other plants of its kind. The mutation is caused by a genetic change that is spontaneous or accidental, or induced intentionally. *Nymphaea* 'Joanne Pring' is considered by some to be a sport of *N*. 'Helvola.'

Stamen—A flower's male reproductive organ, which consists of one or more anthers and filaments.

Staminodes—The colored, petal-like organs located just outside the stamens in water lilies and lotuses; characterized by broad bases and anther-like sacs at the tips.

Standard—The upright petals of an iris flower.

Star lily—Tropical perennial herb, mostly resulting from crosses of *Nymphaea flavovirens* (syn. *N. gracilis*) with its own variations or with *N. capensis* var. *zanzibariensis*.

Sterile—Unable to generate seed.

Stigma—Part of the female reproductive organ of a flower, the stigma is located at the top of the style, and becomes sticky to receive ripe pollen grains during fertilization.

Stellate—Star-shaped, usually referring to flower shape.

Stolon—Stem that grows horizontally above ground or hangs downward, and roots when the tip touches the ground, forming a new plant. Also known as a runner.

Stomate (plural, stomata)—Pore in a leaf through which carbon dioxide, oxygen, and water vapor pass during photosynthesis and transpiration. In terrestrial plants, the underside of leaves contains stomata; in water lily leaves, for example, the stomata are on the upper side.

Stratify—Place seeds in a cold environment to break their dormancy and enable them to germinate. Necessary for most perennial plants.

Striations—Fine stripes.

Style—Part of the female reproductive structure of a flower, the style supports the stigma.

Submersed—Growing or remaining under water (submerged).

Taxonomy—The process of classifying organisms in established categories.

Tender—Term describing a plant that is damaged or killed by cold temperatures. Frost-tender describes plants harmed by frost and freezing temperatures.

Terminal—Usually used in reference to the growth at the end of a stem.

Terrestrial—Living or growing on land (not aquatic).

Tip—The staminal appendage in tropical day-blooming water lilies.

Tomentose—Hairy; covered with hairs.

Trifoliate—Compound leaf made up of three leaflets or leaves produced in groups of three. Ex: bogbean, *Menyanthes trifoliata*.

Tuber—A short, thickened, fleshy part of an underground stem.

Tuberosa rhizome—A slender hardy water lily rhizome in which young or new tubers are attached to the parent tuber only by very fragile, thin pieces; the young tubers usually break off and remain underground when the parent tuber is pulled. Tubers may also be broken off by the rooting of fish.

Tropical water lily—Species forming an underwater herb, native to warmer climates; may also refer to a cultivar resulting from crossing two tropical water lily species or crossing a tropical water lily species and a tropical water lily cultivar.

Turion—A terminal overwintering bud, sometimes scaly, often thick and fleshy, growing from a submerged rootstock. Turions are usually formed at the end of the growing season when they settle to deeper water for wintering.

Umbel—A flower cluster in which the individual flower stalks grow from the same point, like the ribs of an umbrella. Ex: *Butomus* and *Cyperus*.

Upright rhizome—A hardy water lily rhizome that grows upright as opposed to horizontally.

Variegated—Referring to plants characterized by striping, mottling, or other coloration in addition to the plant's usual color.

Variety—A variant of a species that originally occurred in nature rather than as a result of intentional breeding.

Variant—A plant displaying variation from the species.

Vegetative—Asexual vegetative propagation methods produce new plants genetically identical to the parent without pollination and seeds. Also used to describe leafy, non-blooming growth. A vegetative filter in a water garden indicates the use of plants to remove nutrients from the water.

Viviparous—Germination that takes place while new plant is still attached to the parent plant. Usually occurs at leaf node of some tropical water lilies, although the hardy cultivar 'Colonel A.J. Welsh' produces plantlets from its flowers.

Whorl—Group of three or more flowers, stems, or branches that radiate from a single point on the stem or branch.

Xerophyte—A plant that grows in and is adapted to an environment deficient in moisture.

Acknowledgments

Editing and publishing a bimonthly, 96-page magazine doesn't leave much time for writing books. This book would never have happened without the patience of Sterling Publishing Company. Thank you, Sheila, and the powers-that-be. Special appreciation goes to John Woodside, who waded through my many disks of photos, and to Judy Morgan, whose creative talents have again designed a beautiful book that is easy to read. Hannah Steinmetz, editor extraordinaire, as usual performed all those tedious chores of working the words into their proper form and format. A dear friend, of sparkling humor and warmth, she has a much appreciated talent for taking the drudgery out of the mundane side of writing. Both she and Judy deserve to have their names on the cover of this book.

The primary instigator of this project is Steve Stroupe, a special friend who just wouldn't let the idea drop. Notwithstanding his protests to the contrary, his ideas, information, and rereadings were invaluable. He is even using part of the royalties from this book to create an educational fund at *Watergardening Magazine,* to encourage water-related education and projects for inner-city elementary schoolchildren. No man alive loves and respects the earth, the plants that grow on it, and the children that grow up on it more than Steve. This book is as much his vision as it is mine.

Although this book is dedicated to the incomparable Perry D. Slocum, specific acknowledgment is due Perry for contributing so many of his wonderful photographs. It's easy to see why he is an internationally acclaimed photographer as well as a noted hybridizer and plantsman. This book could never have been written without the extensive body of information in his monumental work *Water Gardening: Water Lilies and Lotuses,* written with Peter Robinson. Thank you, too, to Bob Romar, photographer of plants for Maryland Aquatic Nurseries, who offered wondrous photos. Bob has contributed many photos in previous books of mine, but here his talents are truly showcased. Other photographers, both professional and amateur, shared their much appreciated efforts: Sue Bridges, Marilyn Cook, Michael Duff, Ron Everhart, Rob Gardner, Oliver Jackson, Paul Stetson, Bob Strawn, Kirk Strawn, Bill Marocco, Brad McLane, and Harry Hooper of England.

A special note of appreciation goes to Rob Gardner, of the North Carolina Botanical Garden at the University of North Carolina at Chapel Hill for his photographs and information, and for proofreading the section on carnivorous plants. His interest in and enthusiasm for these unique plants is contagious! Also, heartfelt thanks to Tim Jennings, curator of aquatic plants at Longwood Gardens, in Pennsylvania. Tim's input on starting lotuses and Victorias from seed adds another dimension to our enjoyment of these exquisite plants. Much appreciation goes to the many people who have shared in creating the body of knowledge of the plants we grow in our water gardens: Scott Bates, of Grass Roots Nursery, Michigan; Don and Shirley Bryne, of Suwanee River Laboratories, Florida; Barbara and Ray Davies, of Stapeley Water Gardens, England; Michael Duff, former New Zealander now in Bloomington, Indiana; Ben and Debbie Gibson, of Perry's Water Gardens, North Carolina; Clair Henley, of Wychwood Waterlily Farm, England; Harry Hooper, of Mill Lane Nursery and Water Gardens, England; Tim Jennings and Patrick Nutt, of Longwood Gardens, Pennsylvania; Kenneth Landon, hybridizer and present-day "Indiana Jones"; Jim Leonard, of Louisiana Iris Farms, Louisiana; Brad and Bruce McLane, of Florida Aquatic Nurseries, Florida; Rolf and Anita Nelson, of Nelson Water Gardens and Nursery, Texas; Brian and Stuart Schuck, of Charleston Aquatic Nurseries, South Carolina; Richard Schuck and Kelly Billing, of Maryland Aquatic Nurseries, Maryland; Peter Slocum, of Slocum Water Gardens, Florida; Nancy and Trey Styler, of Colorado; Charles B. Thomas, of Lilypons Water Gardens, Maryland, Texas, and California; and Joe Tomocik, of the Denver Botanic Gardens. Thank you all for your love of plants that grow in water!

Finally, this book would not have come about without the critical editorial review by my husband, Dave, as well as his understanding, household help, magazine help, and phone-fielding. My sister, Marilyn Cook, also assisted with the magazine and with book research, typing, and proofreading, and spent many hours on drawings. I love you both!

Index